AJPH

A PUBLICATION OF THE
AMERICAN PUBLIC HEALTH ASSOCIATION

AMERICAN JOURNAL of PUBLIC HEALTH
JANUARY 2025
Issue 1

DISPLACEMENTS TO ESCAPE NATURAL DISASTERS IN THE UNITED STATES

The Path Forward Is Health, p. 4
Drivers and Disparities, p. 52
Prevalence, Correlates, p. 55

Also in this issue:

NALOXONE DISTRIBUTION
Cluster Randomized Wait-List Controlled Trial, p. 83
Overdose Education, pp. 6 and 83
Population-Level Impact, p. 9

URBAN REFORESTATION
Manhattan's Street Trees, p. 66

HEALTH MONITORING DATA
Adding Nativity, Citizenship, and Immigration, p. 75

LONG-ACTING REVERSIBLE CONTRACEPTION
Births and Birth Intendedness, p. 95

Standard Methods for the Examination of Dairy Products, 18th edition

Edited by Jeffrey L. Kornacki, PhD, Elliot T. Ryser, PhD, and Cynthia M. Mangione; Managing Editor: H. Michael Wehr, PhD

Standard Methods for the Examination of Dairy Products is a widely-recognized source of methods to assess the safety and quality of dairy products. It is an overview of microbiological, chemical and physical methods for analyzing milk and dairy products, designed for use by regulatory, industry and commercial laboratories. As with earlier editions, the 18th edition of Standard Methods for the Examination of Dairy Products:

9780-887553-3421, SOFTCOVER,
1144 PP, 2024

- Highlights test methods that are a critical component of both government and industry analytical programs.
- Provides methods that foster uniformity in the testing of milk and milk programs.

This new 18th Edition of SMEDP updates and expands upon earlier editions of this authoritative reference, including:

- Comprehensive revision to chapters on antibiotic drug residues, pathogens, chemical and physical methods, and methods for heat process verification.
- Updates on both automated, and molecular-based methods.

APHABOOKSTORE.ORG

APHA PRESS

AN IMPRINT OF **AMERICAN PUBLIC HEALTH ASSOCIATION**

AMERICAN PUBLIC HEALTH ASSOCIATION
For science. For action. For health.

AJPH®, published monthly, is the official Journal of the American Public Health Association®, 800 I St NW, Washington, DC 20001-3710; (202) 777- APHA; TDD (202) 777-2500. APHA is a nongovernmental professional society founded in 1872, representing all disciplines and specialties in public health.

The *American Journal of Public Health*® (*AJPH*) (print ISSN: 0090-0036; electronic ISSN: 1541- 0048), first published in 1911, is the official journal of the American Public Health Association® (APHA). The oldest and largest organization of public health professionals in the world, APHA represents approximately 30 000 members from more than 50 occupations of public health.

Submissions: Visit www.editorialmanager.com/ajph or ajph.edmgr.com for online manuscript preparation and submission guidelines. Contributions of original unpublished research, social science analyses, scholarly essays, critical commentaries, departments, and letters to the editor are welcome. Questions? Write ajph.submissions@apha.org or call APHA at (202) 777-2469.

Print plus online subscriptions: Institutional price (print copy with online access for a single institution and all authorized users, regardless of geographic location) varies by size of organization and ranges from \$993–\$1445 for US organizations, and \$1073–\$1526 for international organizations (air delivery); multiple campuses not permitted without special arrangement. Details of the tiered pricing system at https://subscriptionoffice.com/pages/apha-landing-page. To order, write apha.subscriptions@apha.org.

Online-only subscriptions: Institutional price for one institution and its authorized users (regardless of geographic location) is \$878–\$1307. To order, write apha.subscriptions@apha.org. For academic consortia or multisite corporate subscriptions, contact apha.subscriptions@apha.org.

Print-only subscriptions: Institutional price is US \$701, \$782 international.

Back print issues: A limited number of print issues are for sale. Single copies are US \$49, \$55 international (air delivery). Shipping included; prepay only. To order, write apha.subscriptions@apha.org.

Reprints: For prices and ordering information on 50 or more reprints, check the Reprints section at www.ajph.org. To order smaller quantities of reprints (rush delivery), use the "Purchase Article" link on the article site itself.

Electronic access: Online articles more than 10 years old are available free for personal use at www.ajph.org. Recent articles are available through pay-per-view: single PDF article for \$24, single issue access for 24 hours for \$33, or entire site access for 24 hours for \$38.

Postal information: Periodicals postage paid at Washington, DC, and additional mailing offices. Postmaster: Send address changes to American Journal of Public Health, 800 I St NW, Washington, DC 20001-3710.

Address changes: Send to AJPH, Membership Department (members) or AJPH Subscriptions (subscribers), APHA, 800 I St NW, Washington, DC 20001-3710. Or write to membership.mail@apha. org (members) or apha.subscriptions@apha.org (subscribers).

Indexes: Publications that index or abstract articles from *AJPH* include the following: Ageline, Assia (Applied Social Science Index and Abstracts), Biological Abstracts, Chemical Abstracts, CINAHL, Criminal Justice Abstracts, EMBASE, EMCare, Environmental Abstracts, e-psyche, ERIC, ETOH (Alcohol and Alcohol Problems Science Database), Excerpta Medica, Food Science and Technology, General Science Index, Grateful Med, Hospital Literature Index, Human Resources Abstracts, International Pharmaceutical Abstracts (IPA), Medline, Physical Education Index, Pollution Abstracts, Psychological Abstracts, PsychINFO, Safety Science Abstracts, Sage Family Studies Abstracts, Sage Human Resources Abstracts, Science Citation Index, SCOPUS, SIIC Data Bases, Social Work Research and Abstracts, and Statistical Reference Index (SRI)/LexisNexis.

AJPH

A PUBLICATION OF THE
AMERICAN PUBLIC HEALTH ASSOCIATION

COVER: A dog can be seen sitting on a front stoop of a home in the Allen Circle neighborhood where many homes and cars have been flooded because of excessive rain on August 7, 2024 in Statesboro, Georgia. Tropical Storm Debby stalled over the Southeast, causing flooding and power outages throughout the region.

Cover concept and design by Aleisha Kropf. Photo by Megan Varner/Getty. Printed with permission.

APHA
AMERICAN PUBLIC HEALTH ASSOCIATION
For science. For action. For health.

Promoting public health research, policy, practice, and education is the *AJPH* mission. As we widen our scope to embrace global issues, we also sharpen our focus to support the needs of public health practitioners. We invite contributions of original unpublished research, opinion and commentary, and letters to the editor.

The *Journal* is printed on acid-free recycled paper.

OPEN ACCESS ONLINE ONLY PODCAST DATA SUPPLEMENT AVAILABLE

EDITOR'S CHOICE

4 The Path Forward Is Health
B. Selzer

OPINIONS, IDEAS, & PRACTICE

EDITORIALS

6 Overdose Education and Naloxone Distribution: An Evidence-Based Practice That Warrants Course Correcting
M. Doe-Simkins and E. J. Wheeler

9 Strategies to Increase the Population-Level Impact of Naloxone Distribution in Communities Highly Affected by the Overdose Crisis
B. D. L. Marshall

12 Moving Targets: The Dynamic Nature and Imperfect Measurement of Social Constructs
R. L. Sell

15 Planning and Accommodating the Micromobility Revolution and Its Impact on Public Health
D. A. Quistberg and D. A. Rodriguez

PERSPECTIVES

18 Recommitting to Housing and Health Care Justice After *City of Grants Pass v Johnson*
A. R. Habib, S. A. Stella, E. K. Farkouh, C. M. Grenko, D. Hart, and A. S. Pasha

23 Names Matter: Affirming Our Commitment to Equity in Publishing
H. M. Brandt, L. M. Schwab-Reese, C. Voyles, M. A. Guest, and A. Hagopian

26 Don't Forget Fido: A Call to Include Pets in Public Health Research and Policy to Support Families and Communities
E. D. Dolan, B. Wyker, E. A. Berliner, M. Goldweber, and A. Hernandez

30 Federal Policy Platforms and Public Health: Reinforcing the Benefits of Air Pollution Control Devices at Power Plants in the United States
J. J. Buonocore, J. Fisher, D. Prull, M. D. Willis, S. Arunachalam, F. Perera, P. Kinney, B. Sousa, and J. I. Levy

34 Community Health Workers as Catalysts for Mental Health Promotion in Transgender and Nonbinary Communities
A. J. Restar, K. Baker, G. Wang, K. Ashley, and A. J. Damian

37 Safeguarding SNAP as an Effective Antihunger Program: Myths and Potential Harms of Adding Diet Quality as a Core Objective
D. M. Krobath, J. A. Lawrence, B. W. Chrisinger, and A. G. Cuevas

NOTES FROM THE FIELD

42 Prior Authorization Requirements and Medicaid Enrollees' Use of Tobacco Cessation Medications, Colorado, 2023
M. Dillender and R. Mermelstein

47 Equity Zones: Building the Bridge to Transformation
C. Ausura, G. Turner, J. Latham, N. Marcus, S. Schnell, and B. Edmiston

ESCAPING DISASTER

52 Escaping Disaster: Understanding the Drivers and Disparities in Disaster Displacement in the United States
K. W. Kintziger and S. E. Scales

RESEARCH & ANALYSIS

ESCAPING DISASTER

55 Prevalence, Correlates, and Impacts of Displacement Because of Natural Disasters in the United States From 2022 to 2023
T. W. Aung and A. R. Sehgal

HISTORY

66 Manhattan's Street Trees: An Unfinished Public Health Story
J. M. Harris Jr

HEALTH MONITORING

75 Adding Nativity, Citizenship, and Immigration Status to Health Monitoring and Survey Data
F. E. Marouf, K. M. Perreira, and H. Pham

OPEN-THEMED RESEARCH

83 Effect of the Communities That HEAL Intervention on Overdose Education and Naloxone Distribution: A Cluster-Randomized, Wait-List Controlled Trial
P. R. Freeman, A. Y. Walley, T. J. Winhusen, E. A. Oga, J. Villani, T. Hunt, R. K. Chandler, D. R. Oyler, B. Reilly, K. Gelberg, C. Douglas, M. S. Lyons, J. Holloway, N. A. Vandergrift, J. W. Adams, K. Asman, T. J. Baker, C. J. Brancato, D. M. Cheng, J. E. Childerhose, J. L. David, D. J. Feaster, L. Gilbert, L. M. Glasgow, D. A. Goddard-Eckrich, C. Knott, H. K. Knudsen, M. R. Lofwall, K. R. Marks, J. T. McMullan, C. B. Oser, M. F. Roberts, A. B. Shoben, M. D. Stein, S. T. Walters, J. Watson, G. A. Zarkin, R. D. Jackson, J. H. Samet, S. L. Walsh, and N. El Bassel

95 Long-Acting Reversible Contraception (LARC) and Early Childbearing Revisited: Births and Birth Intendedness After LARC Removal in a State Medicaid Population (2012–2020)
M. S. Rendall, M. C. W. Eeckhaut, K. Gifford, and C. Hurtado-Acuna

BACKMATTER

OTHER DEPARTMENTS

104 Subscription Form

The Path Forward Is Health

Brian Selzer, BA
Director of Publications
American Public Health Association

With the passing of the 2024 election cycle, the language of hate, racism, indifference, and cruelty is becoming emboldened once again (https://bit.ly/3ZgkNEh), as are threats of violence (https://bit.ly/3Zg6ZJT). Immigrants and sexual minorities are afraid of what will come next (https://bit.ly/3V2mgfc; https://bit.ly/40RVj1o), and potential appointees to the new administration are already espousing the changes they plan to make post-inauguration (https://bit.ly/3AVbC2T).

We will continue to witness in real-time attempts to dismantle trust in medicine and the public health infrastructure, and we could very well see some infrastructure removed. The future is not certain, however, and although it seems bleak, I feel that championing and safeguarding health for everyone is the surest path forward.

As the Publications Director at the American Public Health Association, my department will continue to work with our *AJPH* and book editors and authors to provide the best science and authoritative knowledge on public health policy and initiatives. We will strive to ensure these necessary resources are available to support the public health workforce and researchers, educate our students, and promote equitable access to health for all.

AJPH has been published for more than 100 years and will continue to showcase the top science in the field. The journal will not hesitate to explore and confront those issues that impact and threaten the public's health and safety. It will continue to provide the necessary research to shape policy and promote health, well-being, and equity in care and access to care for all.

Likewise, APHA Press will continue to produce standards to ensure we have trusted methods to produce clean, drinkable water; disease-free foods; and safe dairy products. We will maintain the highest rigor in developing guidelines and reference material needed to respond to and swiftly contain disease outbreaks and public health emergencies.

Both programs will continue to provide the science and tools required to confront the racist power structures and address racial/ethnic inequities that continue to harm minorities. They also will promote skills-building for effective policy and community

Continued on page 5...

HISTORY CORNER

47 YEARS AGO

Health Consequences of a Snow Disaster

Public health interventions can diminish adverse health consequences of a disaster. Interventions taken before a predicted severe storm can save lives and minimize inconvenience. In Connecticut, early cancellation of work and a ban on traffic prevented drivers from being stranded on the road and probably alleviated this source of mortality. Establishment of a "rumor clearing house" after a disaster can speed the investigation of reported disease outbreaks, identify areas in need of emergency health services or supplies, and dispel false rumors before they have time to circulate. . .. [T]he uniform collection of data on the number, causes, and circumstances of death can be useful in assessing whether the disaster's effects are ongoing, relief policies are adequate (e.g., emergency transportation), and high-risk groups (i.e., dialysis patients) are receiving proper care. The number of deaths remains the most publicized health measure of a disaster but no agency currently records this information.

From *AJPH*, October 1979, pp. 1048–1049

engagement, advocating for improving sexual and reproductive health, assuring equality for racial and sexual minorities, and combating misinformation, chronic disease, and the harms from alcohol, tobacco, and drugs.

Despite the dark clouds hovering above, our mission will not change. During my time with APHA and *AJPH*, I've come to admire the strength, passion, and dedication of those who take on the challenge of improving and safeguarding access to health and equality for all. Despite the roadblocks placed in front of you, you continue to push policies that improve access to low-cost, high-quality health care and medicines for men, women, and children; support the rights of women, racial minorities, and sexual minorities; call for laws and regulations to ensure clean water, clean air, and environmental protections; ensure access to healthy and nutritious foods; and push to codify into law sexual and reproductive rights.

You can only keep moving forward, and we will continue to support those efforts. The future is uncertain, but our commitment to serving our members and community is not. More must be done, however, and APHA's Publications department will enhance the way in which we communicate science to include the nonscientist and non–public health expert, who may disagree with the science we are presenting. As this election cycle has demonstrated, when messaging does not resonate, a significant proportion of the US population stops listening. It is imperative that public health messaging be as diverse as the populations we are trying reach so that we can strengthen trust in science and America's safety nets, and so we all better understand how our health and well-being are impacted when public health programs are robust versus under attack or removed. In this way, I hope that the voice of hate and division can shift back to one of inclusivity and understanding, with a shared goal of ensuring the health and welfare of all. AJPH

DOI: https://doi.org/10.2105/AJPH.2024.307915

HISTORY CORNER

39 YEARS AGO

Preparing for Disaster

In December 1984, a lethal cloud of methyl isocyanate was released from the Union Carbide plant in Bhopal, India-killing over 1,700 community residents and leaving thousands more severely injured. While it was maintained that this could not occur in the United States, late in the summer of 1985 "pressure build-up" in a 500-gallon storage tank resulted in the release of a toxic cloud of aldicarb oxime, a less toxic chemical derivative of methyl isocyanate, from a Union Carbide plant in Institute, West Virginia, sending 125 residents to area hospitals for treatment and confining thousands more to their homes without clear immediate warning or understanding of the toxicity of this chemical plant emission. . .. The specter of Bhopal has stimulated the US Congress, EPA, and the chemical industry to come forward with new or revised emergency response proposals. . .. Among them are requirements that each covered major manufacturer develop a comprehensive evacuation and emergency response plan. . .

From *AJPH*, March 1986, p. 233

Overdose Education and Naloxone Distribution: An Evidence-Based Practice That Warrants Course Correcting

Maya Doe-Simkins, MPH, and Eliza J. Wheeler, MS, MPA

ABOUT THE AUTHORS

Maya Doe-Simkins is with Remedy Alliance, Traverse City, MI. Eliza J. Wheeler is with Remedy Alliance, Berkeley, CA.

See also Marshall, p. 9, and Freeman et al., p. 83.

In this issue of *AJPH*, Freeman et al.'s study "Effect of the Communities That HEAL Intervention on Overdose Education and Naloxone Distribution: A Cluster Randomized Wait-List Controlled Trial" (p. 83) is the largest analysis of a well-funded, broadly supported, bipartisan, popular initiative: overdose education and naloxone distribution (OEND). We were pleased to see affirmation of the study hypothesis that well-resourced Communities That HEAL (CTH) intervention communities will distribute, overall, significantly higher rates of naloxone units compared with less well-resourced and less-participatory initiatives (i.e., usual care).

The large budget and a research component make OEND via the HEALing Communities Study unique. Nonetheless, in response to increasing numbers of opioid-involved polydrug overdoses, an expansion of community-based naloxone provision is a shared experience across the country, albeit at rates related to resource investment.

Unfortunately, a considerable majority of the expansion efforts—including certain components of the HEALing Communities Study—have strayed from the existing evidence base. The evidence base for broader bystanders and passive distribution is minimal and would not be expected to affect overdose mortality rates directly. Conflating evidence-based OEND and general community-based naloxone provision can be disingenuous and dangerous, especially when making resource allocation decisions.

OEND as an evidence-based practice refers to three very specific models: (1) naloxone distribution directly to people who use drugs (PWUD) via syringe services programs (SSPs),[1] (2) naloxone provision upon release from incarceration,[2] and (3) coprescribing naloxone with opioids to people at high risk.[3]

However, there is a measurable implementation gap between community-based naloxone provision and evidence-based OEND. Remedy Alliance is a nonprofit wholesale distributor of naloxone to SSPs, harm reduction programs, and state and municipal government programs that are prioritizing SSPs with the naloxone they purchase and that are operating with fidelity to the evidence base.[4] Using a tiered pricing system, better-resourced customers pay a higher price than the partially funded programs, and unfunded entities are eligible for naloxone at no cost. There are nearly 500 programs—representing all but three states—that order naloxone from Remedy Alliance, which has sent out 3.4 million doses since August 2022, a considerable majority of which were injectable naloxone.

Figure 1 shows the number of doses sent to programs in each state or territory, including the number and percentage sent at no cost from August 2022 to August 2024. The states that received more than 100 000 doses are Minnesota, North Carolina, Washington, Arizona, Missouri, Indiana, Illinois, Wisconsin, Georgia, and Oregon. The states and territories that received more than 90% of the naloxone at no cost include Alabama, Alaska, Hawaii, Louisiana, Massachusetts, Mississippi, Nebraska, New York, Puerto Rico, Tennessee, and Virginia. (For data on all states and territories, see Table A, available as a supplement to the online version of this article at http://www.ajph.org.) By keeping in mind these otherwise unpublished data, which are unaccounted for in other data sets, future research might consider a wide range of hypotheses:

Hypothesis 1. Higher proportions of no-cost naloxone are negatively associated with government investment in evidence-based OEND.

Hypothesis 2. Higher numbers of naloxone doses are positively associated with governmental investment

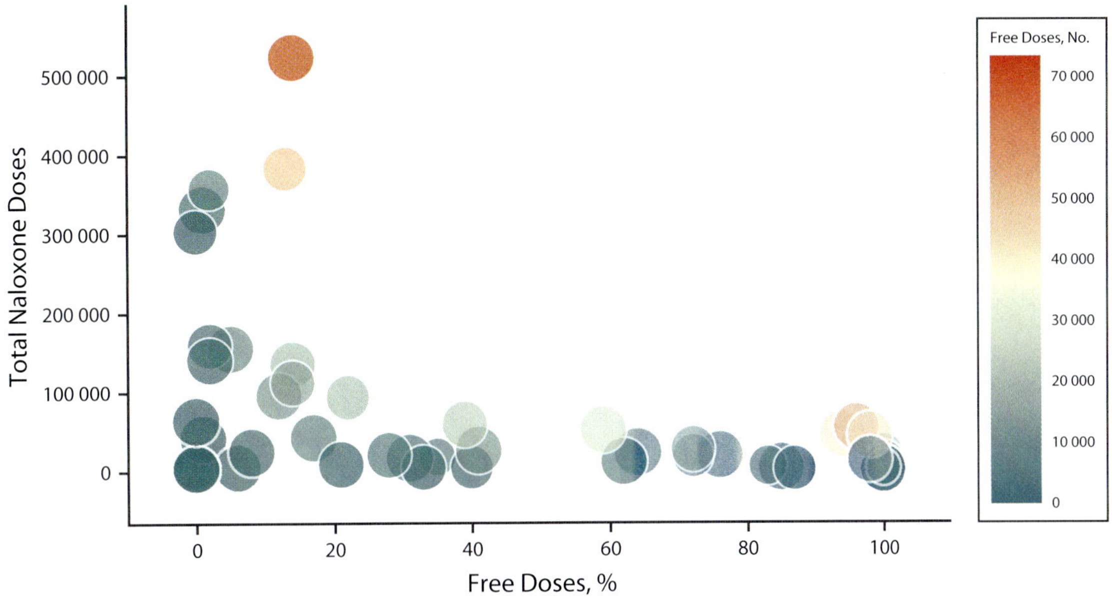

FIGURE 1— Total Naloxone Doses and No-Cost Naloxone Shipped to US States or Territories by Remedy Alliance: August 2022–August 2024

Note. Each circle represents a US state or territory. Along the vertical axis is total volume of naloxone. Along the horizontal axis is percentage free or at no cost to the organizations or health departments. Red circles represent the highest volume of no-cost naloxone, and darker green circles represent states that received a lower volume of no-cost naloxone.

in expensive nasal naloxone products only.

Hypothesis 3. States with a direct purchase agreement with Remedy Alliance will have a significantly higher volume of naloxone sent to the state.

Hypothesis 1 may be influenced by SSPs needing more naloxone than their state or municipality provides. Hypothesis 2 could be influenced by naloxone budget lines that are depleted before the end of the fiscal year, causing gaps in naloxone access for SSPs, or perhaps SSPs want an injectable naloxone offering but are unable to acquire it from state sources. Hypothesis 3 may be influenced by local stigma or restrictive state level systems.

DILUTION OF THE IMPACT OF NALOXONE DISTRIBUTION

In 2013, OEND was confirmed to be an evidence-based practice that reduces fatal opioid overdose, but there was not explicit national federal funding for naloxone until the 2017 rollout of the 2016 CARA Act.[5] When federal funding did become available, it was considerable and rapidly disseminated. As more dollars became available, public health infrastructures expanded, the dedicated workforce drastically increased, and competing interests emerged.

Two competing interests influence community naloxone access. The first is the marketing of new products. This includes the emergence of branded and more expensive naloxone products and also adjacent markets like vending machines, naloxone display boxes, drug disposal packets, "fentanyl protection products," and others that rapidly enter the landscape. These entities are engaged in marketing practices that are compelling to the decision-makers who are inexperienced in resource allocation and evidence-based OEND.

The second category of interests that influence community naloxone access is a sociological inevitability of an ongoing overdose epidemic: broader investment from groups of people with a personal or professional interest in the topic. Freeman et al. describe the first component of the CTH intervention as "a coalition-driven community engagement process to select and support the implementation of strategies to facilitate the uptake of EBPs [evidence-based practices]." For any public health problem, this is an excellent strategy to ensure broad support at a community level. However, an unintended outcome of this coalition-based decision-making is that the voice, needs, and priorities of SSPs and PWUD have become just one of many. Indeed, the originators of the OEND evidence-based intervention are minimally included at best and frequently disregarded completely in "coalition-driven community engagement process[es]."

OPPORTUNITIES FOR COURSE CORRECTION

There are several strategies that resource allocation decision-makers can consider to better align efforts with the OEND evidence base.

Investing in a mix of different naloxone products, including inexpensive generic injectable versions, can help maintain budgets while increasing volume. Spending half a budget on nasal and half on injectable would result in a 36% greater volume of naloxone than nasal alone.

SSPs should be fully resourced, with as much naloxone as they need to develop an abundance mindset that allows organizations to confidently provide as much naloxone as PWUD request. Importantly, SSPs also need funding for staff time for OEND to capitalize on existing social networks by encouraging secondary distribution through drug-using social networks. In the HEALing Communities Study, this practice successfully included paying PWUD to attend to their social networks' naloxone access needs.[6]

To reach people who use drugs by routes other than injection, and to expand the reach of trusted harm reduction services, it is necessary to provide services and supplies that PWUD want.[7] Examples include smoking supplies, snorting supplies, advanced technology drug-checking services, overdose prevention centers, food, and toiletries.

Finally, states and municipalities should triage requests for naloxone in a way that ensures that the venues and organizations most likely to use the naloxone are well stocked.[8] We have numerous examples of historical experiences with this type of rollout; we can look to the prioritization scheme that was deployed with COVID-19 vaccination eligibility as a recent example.

Although there are some excellent and exciting OEND adaptations, there are also some adaptations that deviate dramatically from the evidence base, and those resources may be better directed elsewhere. We applaud adaptation and innovation in public health, particularly for people who have had tenuous or even harmful interfaces with medical, mental, and public health services—for example, people who use drugs, people experiencing homelessness, people who do sex work, and Black, Indigenous, and Latine people. At the same time, the urgency of the overdose crisis demands that the evidence-based models (OEND via SSPs) be fully resourced to achieve maximum benefit. AJPH

CORRESPONDENCE

Correspondence should be sent to Maya Doe-Simkins, 13414 S. W. Bayshore Dr, Traverse City, MI 49684 (e-mail: maya@remedyallianceftp.org). Reprints can be ordered at https://www.ajph.org by clicking the "Reprints" link.

PUBLICATION INFORMATION

Full Citation: Doe-Simkins M, Wheeler EJ. Overdose education and naloxone distribution: an evidence-based practice that warrants course correcting. *Am J Public Health*. 2025;115(1):6–8.

Acceptance Date: September 30, 2024.

DOI: https://doi.org/10.2105/AJPH.2024.307893

ORCID iDs:

Maya Doe-Simkins https://orcid.org/0009-0003-4143-2774

Eliza J. Wheeler https://orcid.org/0000-0002-6643-0607

CONTRIBUTORS

M. Doe-Simkins and E. J. Wheeler developed the concept, analyzed the data, and wrote the manuscript.

ACKNOWLEDGMENTS

We thank Bradly Ray for editorial feedback and the programs that Remedy Alliance works with for performing lifesaving work.

CONFLICTS OF INTEREST

M. Doe-Simkins and E. J. Wheeler are codirectors of the 501(c)(3) nonprofit Remedy Alliance.

REFERENCES

1. Walley AY, Xuan Z, Hackman HH, et al. Opioid overdose rates and implementation of overdose education and nasal naloxone distribution in Massachusetts: interrupted time series analysis. *BMJ*. 2013;346:f174. https://doi.org/10.1136/bmj.f174
2. Bird SM, McAuley A, Perry S, Hunter C. Effectiveness of Scotland's National Naloxone Programme for reducing opioid-related deaths: a before (2006–10) versus after (2011–13) comparison. *Addiction*. 2016;111(5):883–891. https://doi.org/10.1111/add.13265
3. Coffin PO, Behar E, Rowe C, et al. Nonrandomized intervention study of naloxone coprescription for primary care patients receiving long-term opioid therapy for pain. *Ann Intern Med*. 2016;165(4):245–252. https://doi.org/10.7326/M15-2771
4. Remedy Alliance for the People, Wheeler EJ, Doe-Simkins M, Dasgupta N. Remedy Alliance for the People Annual Report 2023. https://doi.org/10.17615/ymxe-6x08
5. National Academies of Sciences, Medicine Division, Board on Population Health and Public Health Practice, Committee on the Review of Specific Programs in the Comprehensive Addiction and Recovery Act. *Measuring Success in Substance Use Grant Programs: Outcomes and Metrics for Improvement*. Washington, DC: National Academies Press; 2020.
6. Lewis NM, Smeltzer RP, Baker TJ, et al. Feasibility of paying people who use drugs cash to distribute naloxone within their networks. *Harm Reduct J*. 2024;21(1):42. https://doi.org/10.1186/s12954-024-00947-6
7. Tapper A, Ahern C, Graveline-Long Z, Newberger NG, Hughto JM. The utilization and delivery of safer smoking practices and services: a narrative synthesis of the literature. *Harm Reduct J*. 2023;20(1):160. https://doi.org/10.1186/s12954-023-00875-x
8. National Association of State and Territorial AIDS Directors (NASTAD). Recommendations for federal partners and health departments navigating naloxone supply. July 8, 2021. Available at: https://nastad.org/resources/recommendations-federal-partners-and-health-departments-navigating-naloxone-supply. Accessed September 5, 2024.

Strategies to Increase the Population-Level Impact of Naloxone Distribution in Communities Highly Affected by the Overdose Crisis

Brandon D. L. Marshall, PhD

ABOUT THE AUTHOR

The author is with the Brown University School of Public Health, Providence, RI.

See also Doe-Simkins and Wheeler, p. 6, and Freeman et al., p. 83.

Naloxone distribution is a proven public health strategy to reduce overdose deaths.[1] With the nation's overdose crisis claiming more than 100 000 lives annually,[2] comprehensive, multifaceted strategies are urgently needed to increase access to naloxone such that the medication is readily available and rapidly administered whenever an overdose occurs. Federal agencies, including the Substance Abuse and Mental Health Services Administration, have strongly endorsed naloxone distribution as a key component of the nation's response to the overdose crisis[3] and have encouraged jurisdictions to develop naloxone "saturation" plans, often defined as a benchmark of having naloxone available at 80% of witnessed overdose deaths.[4] Federal policy changes, including the US Food and Drug Administration's approval of the first over-the-counter naloxone product in March 2023, have further aimed to ensure that naloxone is broadly available in communities across the country.

Despite these laudable efforts, overdose deaths have not decreased significantly, even in states with high rates of naloxone distribution,[5] and modeling studies have demonstrated that increasing naloxone access must be paired with other interventions to achieve sustained reductions in overdose deaths at the population level.[6,7] In this issue of *AJPH*, Freeman et al. (p. 83) report the results of the HEALing Communities Study—a cluster-randomized, parallel-arm, wait-list-controlled implementation science trial—on naloxone distribution across 67 highly affected countries in 4 US states (Kentucky, Massachusetts, New York, and Ohio).

The study authors found a 79% increase in naloxone distribution in counties that received the Communities That HEAL (CTH) intervention relative to those in the wait-list control arm and a more than twofold increase in naloxone distributed through community programs. The communities randomized to the CTH intervention implemented more than 250 strategies to increase naloxone access, including a focus on "active" strategies, defined as proactive delivery to at-risk individuals and their social networks or delivery in high-risk venues, including behavioral health settings, criminal justice settings, and health care sectors.

Despite the rapid and substantial increase in naloxone distribution as a result of the CTH intervention, the HEALing Communities Study Consortium recently reported that opioid-related overdose deaths were only 9% lower in communities implementing the CTH intervention relative to usual care, and the difference was not statistically significant.[8] The consortium has hypothesized possible explanations for the lack of effect, and these explanations include delayed implementation of many of the intervention packages (largely owing to the COVID-19 pandemic), the relatively short trial follow-up period, and a rapidly evolving, unregulated drug market, which may have reduced the effectiveness of the intervention.[8] Nonetheless, the small, nonsignificant reduction in overdose deaths despite a rapid increase in naloxone distribution reported by Freeman et al. is notable and warrants analysis. Here I offer three possible explanations that should be interrogated further, all with the goal of maximizing the effectiveness of increased naloxone distribution in highly affected communities.

DELAYED EFFECTS OF NALOXONE DISTRIBUTION

First, unlike many public health programs in which the desired impact is (relatively) immediate and beneficial to the individual receiving the intervention (e.g., vaccination), the effect of naloxone distribution on preventing overdose deaths is both delayed and indirect; that is, the mechanism of action (i.e., the medication being administered to

AJPH January 2025, Vol. 115, No. 1

reverse overdose symptoms) is conditional on a number of other factors. Specifically, naloxone must not only be distributed in communities but be immediately accessible to a bystander who directly witnesses an overdose event. For these reasons, community-based naloxone distribution programs should prioritize the populations most likely to be present in the event of an overdose: friends and family members of people who use drugs and, of course, people who use drugs themselves.

The distinction here is a subtle yet important one. For example, programs that provide naloxone to people who are being released from correctional settings are certainly valuable given the extraordinarily high risk of overdose after release from prisons and jails, but equally so might be interventions distributing naloxone to the social and drug-using networks of those involved in the criminal justice system. For example, Clark County Jail Services in Washington State has installed naloxone vending machines in the jail's public lobby,[9] with the goal of making naloxone broadly available to friends, loved ones, and family members of people being released from the correctional system.

OVERDOSE DETECTION

A second (related) point is that naloxone is effective only when an overdose is witnessed by a bystander who can identify opioid overdose symptoms and administer the medication in a timely manner. A corollary to this fact is that the population-level impact of naloxone on reducing opioid overdose mortality rates is dependent on the proportion of overdoses that are witnessed. Therefore, public health approaches to increase the effectiveness of naloxone should consider combining these strategies with interventions designed to increase the proportion of overdoses that are witnessed. Some promising approaches in this domain include overdose detection technologies, toll-free overdose prevention hotlines (e.g., Never Use Alone), overdose prevention centers, and public health campaigns encouraging people to use drugs with others around.

Our research team has demonstrated that combination strategies are likely synergistic; that is, interventions to reduce solitary drug use increase the population-level impact of further scaling naloxone access, particularly in communities with historically high rates of naloxone distribution.[10] As jurisdictions across the country make decisions about how best to spend newly available resources provided through opioid settlements, combination approaches that explicitly pair naloxone distribution with strategies to reduce solitary drug use should be prioritized.

EFFECTS OF STRUCTURAL RACISM

Third, and finally, addressing the downstream effects of structural racism in the criminal justice, health care, and behavioral health delivery systems will be paramount to ensuring equitable access to naloxone across racial/ethnic groups. Our research team and others have shown that naloxone distribution in communities of color often lags behind dissemination in predominantly White neighborhoods[11] and has not kept up with the substantial need, particularly in light of rapidly increasing overdose rates among Black, Hispanic/Latino, and Indigenous people who use drugs.[12] Racial equity should be a core principle of any naloxone distribution strategy, including full, meaningful engagement from the communities of color most heavily affected by structural racism and the nation's overdose crisis.

Although these and other challenges are considerable, they should not prevent policymakers and public health leaders from working toward the "North Star" of naloxone distribution: the medication should be readily available whenever and wherever an overdose occurs. However, much like helmets, seat belts, and automated external defibrillators, naloxone is ultimately a lifesaving intervention of last resort. We must also work toward a world in which naloxone is rarely needed in the first place, one where the drug supply is safe, overdoses are uncommon, and people who use drugs are free from criminalization, stigma, and discrimination. AJPH

CORRESPONDENCE

Correspondence should be sent to Brandon D. L. Marshall, PhD, 121 South Main St, Box G-S-121-2, Providence, RI 02912 (e-mail: brandon_marshall@brown.edu). Reprints can be ordered at https://www.ajph.org by clicking the "Reprints" link.

PUBLICATION INFORMATION

Full Citation: Marshall BDL. Strategies to increase the population-level impact of naloxone distribution in communities highly affected by the overdose crisis. *Am J Public Health*. 2025;115(1):9–11.

Acceptance Date: September 27, 2024.

DOI: https://doi.org/10.2105/AJPH.2024.307887

ORCID iD:

Brandon D. L. Marshall https://orcid.org/0000-0002-0134-7052

ACKNOWLEDGMENTS

I express gratitude to the PROFOUND research team for many years of productive collaboration.

CONFLICTS OF INTEREST

The author has no conflicts of interest to report.

REFERENCES

1. Walley AY, Xuan Z, Hackman HH, et al. Opioid overdose rates and implementation of overdose education and nasal naloxone distribution in Massachusetts: interrupted time series analysis. *BMJ*. 2013;346(5):f174. https://doi.org/10.1136/bmj.f174

2. Centers for Disease Control and Prevention. US overdose deaths decrease in 2023, first time since 2018. Available at: https://www.cdc.gov/nchs/pressroom/nchs_press_releases/2024/20240515.htm. Accessed September 16, 2024.
3. US Department of Health and Human Services. Harm reduction. Available at: https://www.hhs.gov/overdose-prevention/harm-reduction. Accessed July 24, 2024.
4. Irvine MA, Oller D, Boggis J, et al. Estimating naloxone need in the USA across fentanyl, heroin, and prescription opioid epidemics: a modelling study. *Lancet Public Health.* 2022;7(3):e210–e218. https://doi.org/10.1016/S2468-2667(21)00304-2
5. Morgan JR, Freibott CE, Jalali A, et al. The role of increasing pharmacy and community distributed naloxone in the opioid overdose epidemic in Massachusetts, Rhode Island, and New York City. *Drug Alcohol Depend Rep.* 2022;4:100083. https://doi.org/10.1016/j.dadr.2022.100083
6. Zang X, Bessey SE, Krieger MS, et al. Comparing projected fatal overdose outcomes and costs of strategies to expand community-based distribution of naloxone in Rhode Island. *JAMA Netw Open.* 2022;5(11):e2241174. https://doi.org/10.1001/jamanetworkopen.2022.41174
7. Linas BP, Savinkina A, Madushani RWMA, et al. Projected estimates of opioid mortality after community-level interventions. *JAMA Netw Open.* 2021;4(2):e2037259. https://doi.org/10.1001/jamanetworkopen.2020.37259
8. HEALing Communities Study Consortium. Community-based cluster-randomized trial to reduce opioid overdose deaths. *N Engl J Med.* 2024;391(11):989–1001. https://doi.org/10.1056/NEJMoa2401177
9. Corrections1. Washington sheriff's office installs naloxone vending machine in jail lobby. Available at: https://www.corrections1.com/drug-issues/wash-sheriffs-office-installs-naloxone-vending-machine-in-jail-lobby. Accessed September 16, 2024.
10. Zang X, Skinner A, Krieger MS, et al. Evaluation of strategies to enhance community-based naloxone distribution supported by an opioid settlement. *JAMA Netw Open.* 2024;7(5):e2413861. https://doi.org/10.1001/jamanetworkopen.2024.13861
11. Nolen S, Zang X, Chatterjee A, et al. Evaluating equity in community-based naloxone access among racial/ethnic groups in Massachusetts. *Drug Alcohol Depend.* 2022;241:109668. https://doi.org/10.1016/j.drugalcdep.2022.109668
12. Jones A, Santos-Lozada A, Perez-Brumer A, Latkin C, Shoptaw S, El-Bassel N. Age-specific disparities in fatal drug overdoses highest among older black adults and American Indian/Alaska native individuals of all ages in the United States, 2015–2020. *Int J Drug Policy.* 2023;114:103977. https://doi.org/10.1016/j.drugpo.2023.103977

Moving Targets: The Dynamic Nature and Imperfect Measurement of Social Constructs

Randall L. Sell, ScD

ABOUT THE AUTHOR

Randall L. Sell is with the Dornsife School of Public Health, Drexel University, Philadelphia, PA.

The research by Kahn et al. in the December 2024 issue of *AJPH* highlights a fundamental truth in survey research that extends beyond their investigation of sexual orientation measurement to all of measurement, and in particular demography: when questions delve into self-perception (e.g., "How do you think about yourself?"), response options must accurately mirror how people perceive themselves.[1] This ensures that data reflect reality, not researcher assumptions or unproven theories. Moreover, the purpose of collecting such data should extend beyond mere statistics: it must be able to guide public health strategies and interventions. These considerations need to be at the forefront when creating and selecting measures, not just in the case of sexual orientation but for all demographic measures. Furthermore, it is essential to recognize that most of these constructs are not static but moving targets that evolve over time.

In a 2001 article in this Journal, I argued that the lack of scientific information on the health of lesbian, gay, and bisexual Americans posed a significant threat to their well-being and hindered progress in civil rights and health care access.[2] That and a later article advocated sexual orientation data collection and outlined a plan to address methodological challenges in this area, similar to those explored by Kahn et al. in their current research.[3]

Kahn et al. inform some key aspects of developing and selecting appropriate sexual orientation measures for health surveys. Their study focuses on two common survey questions, one from the National Health Interview Survey (NHIS) and the other from the National Longitudinal Study of Adolescent to Adult Health (Add Health), both ostensibly aiming to assess sexual orientation. Despite their shared goal, these questions differ in their prompts and, more significantly, in their response options—a distinction that has major implications. The variations in wording and response choices influence how individuals interpret the questions and ultimately how they self-identify.[4] As a result, as Kahn et al. show, the two questions effectively capture different, although overlapping, segments of the sexual minority population, each with its own distinct patterns of mental health outcomes. This highlights the challenge of accurately measuring and labeling sexual orientation, even when operating under the same broad conceptual umbrella. The findings of Kahn et al., however, do not clearly indicate which of these measures would be more effective for addressing the mental health of sexual minorities.

Both the NHIS and the Add Health "sexual orientation" questions ask the respondent to consider "how you think about/of yourself." Neither question explicitly indicates that it is assessing sexual orientation, and it is from the response categories that a respondent can deduce that they are being asked about their sexuality (as many other demographic variables are measured). The response categories from the NHIS question were selected after engaging with the public to determine how people thought about their sexual orientation and the language they used to describe their sexual orientation identities to researchers.[5] This is why the NHIS question includes discrete categories to choose from, one of which is "straight, that is, not gay, lesbian, or bisexual." This response option was created after it was determined that many people in the general population identified not as "heterosexual" or "straight" but rather as "not gay." The response options to the NHIS sexual orientation question were created to reflect the reality of people's experiences and were further tested before fielding.[5]

It is plausible that the NHIS question, with its clear-cut categories based on research showing that people perceive sexual orientations as distinct categories, is easier for respondents to answer than the Add Health question's bipolar continuum ranging from "100% heterosexual (straight)" to "100% homosexual (gay)," which has not been shown to reflect sexual orientation self-perceptions. That is, the Add Health continuum may not accurately reflect

AJPH January 2025, Vol. 115, No. 1

how people conceptualize their sexuality, whereas the NHIS question does. Previous attempts to measure sexual orientation on an Add Health–like continuum, although grounded in influential work such as Alfred Kinsey's and Sandra Bem's, have sometimes included a struggle to capture the lived experiences of diverse populations.[6] This highlights the crucial need for future measures to prioritize reflecting how individuals understand and express their sexuality. Researchers must also consider cultural factors, potential social desirability bias, and the dynamic nature of self-identity when designing sexual orientation questions.

When choosing a sexual orientation measure, it is also vital to consider how it fits with the research goals and potential applications of the data. For instance, if the NHIS data reveal mental health concerns among gay and bisexual men, an intervention could specifically target this group with materials titled "Are You a Gay or Bisexual Man?" By contrast, using Add Health data, a similar intervention might need a title like "Are You Anything but 100% Heterosexual?" to reflect the measure's response options.

Furthermore, although the Add Health measure's continuum of categories identifies a larger sexual minority population, this alone does not make it the better choice. The debate over ideal sexual orientation measures and their impact on population estimates has existed since Kinsey's pioneering work.[7] Importantly, Kinsey's approach involved assigning individuals to categories on his scale based on extensive interviews, not self-identification.[8] It was not until the 1980s that the first and only population-based study that entire decade allowed subjects to self-report their sexual orientation.[9]

It is important to critically examine the sexual orientation measures commonly used today (as we should with all other demographic variables), and it is acceptable to acknowledge their inherent limitations. No instrument can perfectly capture the full complexity of these constructs, nor can any measure remain static in the face of evolving social understandings. Race and ethnicity serve as prime examples of this fluidity.[10] The US census, for example, has evolved significantly in its race data collection over the centuries, moving from a few broad categories to more nuanced ones reflecting changing demographics and social views. This evolution of measures, often influenced by political and social climate, has rarely remained static from any census to the subsequent one and the census now includes the option of multiracial identification. Therefore, instead of striving for an unattainable perfect measure, we should focus on evaluating the "utility" of existing measures at a point in time, recognizing that each may capture different aspects of the construct and offer unique insights to inform public health practice.

This utility or pragmatic approach to sexual orientation measurement allows us to live with measurement imperfections and limitations. Kahn et al. demonstrate this by highlighting how the two different measures investigated capture distinct aspects of sexual orientation. Although both the Add Health and the NHIS questions are framed as measuring sexual orientation, they tap into different underlying constructs. The Add Health question, with its nuanced response options, identifies a broader range of individuals who might consider themselves among sexual minorities, whereas the NHIS question has more limited categories. This discrepancy can lead to underestimation of health disparities among sexual minorities when using the NHIS question, but it might also offer a more precise identification of specific subgroups (e.g., those identifying as gay, lesbian, or bisexual) for targeted interventions, as previously mentioned.

In conclusion, the quest for perfect measures, of which sexual orientation is just one example, remains an ongoing endeavor. We must acknowledge the inherent limitations of measures while recognizing their potential utility in shaping public health initiatives. A robust ongoing research process—such as has been used to study race and ethnicity data collection—employing mixed methods in which qualitative and quantitative data continuously inform each other offers the most promising path forward. The dynamic nature of social constructs necessitates that our measurement tools evolve alongside them. By embracing this fluidity and documenting the utility of imperfect measures, we can continuously improve data collection practices while simultaneously addressing the health needs of all individuals irrespective of their sexual orientation. AJPH

CORRESPONDENCE

Correspondence should be sent to Randall L. Sell, ScD, Dornsife School of Public Health, Drexel University, 3215 Market St, Room 414, Philadelphia, PA 19104 (e-mail: Randy@Drexel.edu). Reprints can be ordered at https://www.ajph.org by clicking the "Reprints" link.

PUBLICATION INFORMATION

Full Citation: Sell RL. Moving targets: the dynamic nature and imperfect measurement of social constructs. *Am J Public Health*. 2025;115(1):12–14.

Acceptance Date: October 9, 2024.

DOI: https://doi.org/10.2105/AJPH.2024.307901

ORCID iD:

Randall L. Sell https://orcid.org/0009-0008-3377-0155

CONFLICTS OF INTEREST

The author has no conflicts of interest to declare.

REFERENCES

1. Kahn NF, Halpern CT, Burshell DR, Hernandez SM, Conron KJ. Assessment of health disparities and sexual orientation response choices used in two US national population-based health surveys, 2020–2021. *Am J Public Health*. 2024;114(12):1375–1383. https://doi.org/10.2105/AJPH.2024.307839
2. Sell RL, Becker JB. Sexual orientation data collection and progress toward Healthy People 2010. *Am J Public Health*. 2001;91(6):876–882. https://doi.org/10.2105/AJPH.91.6.876
3. Sell RL. Challenges and solutions to collecting sexual orientation and gender identity data. *Am J Public Health*. 2017;107(8):1212–1214. https://doi.org/10.2105/AJPH.2017.303917
4. Miller K, Willson S, Chepp V, Padilla JL, eds. *Cognitive Interviewing Methodology*. Hoboken, NJ: Wiley; 2014. https://doi.org/10.1002/9781118838860
5. Miller K, Ryan JM. Design, development and testing of the NHIS sexual identity question. Available at: https://wwwn.cdc.gov/qbank/report/Miller_NCHS_2011_NHIS%20Sexual%20Identity.pdf. Accessed October 18, 2024.
6. Sell RL. The Sell assessment of sexual orientation: background and scoring. *J Gay Lesbian Bisex Identity*. 1996;1(4):295–310. https://doi.org/10.1007/BF03372244
7. Sell RL. Defining and measuring sexual orientation for research. In: Meyer IH, Northridge ME, eds. *The Health of Sexual Minorities: Public Health Perspectives on Lesbian, Gay, Bisexual and Transgender Populations*. New York, NY: Springer; 2007:355–374. https://doi.org/10.1007/978-0-387-31334-4_14
8. Kinsey AC, Pomeroy WR, Martin CE. Sexual behavior in the human male. *Am J Public Health*. 2003;93(6):894–898. https://doi.org/10.2105/AJPH.93.6.894
9. Sell RL, Wells JA, Wypij D. The prevalence of homosexual behavior and attraction in the United States, the United Kingdom and France: results of national population-based samples. *Arch Sex Behav*. 1995;24(3):235–248. https://doi.org/10.1007/BF01541598
10. Bulmer M. Measuring race and ethnicity. In: Bulmer M, Gibbs J, Hyman L, eds. *Social Measurement Through Social Surveys*. London, UK: Routledge; 2016:109–126. https://doi.org/10.4324/9781315609492

Planning and Accommodating the Micromobility Revolution and Its Impact on Public Health

D. Alex Quistberg, PhD, MPH, and Daniel A. Rodriguez, PhD

ABOUT THE AUTHORS

D. Alex Quistberg is with the Urban Health Collaborative, Drexel University School of Public Health, Philadelphia, PA. Daniel A. Rodriguez is with the Institute of Transportation Studies, University of California, Berkeley.

Micromobility has grown immensely over the past decade, encompassing both public shared systems and private ownership, and, as Burford et al. have found, a surge in user injuries and deaths has accompanied the growth.[1] Micromobility refers to the use of small vehicles, such as bicycles and scooters, that are either human powered or electric.[2] These vehicles are ideal for short trips—although electric-powered micromobility has expanded the potential distance range.

BENEFITS AND CHALLENGES

Micromobility appeals to users—whether they are using a privately owned vehicle or one from a sharing system—because it increases their physical activity, promotes sustainability, replaces car trips, and provides a convenient first- and last-mile connection to public transportation.

Cities have expanded the ecosystem of available mobility options, leading to rapid growth in micromobility modes. Despite the benefits from this expansion, local and state governments have not made adequate investments to support these modes, leading to major disparities among neighborhoods and racial and ethnic groups in the risks faced while using micromobility.

Considering micromobility's current and predicted future growth, it is urgent for cities and states to ensure the safety of micromobility users and nonusers (e.g., pedestrians). Injuries and deaths related to micromobility have substantial impacts on health care delivery and costs, including millions of dollars annually in direct costs to private and government insurance. Switching to micromobility can help households save on car payments, insurance, maintenance, and fuel, while also reducing costs for local, state, and federal governments on building and maintaining transportation infrastructure.

States and cities should consider where, when, and how many people are riding these transportation modes to better accommodate and promote their usage. Unfortunately, most cities lack adequate infrastructure to support micromobility growth. Many states and cities have either required micromobility modes to share bicycle infrastructure or encouraged their use on sidewalks.[3] Most bicyclists and e-bicyclists use existing bicycle infrastructure, such as separated bicycle lanes, although they may resort to using sidewalks when there is no bicycle infrastructure, especially on higher volume, higher speed roads.[4,5] Those riding e-scooters, hoverboards, and other micromobility vehicles use a mix of sidewalks and bicycle infrastructure; this is not ideal, considering the growth of micromobility and the speed differential between pedestrians, bicycles, e-bicycles, and e-scooters.

Despite the growth in both bicycling and other micromobility modes since the start of the COVID-19 pandemic, most cities and states have not kept up with micromobility demand. City transportation infrastructure is mostly dedicated to motor vehicle travel and parking, which does nothing to decrease collision risks for vulnerable road users such as pedestrians and bicyclists[6] and discourages alternative transportation modes.[7]

SAFETY AND INFRASTRUCTURE NEEDS

To accommodate the growth of micromobility and encourage its safe use, dedicated travel and storage spaces are needed. The single-file cycling lanes in most cities may put micromobility users at risk on higher volume and higher speed roadways when trying to pass or avoid obstacles.[8] Widening bicycle lanes or increasing the separation between bicycle lanes and motor vehicle traffic lanes may help decrease micromobility user conflicts and reduce their need to enter motor vehicle traffic.[9]

Cities and states should also significantly expand micromobility infrastructure by adding bicycle lanes to arterial and collector roads. Also important is improving the quality of the lanes, including ensuring smooth surfaces in areas with high micromobility use, as many of these vehicles have small wheels. Protecting lanes and intersections can help prevent motor vehicles from using these spaces for driving, parking, or turning, reducing potential conflicts. Additionally, intersection and roadway designs should prioritize the safety of pedestrians and micromobility users over motor vehicle speed and efficiency because these users face the highest injury risks. Traffic-calming measures on multimodal roads can further help reduce these risks.

More aggressive policies can also make a difference, such as limiting motor vehicle access (e.g., in low or no emissions zones) and increasing the price drivers pay for parking where walking, transit, and micromobility use is high. Reducing motor vehicle use in urban areas, where micromobility use is typically most frequent and dense, can help reduce the injuries related to micromobility and other road users observed by Burford et al.[1] Finally, the safety of micromobility vehicles probably needs to be better regulated, considering incidents related to battery fires and other device failures.

PROTECTIVE GEAR AND PERSONAL SAFETY BEHAVIORS

Falls and collisions with other users, pedestrians, and stationary objects are also common causes of injury. Improving the coverage and quality of dedicated infrastructure is a priority for cities to reduce and prevent micromobility user injuries and deaths, followed by increasing personal safety behaviors. Helmets are effective at preventing head injuries among bicyclists depending on the type of collision, and specialized helmets are available for motorized micromobility users to offer protection at higher impact speeds.[10] The limited research on helmet efficacy suggests it can protect e-scooter users during falls, which are a common cause of injury in this group.[11]

Some localities have laws that require helmets, but these laws have not always proven effective at increasing helmet use or reducing head injuries among micromobility users. This may be because of poor, selective, or inequitable enforcement. To address this, additional public health strategies are needed to promote helmet use, such as incentivizing it through workplaces, schools, health care facilities, and community events or including helmets with every micromobility-sharing service or commercial sale.[3]

Government research agencies and other organizations could incentivize the development of innovative helmet designs and protective gear that better aligns with user preferences and needs via grants, challenges, commercial initiatives, or other opportunities. Similar support, including the development of automated lighting solutions, could encourage micromobility users to adopt reflective and lighting gear.

Findings by Burford et al. suggest that drug and alcohol use by micromobility users, particularly among e-scooter users, is a risk factor for injuries and accounts for nearly 10% of injuries.[1] Additionally, according to 2022 National Highway Traffic Safety Administration data, 20% of the pedalcyclists in fatal collisions were riding under the influence of alcohol, with blood alcohol levels greater than 0.08 grams per deciliter. Awareness campaigns about the risks of riding under the influence of drugs or alcohol hold promise for shifting risk perception, especially when paired with programs that encourage safer alternatives when intoxicated, such as taking taxis or public transportation. Limited enforcement, if focused on areas and times of alcohol consumption, may be a consideration, but there has been little evaluation of such programs for micromobility and they may result in unequal application, as seen with similar policies.[10]

One other safety behavior to consider is the travel speed of micromobility users, including in shared spaces with slower modes, such as walking. Most shared micromobility modes have a maximum set speed, as do many privately owned vehicles, but they can be modified to allow faster speeds. Many states have a speed limit for micromobility, including for travel on sidewalks, if allowed, but they are inconsistent, and their enforcement likely is as well.[3] Addressing speeding in a consistent, equitable way for these modes may be challenging because they are not registered and do not carry license plates, and automated speed enforcement is unlikely. Providing ample travel spaces for micromobility would probably better address this problem and reduce sidewalk usage.

DATA COLLECTION AND POLICY SUPPORT

It is impossible to address many of the safety issues surrounding micromobility without adequate data about the users (e.g., age, gender, race/ethnicity), user density and frequency, where they ride, and comprehensive collision data, as Burford et al. note.[1] Regular, consistent measurement of use would help researchers, advocates, and policymakers make better decisions about how to more fully integrate these modes into the mobility offerings of cities. Federal and state incentives to collect these data, as with motor vehicle traffic volumes and transit passenger data, would help increase our understanding of these modes. Additionally, public health data collection needs improvements to capture specific micromobility modes to better link modes to injuries and outcomes. If we cannot reliably track trends in use, understanding the context in which injuries are occurring will make reducing and preventing those injuries very challenging.

Micromobility provides valuable opportunities to make transportation more sustainable, healthy, cost effective, and equitable by replacing automobile trips and complementing other modes, such as public transportation and walking.[12,13] Implementing supportive infrastructure and promoting safe behaviors among motorists and micromobility users can help prevent injuries and deaths. City, state, and federal officials can enable many of these changes via policies and directing funding to these activities. AJPH

CORRESPONDENCE

Correspondence should be sent to D. Alex Quistberg, Associate Research Professor, Drexel University School of Public Health, Urban Health Collaborative, 3600 Market St, 7th Floor, Office 717C, Philadelphia, PA 19104 (e-mail: daq26@drexel.edu). Reprints can be ordered at https://www.ajph.org by clicking the "Reprints" link.

PUBLICATION INFORMATION

Full Citation: Quistberg DA, Rodriguez DA. Planning and accommodating the micromobility revolution and its impact on public health. *Am J Public Health*. 2025;115(1):15–17.

Acceptance Date: October 28, 2024.

DOI: https://doi.org/10.2105/AJPH.2024.307909

ORCID iDs:

D. Alex Quistberg https://orcid.org/0000-0001-9730-2686

Daniel A. Rodriguez https://orcid.org/0000-0001-6550-5518

CONTRIBUTORS

D. A. Quistberg drafted the initial version of the editorial. The authors contributed equally to conceptualizing, revising, and approving the editorial.

ACKNOWLEDGMENTS

D. A. Quistberg was supported by the Fogarty International Center, National Institutes of Health (NIH; award K01TW011782).

Note. The content of this editorial is solely the responsibility of the authors and does not necessarily represent the official views of the NIH.

CONFLICTS OF INTEREST

The authors have no conflicts of interest to declare.

REFERENCES

1. Burford KG, Itzkowitz NG, Rundle AG, DiMaggio C, Mooney SJ. The burden of injuries associated with e-bikes, powered scooters, hoverboards, and bicycles in the United States: 2019–2022. *Am J Public Health*. 2024;114(12):1365–1374. https://doi.org/10.2105/AJPH.2024.307820
2. Price J, Blackshear D, Blount W Jr, Sandt L. Micromobility: a travel mode innovation. *Public Roads Magazine*. 2021;85(1):8–12. Available at: https://highways.dot.gov/public-roads/spring-2021/02. Accessed November 1, 2024.
3. Fluid Freeride. Complete US electric scooters laws guide 2024. Available at: https://fluidfreeride.com/blogs/news/electric-scooter-laws. Accessed August 23, 2024.
4. Lanza K, Burford K, Ganzar LA. Who travels where: behavior of pedestrians and micromobility users on transportation infrastructure. *J Transp Geogr*. 2022;98:103269. https://doi.org/10.1016/j.jtrangeo.2021.103269
5. Zuniga-Garcia N, Ruiz Juri N, Perrine KA, Machemehl RB. E-scooters in urban infrastructure: understanding sidewalk, bike lane, and roadway usage from trajectory data. *Case Stud Transp Policy*. 2021;9(3):983–994. https://doi.org/10.1016/j.cstp.2021.04.004
6. Thompson J, Stevenson M, Wijnands JS, et al. A global analysis of urban design types and road transport injury: an image processing study. *Lancet Planet Health*. 2020;4(1):e32–e42. https://doi.org/10.1016/S2542-5196(19)30263-3
7. Lee K, Sener IN. E-bikes toward inclusive mobility: a literature review of perceptions, concerns, and barriers. *TRIP*. 2023;22:100940. https://doi.org/10.1016/j.trip.2023.100940
8. Schepers P, Theuwissen E, Nuñez Velasco P, et al. The relationship between cycle track width and the lateral position of cyclists, and implications for the required cycle track width. *J Safety Res*. 2023;87:38–53. https://doi.org/10.1016/j.jsr.2023.07.011
9. National Association of City Transportation Officials. Urban bikeway design guide, 3rd ed. 2024. Available at: https://nacto.org/program/cities-for-cycling/#:~:text=In-,2010,-%2C%20cities%20banded. Accessed September 7, 2024.
10. Jackson S, Retting R, Miller S. Impact analysis of bicycle safety laws. August 1, 2021. Available at: https://rosap.ntl.bts.gov/view/dot/57149. Accessed November 1, 2024.
11. Wei W, Petit Y, Arnoux P-J, Bailly N. Head-ground impact conditions and helmet performance in e-scooter falls. *Accid Anal Prev*. 2023;181:106935. https://doi.org/10.1016/j.aap.2022.106935
12. Guo Y, Zhang Y. Understanding factors influencing shared e-scooter usage and its impact on auto mode substitution. *Transp Res Part D Transp Environ*. 2021;99:102991. https://doi.org/10.1016/j.trd.2021.102991
13. Abduljabbar RL, Liyanage S, Dia H. The role of micro-mobility in shaping sustainable cities: a systematic literature review. *Transp Res Part D Transp Environ*. 2021;92:102734. https://doi.org/10.1016/j.trd.2021.102734

Recommitting to Housing and Health Care Justice After *City of Grants Pass v Johnson*

Anand R. Habib, MD, MPhil, Sarah A. Stella, MD, Elizabeth K. Farkouh, BS, Caleb M. Grenko, BS, Dionne Hart, MD, and Amirala S. Pasha, DO, JD

ABOUT THE AUTHORS

Anand R. Habib is with the Section of General Internal Medicine, Yale School of Medicine, New Haven, CT. Sarah A. Stella is with the Division of Hospital Medicine, University of Colorado School of Medicine, Aurora. Elizabeth K. Farkouh and Caleb M. Grenko are with the Alix School of Medicine, Dionne Hart is with Department of Psychiatry and Psychology, and Amirala S. Pasha is with Division of General Internal Medicine, Mayo Clinic, Rochester, MN.

In 2023, on any given night, more than 653 000 individuals in the United States were unhoused, defined as being unsheltered, residing in shelters and temporary housing, at imminent risk of housing loss, or fleeing interpersonal violence.[1,2] This figure includes individuals from households with and without children. Houselessness disproportionately affects racially and ethnically minoritized groups, gender minorities, veterans, disabled persons, and those with severe mental illness and substance use disorders.[1,3] Approximately 37% of people experiencing houselessness (PEH) identify as Black, although this demographic constitutes only 13% of the overall US population.[1] Throughout this editorial, we use the person-first term "houseless" rather than "homeless" to lessen the stigma that "homeless" can evoke, and to distinguish between a house (i.e., a physical structure purpose-built for safe, stable human habitation) and a home, which can encompass social connection and rootedness to a geography that goes beyond shelter.

Affordable, quality housing and health care are basic human needs and human rights. However, the bidirectional relationship between houselessness and health outcomes colludes to produce a persistent gap of up to 30 years in life expectancy between unhoused and housed individuals.[4] With a shortage in affordable housing and more than 42 million households burdened by rising rents and mortgage payments, the number of individuals falling into this life expectancy chasm will grow.[5]

Although the proximate causes of houselessness are numerous and unique to each individual's circumstances, structural factors such as inadequate affordable housing, wealth inequality, historical redlining, and exclusionary zoning distally and synergistically drive houselessness.[6] Consequently, clinicians and health care systems cannot address houselessness on their own. Reducing the number of PEH will ultimately require significant investments to increase the supply of affordable housing, in tandem with prevention strategies. Still, we believe that clinicians and health care systems have an important role in addressing the harms associated with houselessness and advocating for dignity-driven solutions. In this editorial, considering the recent US Supreme Court decision in *City of Grants Pass v Johnson*,[7] we argue that the criminalization of houselessness adds insult to the indignity that PEH encounter and worsens preexisting health inequities associated with houselessness. We discuss the strong link between houselessness and poor health outcomes; the legal aspects of criminalizing houselessness; the need for clinicians and health care systems to partner in identifying houseless individuals and connecting them to available permanent supportive housing through relationships with community-based organizations; and innovative strategies, including Housing First approaches.

CONNECTION BETWEEN HEALTH AND HOUSING

Evidence consistently demonstrates that PEH suffer from worse physical and mental health outcomes, even compared with low-income populations who are housed.[8] Consequently, when demographic and geographic differences are accounted for, PEH have mortality rates eight to 16 times greater than standardized mortality rates in the general population.[4]

Psychiatric conditions particularly afflict PEH.[3] Sixty-nine percent endorse having psychiatric symptoms such as anxiety and depression, and 27% report requiring psychiatric hospitalization.[3] Likewise, high-risk alcohol use and other substance use are highly prevalent among PEH, with lifetime prevalence estimates of 62% and 65%, respectively.[3] In addition to experiencing high rates of psychological distress,

AJPH January 2025, Vol. 115, No. 1

PEH also suffer from increased cognitive impairment, complicating their ability to traverse a labyrinthine and patchy social service safety net.[9]

Unhoused individuals also suffer from earlier onset and a higher burden of chronic physical health disorders, including, but not limited to, chronic obstructive pulmonary disease; liver disease, including hepatitis; cardiovascular disease; infectious diseases, including tuberculosis and HIV; unintentional weight loss; and debility, including paralysis.[10] Experiencing houselessness also increases the risk of traumatic events such as physical and sexual assault.[3] A high risk of exposure to adverse environmental conditions and a high risk of victimization exacerbate the health issues of PEH.

Beyond the devastating personal consequences, these conditions, coupled with structural barriers to accessing high-quality health care, all contribute to a significant burden on an already fragmented health care system, leading to hopelessness, distrust, self-treatment, and overuse of emergency services. Annually, two thirds of unhoused individuals will visit the emergency department and one third will be hospitalized—rates three to four times higher than those of the average American.[11] Collectively, total annual Medicaid spending is approximately $11 200, or 2.5 times greater per capita for PEH compared with those with stable housing.[12]

LEGAL ASPECTS OF CRIMINALIZING HOUSELESSNESS

In response to the national rise in unsheltered houselessness, various US jurisdictions have passed vagrancy laws to mask signs of houselessness by removing houseless individuals from public areas. These laws typically criminalize life-sustaining activities such as asking for help, sleeping outdoors or in a vehicle, or sheltering in public places. Between 2006 and 2019, city-wide camping bans approximately doubled while bans on living in vehicles increased by 213%.[13] In 2019, the National Law Center on Homelessness and Poverty found that 187 urban and rural cities nationwide had laws against houselessness with varying degrees of punitiveness.[13]

Consistent with these trends, Grants Pass, Oregon, where the number of PEH outnumbered the total number of shelter beds, passed a law in 2019 banning unhoused individuals from using any material for bedding purposes to maintain a temporary place to live on public property within the city limits, effectively banning the presence of houseless individuals. Plaintiffs objected to this law on constitutional grounds in *City of Grants Pass v Johnson*.[7] Although litigants chose this particular law to challenge the constitutionality of criminalizing houselessness, Grants Pass's law is neither novel nor unique.

The question the Supreme Court faced in *Grants Pass* was whether the inherent cruelty of the enforcement of generally applicable laws criminalizing sheltering on public property constitutes "cruel and unusual punishment," which is prohibited by the Eighth Amendment. Previously, in *Robinson v California*, which involved a law criminalizing addiction, the Supreme Court held that laws criminalizing a "status" (e.g., addiction) rather than a "conduct" (e.g., drug use) violated the Eighth Amendment.[7] Therefore, in *Grants Pass*, since the criminalized conduct involved activities necessary to sustain life, especially in localities that lacked sufficient publicly available shelter beds, the pivotal question was whether the challenged law criminalized the mere status of being houseless or the conduct of houseless individuals.

In *Grants Pass*, in a majority opinion authored by Justice Gorsuch, the Court ruled along ideological lines in a 6–3 decision that enforcing generally applicable laws regulating camping on public property does not violate the Eighth Amendment's prohibition on cruel and unusual punishment.[7] Moreover, the Court found that the Eighth Amendment's ban is typically limited to the method or kind of punishment rather than what conduct could be punished in the first instance. Effectively, the majority concluded that so long as the statute criminalizes a "conduct" and not a "mere status," regardless of how involuntary or essential that conduct may be to sustaining life, as camping may be for PEH, it does not run afoul of the Eighth Amendment, leaving Grants Pass's law intact.

Notwithstanding the Court's opinion, the misguided practice of criminalizing houselessness is the most expensive and least effective solution to houselessness, turning a public health concern into a policing matter. In 2015, for example, the city of Los Angeles spent $87 million on law enforcement related to houselessness and only $13 million on housing for PEH.[13] Criminalizing houselessness worsens preexisting inequities in health outcomes and the criminal justice system while costing taxpayers significant sums to incarcerate PEH, leading to further suffering without addressing the underlying causes of houselessness.[13] Furthermore, by creating an environment hostile to PEH, communities enacting vagrancy laws unfairly place the financial burden of supporting PEH on neighboring communities to which PEH may move to avoid penalties.

NEW REQUIREMENTS TO SCREEN FOR HOUSING INSECURITY

Because legal structures fail to protect PEH and systematically exacerbate this public health crisis, and given unhoused individuals' frequent contact with the health care system, clinicians and health care systems can play an essential role in screening to identify individuals with housing needs.

Although rates of screening patients for housing insecurity and referral to community-based housing support services have been suboptimal, advancements are being made. In 2023, the Centers for Medicare and Medicaid Services (CMS) and The Joint Commission implemented new reporting requirements around health-related social needs screening.[14,15] These requirements acknowledge the limited effect that increased spending on direct medical care has had on addressing health outcomes disparities and are consistent with attempts to incentivize health care systems to accept accountability for population-level health care costs and outcomes.

Existing studies of the effectiveness of systematic and comprehensive health-related social needs screening are heterogeneous in quality and report mostly on process measures rather than on health care utilization, costs, or clinical outcomes. Nevertheless, they suggest that patients are receptive to screening, that clinicians believe health-related social needs screening should be the standard of care, that rates of unmet health-related social needs are high (in many cases > 50%), and that screening and referral improve patients' access to community-based resources.[16–18]

Although changing the requirements of the CMS and The Joint Commission may help to realign operational priorities currently focused on throughput and clinical volume to those focused on whole-person care, extant studies highlight the challenges of effectively addressing unmet health-related social needs. Clinicians underline the need for more time, improved training on how to efficiently screen and effectively refer, and the inadequacy of the existing social safety net. In turn, patients emphasize the importance of stigma-free screening, privacy, care coordination, and follow-up.[17]

Screening and referral are necessary, but insufficient. For screening efforts to be truly impactful, they must be paired with meaningful connection to evidence-based interventions to address houselessness through partnerships with community-based organizations. There must also be sustained, communitywide investment in community-based organizations' capacity to manage increased referrals and concomitant governmental policies and financing to increase affordable, transitional, and long-term housing supply so that referrals lead to reductions in the number of PEH. Without this, screening efforts may simply serve to check another box, burn already fragile trust with PEH, and contribute to further hopelessness in systems.

HOUSING FIRST POLICIES

Beyond screening and referral, as a society, we must continue to invest in evidence-based approaches to reduce houselessness. The relationship between health and houselessness is complex, as health conditions can act as both a risk factor for and a consequence of houselessness. However, evidence from studies examining housing interventions further supports the notion that addressing houselessness can improve health outcomes. For example, an examination of inclusionary zoning policies, which promote affordable housing, found that communities with such policies had improved cardiovascular outcomes, including reduced blood pressure and cholesterol levels.[19]

Previous research has also shown that permanent supportive housing—delivered through a Housing First approach, in which people can access housing without prerequisites and receive low-barrier wraparound supportive services—is a proven, long-term solution to chronic houselessness.[20] The Housing First model was developed in the 1990s as an alternative to the Treatment First approach, which instead required that people engage in substance use or behavioral health treatment to be eligible for housing.[20] In the decades since its introduction, Housing First has consistently been shown to expedite exits from houselessness and to increase housing stability among PEH, including those with serious mental illness, those with chronic disabling medical conditions such as HIV/AIDS, and those who frequently interact with the criminal justice system and utilize other high-cost services.[20,21] Thus, Housing First is now the gold standard and preferred approach for reducing houselessness in the United States.[20]

Denver, Colorado's Supportive Housing Social Impact Bond Initiative, implemented in 2016, provided supportive housing via a Housing First approach to PEH who had frequent interactions with the criminal justice system (i.e., had eight or more arrests over three consecutive years prior to enrollment, primarily for nonviolent offenses associated with houselessness).[21] An evaluation of the program's impact on housing stability and criminal justice involvement found high rates of housing stability, with 77% of individuals referred to housing remaining housed at three years.[21] Compared with those who received usual care in the community, those referred for permanent, supportive housing had 34% fewer police contacts and 40% fewer arrests.[21] The program also reduced jail stays and total jail days by 30% and 27%, respectively.[21]

LEVERAGING MEDICAID FOR INNOVATION

States are also increasingly leveraging Medicaid to address unmet health-related social needs, including housing. A number of strategies—including Section 1115 and 1915(b, c, or i) waiver programs and managed-care arrangements—allow state Medicaid agencies to fund housing-related services for their beneficiaries.[22] These waiver programs allow the US Secretary of Health and Human Services to approve state-specific demonstration projects that utilize Medicaid funds to pay for services to address health-related social needs, including certain housing-related expenses.[22] States then have the flexibility to define eligible populations and may cover a range of community-based housing-supportive services.

Many states, including California, Arizona, and Oregon, already have 1115 waivers in place to provide a variety of pretenancy and tenancy-based supportive services, including case management, housing navigation, transition costs, and rent for up to six months.[23] Colorado recently also announced its intention to apply for an amendment to its substance use disorders 1115-waiver demonstration, which, if approved, will provide housing navigation, transition support, and tenancy-sustaining support for individuals with behavioral health or chronic health conditions who are eligible for permanent, supportive housing vouchers.[24]

CONCLUSION

Rather than provoking pessimism, the decision in *Grants Pass* is a clarion call to redouble current efforts to end houselessness. This will require large-scale investments and cross-sector partnerships. Given the mutually reinforcing association between houselessness and poor health, clinicians and health care systems have a vital role to play in these efforts. The new requirements of the CMS and The Joint Commission for health-related social needs screening provide a first step in systematically quantifying the prevalence and drivers of houselessness and housing insecurity in each community. They may also nudge health care systems to think more comprehensively about the upstream structural determinants of health that ultimately lead individuals to seek care.

Screening requirements must be coupled with new financing strategies beyond simple referrals to community-based housing support services and medical respite for those discharged from the hospital. For instance, Medicaid section 1115 and 1915 waivers along with innovative social impact bonds can not only fund community-based case management but also provide broader regulatory flexibility and financing for efforts to reduce houselessness. The success and sustainability of such initiatives ultimately depend upon the increased availability of affordable housing.

In terms of addressing housing supply and demand, numerous policy possibilities exist. Beyond inclusionary zoning, increased federal, project-based funding through National Housing Trust Fund grants and low-income housing tax credits can allow state and local governments to incentivize property developers not only to rehabilitate and maintain existing affordable housing stock or build new lower-income housing, but also to preserve long-term affordability as a condition for obtaining financing. More robust rental subsidies through expanded emergency rental assistance, tenant-focused housing choice voucher programs, needs-based down-payment assistance for first-time, low-income homeowners, and expanded legal protections against eviction, particularly for those experiencing physical disability or multimorbidity, can complement supply side solutions. Here, too, health care systems, as major employers and drivers of community redevelopment, can advocate for policies that provide housing without exacerbating the housing cost burden for lower-income families, invest in affordable housing, lobby for the repeal of vagrancy laws, and assist in evaluating housing-first initiatives that bolster the evidence base driving policymaking.

Although progress in addressing the health outcome gaps between unhoused and housed individuals has been slow and despite the *Grants Pass* decision, the efforts described here, among others, can help advance the fight for housing and health justice. AJPH

CORRESPONDENCE

Correspondence should be sent to Amirala S. Pasha, DO, JD, Mayo Clinic, 200 First Street SW, Rochester, MN 55905 (e-mail: pasha.amirala@mayo.edu). Reprints can be ordered at https://www.ajph.org by clicking the "Reprints" link.

PUBLICATION INFORMATION

Full Citation: Habib AR, Stella SA, Farkouh EK, Grenko CM, Hart D, Pasha AS. Recommitting to housing and health care justice after *City of Grants Pass v Johnson*. *Am J Public Health*. 2025;115(1):18–22.

Acceptance Date: September 15, 2024.

DOI: https://doi.org/10.2105/AJPH.2024.307870

ORCID iDs:

Anand R. Habib https://orcid.org/0000-0002-6629-8749

Elizabeth K. Farkouh https://orcid.org/0000-0002-7379-058X

Amirala S. Pasha https://orcid.org/0000-0002-4474-9502

CONTRIBUTORS

All authors contributed to the conceptualization, drafting, revising, and final approval of the manuscript.

CONFLICTS OF INTEREST

S. A. Stella receives grants from the City of Denver and Caring for Denver Foundation. The other authors report no conflicts of interest.

REFERENCES

1. Dept of Housing and Urban Development. Continuum of care homeless assistance programs homeless populations and subpopulations. 2023. Available at: https://files.hudexchange.info/reports/published/CoC_PopSub_NatlTerrDC_2023.pdf. Accessed July 8, 2024.
2. Dept of Housing and Urban Development, Office of the Assistant Secretary for Community Planning and Development. Homeless emergency assistance and rapid transition to housing: defining "homeless." *Fed Regist.* 2011;76(233):75994–76019.
3. Kushel M, Moore T. Toward a new understanding: The California Statewide Study of People Experiencing Homelessness. UCSF Benioff Homeless and Housing Initiative. 2023. Available at: https://homelessness.ucsf.edu/resources/reports/toward-new-understanding-california-statewide-study-people-experiencing. Accessed July 18, 2024.
4. Funk AM, Greene RN, Dill K, Valvassori P. The impact of homelessness on mortality of individuals living in the United States: a systematic review of the literature. *J Health Care Poor Underserved.* 2022;33(1):457–477. https://doi.org/10.1353/hpu.2022.0035
5. Herbert C. Housing costs strain owners and renters alike; millions priced out of homeownership. Joint Center for Housing Studies of Harvard University. June 20, 2024. Available at: https://www.jchs.harvard.edu/blog/housing-costs-strain-owners-and-renters-alike-millions-priced-out-homeownership. Accessed July 18, 2024.
6. Swope CB, Hernández D. Housing as a determinant of health equity: a conceptual model. *Soc Sci Med.* 2019;243:112571. https://doi.org/10.1016/j.socscimed.2019.112571
7. *City of Grants Pass v Johnson*, 144 S Ct 2202 (2024). Available at: https://www.supremecourt.gov/opinions/23pdf/23-175_19m2.pdf. Accessed July 1, 2024.
8. Lebrun-Harris LA, Baggett TP, Jenkins DM, et al. Health status and health care experiences among homeless patients in federally supported health centers: findings from the 2009 Patient Survey. *Health Serv Res.* 2013;48(3):992–1017. https://doi.org/10.1111/1475-6773.12009
9. Brown RT, Hemati K, Riley ED, et al. Geriatric conditions in a population-based sample of older homeless adults. *Gerontologist.* 2017;57(4):757–766. https://doi.org/10.1093/geront/gnw011
10. Bensken WP, Krieger NI, Berg KA, Einstadter D, Dalton JE, Perzynski AT. Health status and chronic disease burden of the homeless population: an analysis of two decades of multi-institutional electronic medical records. *J Health Care Poor Underserved.* 2021;32(3):1619–1634. https://doi.org/10.1353/hpu.2021.0153
11. Lin WC, Bharel M, Zhang J, O'Connell E, Clark RE. Frequent emergency department visits and hospitalizations among homeless people with Medicaid: implications for Medicaid expansion. *Am J Public Health.* 2015;105(S5, Suppl 5):S716–S722. https://doi.org/10.2105/AJPH.2015.302693
12. Koh KA, Racine M, Gaeta JM, et al. Health care spending and use among people experiencing unstable housing in the era of accountable care organizations. *Health Aff (Millwood).* 2020;39(2):214–223. https://doi.org/10.1377/hlthaff.2019.00687
13. Bauman T, Bal R, Barr K, et al. Housing not handcuffs. National Law Center on Homelessness & Poverty. 2019. Available at: https://homelesslaw.org/wp-content/uploads/2019/12/HOUSING-NOT-HANDCUFFS-2019-FINAL.pdf. Accessed July 19, 2024.
14. FY 2023 Hospital Inpatient Prospective Payment System (IPPS) and Long-Term Care Hospital Prospective Payment System (LTCH PPS) Final Rule—CMS-1771-F. Centers for Medicare & Medicaid Services. Available at: https://www.cms.gov/newsroom/fact-sheets/fy-2023-hospital-inpatient-prospective-payment-system-ipps-and-long-term-care-hospital-prospective. Accessed June 13, 2024.
15. The Joint Commission. New requirements to reduce health care disparities. 2022. Available at: https://www.jointcommission.org/-/media/tjc/documents/standards/r3-reports/r3_disparities_july2022-6-20-2022.pdf. Accessed July 19, 2024.
16. Yan AF, Chen Z, Wang Y, et al. Effectiveness of social needs screening and interventions in clinical settings on utilization, cost, and clinical outcomes: a systematic review. *Health Equity.* 2022;6(1):454–475. https://doi.org/10.1089/heq.2022.0010
17. Trochez RJ, Sharma S, Stolldorf DP, et al. Screening health-related social needs in hospitals: a systematic review of health care professional and patient perspectives. *Popul Health Manag.* 2023;26(3):157–167. https://doi.org/10.1089/pop.2022.0279
18. Sadowski LS, Kee RA, VanderWeele TJ, Buchanan D. Effect of a housing and case management program on emergency department visits and hospitalizations among chronically ill homeless adults: a randomized trial. *JAMA.* 2009;301(17):1771–1778. https://doi.org/10.1001/jama.2009.561
19. Jones A, Squires GD, Nixon C. Ecological associations between inclusionary zoning policies and cardiovascular disease risk prevalence: an observational study. *Circ Cardiovasc Qual Outcomes.* 2021;14(9):e007807. https://doi.org/10.1161/CIRCOUTCOMES.120.007807
20. Housing and Urban Development Office of Policy Development and Research. Housing First: a review of the evidence. 2023. Available at: https://www.huduser.gov/portal/periodicals/em/spring-summer-23/highlight2.html. Accessed July 19, 2024.
21. Cunningham M, Hanson D, Gillespie S, et al. Breaking the homelessness–jail cycle with housing first: results from the Denver Supportive Housing Social Impact Bond Initiative. The Urban Institute. 2021. Available at: https://www.urban.org/sites/default/files/publication/104501/breaking-the-homelessness-jail-cycle-with-housing-first_1.pdf. Accessed July 19, 2024.
22. Chhean E, Wagner R. Medicaid authorities for housing-related services. National Academy for State Health Policy. October 2, 2023. Available at: https://nashp.org/medicaid-authorities-for-housing-related-services. Accessed July 19, 2024.
23. Chhean E. Service definitions and reimbursement approaches for housing-related services under Medicaid. National Academy for State Health Policy. October 2, 2023. Available at: https://nashp.org/state-tracker/service-definitions-and-reimbursement-approaches-for-housing-related-services-under-medicaid. Accessed July 19, 2024.
24. Colorado Dept of Health Care Policy & Financing. Expanding the substance use disorder (SUD) continuum of care waiver. 2024. Available at: https://hcpf.colorado.gov/1115sudwaiver. Accessed July 19, 2024.

Names Matter: Affirming Our Commitment to Equity in Publishing

Heather M. Brandt, PhD, Laura M. Schwab-Reese, PhD, MA, Casper Voyles, PhD, MPH, M. Aaron Guest, PhD, MSW, MPH, and Amy Hagopian, PhD, MHA

ABOUT THE AUTHORS

Heather M. Brandt is with the HPV Cancer Prevention Program, St. Jude Children's Research Hospital, Memphis, TN. Laura M. Schwab-Reese is with the Department of Public Health, Purdue University, West Lafayette, IN. Casper Voyles is with the Department of Social Justice and Social Change, Hamline University, St. Paul, MN. M. Aaron Guest is with the Center for Innovation in Healthy and Resilient Aging, Arizona State University, Phoenix. Amy Hagopian is with the Department of Global Health and Department of Health Systems and Population Health, University of Washington, Seattle. At the time of conceptualization, H. M. Brandt, L. M. Schwab-Reese, and A. Hagopian were members of the AJPH *Editorial Board, and C. Voyles and A. Guest were leaders in the LGBTQ Health Caucus in official relations with the American Public Health Association.*

AJPH has a longstanding history of inclusive practices and progressive thinking. *AJPH* has been a bellwether for publishing emerging trends in public health and advancing the state of public health science. The *Journal* has been recognized for boldly explicating critical social issues, such as racism and discrimination in health.[1] Thus, *AJPH* remains committed to understanding and addressing issues of equity in publishing.

ADDRESSING A GAP IN POLICY AND PRACTICE

Recently, members of the Editorial Board were made aware of a gap in our policies and procedures that was inconsistent with our commitment to inclusive practices. An inquiry was submitted to *AJPH* in 2022 to change an author's name. Although such changes were not allowed under the current policy, it was important to understand ways to make the *Journal*'s policies and practices more inclusive.

In its role as an advisory board for *AJPH*, the Editorial Board defines the long-range vision, strategic plan, and annual priorities for the *Journal*; establishes policies and procedures for the Editorial Board and *AJPH*; and provides guidance to protect the quality and integrity of *AJPH* by monitoring possible opportunities for policy change and make recommendations when policy gaps are identified. As part of this role, members of the Editorial Board formed an ad hoc subcommittee to understand current context and conditions regarding name change requests in the realm of academic publishing, including collaborating with leaders of the LGBTQ Health Caucus. It was clear that academic publishing industry standards were changing and that *AJPH* needed an inclusive name change policy. In July 2023, we began the process of changing policy by submitting a formal letter to APHA Executive Director Georges Benjamin, MD, and copied to *AJPH* Editor-in-Chief Alfredo Morabia, MD, PhD. With their support, we began to develop, and ultimately implement, a new inclusive name change policy.

In this editorial, we describe the important background of our process and offer insight into implications for future inclusive actions. Implementing an inclusive name change policy may be viewed as symbolic or an ethical breach by some, but inclusivity is fundamental to our work in public health and valuing those who contribute to the research and scholarship enterprise of *AJPH*. An inclusive name change policy will leave no question about *AJPH*'s commitment to continuous advancement toward inclusivity in publishing. Such a policy will allow individuals to exert autonomy in their identity through elective name change, regardless of impetus and circumstance.

CHANGING CONTEXT IN PUBLISHING

Author name change requests are not a new phenomenon. However, until recently, publishing standards did not provide actions fundamental to inclusivity in policies and procedures. Until the late 2010s, many publishers cited the 2013 Committee on Publication Ethics (COPE) case 13-02[2] to restrict postpublication name changes. This case vaguely restricted name changes to those with "very valid reasons," a highly ambiguous phrase that few authors acted on and indeed may have been used to restrict name changes. However, rising concerns in 2019 prompted COPE to clarify that the 2013 case should not deny name changes for authors identifying as transgender, nonbinary, or gender diverse. Simultaneously, organizations, including the American Psychological Association, American Chemical Society Publications, and PLOS, revised their policies to accommodate name changes in 2020. After COPE's 2021 update[3] and a significant guest article,[4] many publishers embraced more inclusive guidelines, often incorporating COPE's five key principles: accessibility, comprehensiveness, invisibility, expediency, and recurrence maintenance. Although initial guidance was forthcoming from COPE, it has not yet materialized. In this vacuum, publishers, including Sage Publications,[5] have developed and implemented name change policies informed as per the COPE guidance. These, in turn, have served as models for the *AJPH* name change policy.

ALIGNING POLICIES WITH OUR CORE VALUES

Publication in academic journals is the professional currency with which scholars obtain and maintain job opportunities and prominence in their field. Reasons for initiating name change traverse a range of circumstances. In particular, transgender scholars whose names change during their careers may face a decision that pits desires for career advancement against those related to their desire to live authentically. These are not the only reasons name changes may be required. Name change policies that deny the option for chosen name to be reflected in publications or ones that require public notification of a change to the author's name may cause tension with how discreet one wants to be about this change. Options available to such scholars with publications in journals without inclusive name change policies come with different implications for affirmation of and others' knowledge about their identities.[6] For many, a legal name change is one aspect of gender affirmation, a process associated with lower reports of psychological distress, including in response to gender-based mistreatment.[7] Reflecting the legal name change through the amendment of the scholarly record goes beyond symbolism and promotes health among professionals in our discipline. As the leading journal in public health, *AJPH* represents a discipline focused on social justice that prioritizes the amelioration of inequities and advances holistic well-being. In this spirit, *AJPH* seized this opportunity to align its publishing practices with its mission to champion the health of all people and with our core ethics and beliefs.

A STEP IN THE RIGHT DIRECTION

Adopting an inclusive name change policy is a meaningful step toward our continued quest for health equity that extends beyond lesbian, gay, bisexual, transgender, queer/questioning, and more (LGBTQ+) communities. (Note: Multiple terms exist to describe the infinite diversity that exists within human sexual and gender identity. This is one reason why authors must disclose their interpretation early in their work. For this editorial, we use "sexual and gender–diverse populations.") Removing barriers so that scholars can live authentically without fear of reprisal serves as a beacon that *AJPH* is an affirming space for public health professionals and builds upon our shared history of inclusion. For too long, authors have faced concerns regarding whether they can professionally identify without inviting public scrutiny and confusion. However, it is only one step on the journey. Adopting inclusive practices must be met with additional action by *AJPH* and the public health field at large. We have identified the following next steps for inclusive publishing that should be the aim of our field:

- Encourage authors of all published articles to report the sexual and gender identity of their sample—not only in sexual and gender diverse–specific research—and ideally using self-reported and consistent terms referring to sex, gender, sexual identity, and gender identity.
- Continue the recruitment of reviewers and editors who can advise on emerging areas of sexual and gender–diverse population scholarship.
- Require authors to be specific in their definitions of sexual and gender diversity and use a cultural humility approach to identify terminology that is consistent with the identities of their participants. Sexual and gender–diverse communities are not monolith, and broad terms may obscure the unique experiences across different groups.

As our understanding of the sexual and gender–diverse community continues to evolve, so will the recommendations to ensure their representation in scholarship that aims to improve health. It includes action to allow the self-disclosure of authors' descriptors, such as pronouns, to support gender affirmation within scholarly discourse. Following the principles of universal design, removing barriers for some removes barriers for all and promotes greater participation among all groups.

We thank the authors who brought this issue to our attention and appreciate the support of those who contributed to the development of this inclusive name change policy. We also recognize there is more to do—including actions yet to be acknowledged as identities, terminologies, and best practices related to affirming them continue to shift. We hope *AJPH* and APHA will continue to be at the forefront of inclusive policies and processes to advance the state of equity in publishing. AJPH

CORRESPONDENCE

Correspondence should be sent to Heather M. Brandt, PhD, Director, HPV Cancer Prevention Program, St. Jude Children's Research Hospital, 262 Danny Thomas Place, Memphis, TN 38105 (e-mail: heather.brandt@stjude.org). Reprints can be ordered at https://www.ajph.org by clicking the "Reprints" link.

PUBLICATION INFORMATION

Full Citation: Brandt HM, Schwab-Reese LM, Voyles C, Guest MA, Hagopian A. Names matter: affirming our commitment to equity in publishing. *Am J Public Health*. 2025;115(1):23–25.

Acceptance Date: September 19, 2024.

DOI: https://doi.org/10.2105/AJPH.2024.307876

ORCID iDs:

Heather M. Brandt https://orcid.org/0000-0003-1066-2879

Laura M. Schwab-Reese https://orcid.org/0000-0002-9174-1730

M. Aaron Guest https://orcid.org/0000-0001-7356-3734

CONTRIBUTORS

H. M. Brandt, L. M. Schwab-Reese, and A. Hagopian, as members of the *AJPH* editorial board, and C. Voyles and A. Guest, as leaders in the LGBTQ Health Caucus, in official relations with the American Public Health Association, collaborated on all aspects of the editorial from conceptualization through submission.

ACKNOWLEDGMENTS

This publication was supported by the American Lebanese and Syrian Associated Charities of St. Jude Children's Research Hospital.

We appreciate the support and work of the *AJPH* Editorial Board; LGBTQ Health Caucus, in official relations with the American Public Health Association; and the Institute for Social Science Research at Arizona State University. We extend gratitude to our colleagues on the *AJPH* Editorial Board, especially the assistance of Brian Selzer in his role as director of publications, and leadership and members of the LGBTQ Health Caucus for their support of this effort.

CONFLICTS OF INTEREST

The authors report that they have no conflicts of interest.

REFERENCES

1. Morabia A. Why is *AJPH* publishing more than other major journals about race and racism? *Am J Public Health*. 2021;111(9):1557. https://doi.org/10.2105/AJPH.2021.306461
2. Committee on Publication Ethics. Change in author's name after publication (case number 13-02). 2013. Available at: https://publicationethics.org/case/change-authors-name-after-publication. Accessed September 15, 2024.
3. Committee on Publication Ethics. Update on COPE guidance regarding author name changes. January 13, 2021. Available at: https://publicationethics.org/news/update-cope-guidance-regarding-author-name-changes. Accessed September 15, 2024.
4. Committee on Publication Ethics. A vision for a more trans-inclusive publishing world: guest article. January 13, 2021. Available at: https://publicationethics.org/news/vision-more-trans-inclusive-publishing-world. Accessed September 15, 2024.
5. Sage Publications. Name change policy. October 3, 2023. Available at: https://us.sagepub.com/en-us/nam/name-change-policy. Accessed September 15, 2024.
6. Gaskins LC, McClain CR. Visible name changes promote inequity for transgender researchers. *PLoS Biol*. 2021;19(3):e3001104. https://doi.org/10.1371/journal.pbio.3001104
7. Restar A, Jin H, Breslow A, et al. Legal gender marker and name change is associated with lower negative emotional response to gender-based mistreatment and improve mental health outcomes among trans populations. *SSM Popul Health*. 2020;11:100595. https://doi.org/10.1016/j.ssmph.2020.100595

Don't Forget Fido: A Call to Include Pets in Public Health Research and Policy to Support Families and Communities

Emily D. Dolan, PhD, Brett Wyker, MS, Elizabeth A. Berliner, DVM, DABVP, Matt Goldweber, BA, and Ana Hernandez, MA

ABOUT THE AUTHORS

Emily D. Dolan and Brett Wyker are with the Department of Strategy and Research, Elizabeth A. Berliner is with the Department of Shelter Medicine Services, and Matt Goldweber and Ana Hernandez are with the Department of Community Engagement, American Society for the Prevention of Cruelty to Animals, New York, NY.

AJPH January 2025, Vol. 115, No. 1

The Institute of Medicine describes the mission of public health as "fulfilling society's interest in assuring conditions in which people can be healthy."[1(p7)] This human-centered perspective overlooks the critical importance of companion animal welfare in community health. The powerful interconnectedness of people and their pets means that the health and welfare of families and communities is entwined with the health and welfare of their pets. Because pets are not adequately considered in public health research and policy currently, the onus is disproportionately placed on the animal welfare field to solve community health problems associated with caring for pets. Animal welfare organizations such as humane societies, animal shelters, rescues, and other nonprofits are primarily dependent upon philanthropy; municipal funding is generally limited to a narrow scope, such as providing affordable rabies vaccination and animal control. To comprehensively address the needs of families and communities, recognition of the tangible and meaningful intersections of human and animal health is required in research and policy planning.

Pet ownership in the United States has increased, with pets living in 87 million or 66% of households today.[2] Pet owners find the companionship of pets to be an important source of emotional support.[3,4] There is some evidence of physical health benefits as well, although the literature is mixed. When people are struggling to care for pets, many resort to relinquishment, sometimes to an animal shelter. The American Society for the Prevention of Cruelty to Animals (ASPCA) estimates that nearly 6.3 million pets enter shelters annually and almost a million are euthanized. Involuntary family separation creates stress, grief, and risk of safety for families, is dangerous for pets, and overwhelms the animal welfare social system.[5] Resource burdens on social systems such as animal control and animal shelters are significant. The devastating burden on families and communities is costly, but more importantly, it strikes at the heart of the public health mission to protect the health of people and communities. We describe three notable challenges for families and their pets:

1. The severe shortage of pet-inclusive rental housing negatively affects families;
2. Families are vulnerable during natural disasters; and
3. Families increasingly lack access to veterinary care.

PET-INCLUSIVE RENTAL HOUSING

Lack of access to pet-inclusive housing is cited as a top reason people relinquish their pets to shelters.[6] One survey of renters by Apartments.com found that 65% of respondents who were forced to give up pets said they couldn't find pet-inclusive housing and 27% could not afford the pet deposit. When faced with homelessness, people will refuse assistance if they are unable to stay with their pet.[4] Although pet ownership is reported as a "barrier" to accessing housing and services for homeless youths, it may be protective of health and well-being.[7] Landlord prohibition of pets, restriction of size or breed, and high pet rents and fees are increasingly excluding people from accessing housing in the United States, predominately affecting underserved populations.[8–10]

VULNERABILITY DURING NATURAL DISASTERS

The Louisiana SPCA estimates that 104 000 owned pets were unable to be evacuated during hurricane Katrina; 50 000 to 70 000 ultimately died.

During the Marshall Fire in Colorado in 2021, 30 000 residents were displaced, and more than 1000 pets died because residents were unable to retrieve them.[4] Many pet owners facing impending disasters and extreme weather events may not evacuate if they cannot take pets with them.[11,12]

Yet emergency shelters, temperature control centers, and hotels may prohibit pets. When facilities do allow pets, the policies may be restrictive and create additional barriers for owners, such as documentation of vaccination, specific containment requirements, or restriction of species or breed. Response efforts may disproportionately affect vulnerable families who have fewer options for transportation and housing away from the disaster area.[13,14] Planning that incorporates pet-inclusive evacuations increases the likelihood of pet owners' compliance; the Federal Emergency Management Agency's best practice guidelines already capture health and safety considerations, including for pets. Moreover, animal welfare organizations have expertise in designing shelters to increase safety and ensure legal compliance.

ACCESS TO VETERINARY CARE

The American Pet Products Association estimates that approximately 87 million households include one or two dogs or cats. Further, the Humane Society of the United States estimates that 20 million pets may be living in poverty. An unpublished 2022 study by the ASPCA on a sample of American households found that about 25% of pet owners reported that there was a time in the past two years when they needed veterinary care and were unable to attain it. Forty-three percent reported they could not obtain care because they could not afford it. Lack of access is exacerbated by a national veterinarian shortage and increased corporate consolidation. People who surrender sick pets to a shelter may hope the shelter will provide care. Many animal welfare organizations are responding with alternatives, such as expanding their scope to provide health care to owned pets without requiring that the pet be relinquished. These programs often struggle because of low funding, lack of access to veterinarians, and insufficient staffing support. However, integrating these programs in a One Health model can be a gateway for people to receive human support services as they access care for pets.[15] Furthermore, basic access to preventive veterinary care reduces the risk of zoonotic transfer of disease between pets and people and improves family well-being.

WHERE DO WE GO FROM HERE?

Recognizing the interconnectedness of animal welfare and public health, McDowall et al.[16] presented modifications to the US Department of Health and Human Services' domains model, highlighting where animal welfare is inextricably bound with public health. The model shows the downstream effects on pets from social determinates related to human health, including environment, community, and economic stability.[17] A comprehensive approach to community well-being, including public health research and policy planning for families, can help keep people and their pets together.[17]

Tendrils of intersection between public health and animal welfare are beginning to strengthen, primarily driven by the efforts of animal welfare organizations to draw in public health professionals. Pioneering movements like Pets for Life, Human Animal Support Services (HASS), Companions and Animals for Reform and Equity (CARE), and People and Animals in Community Together (PACT) are utilizing community-based outreach and interventions to keep families together, recognizing pet relinquishment as an unacceptable result of health and economic disparities. Animal welfare organizations are making connections to human health entities such as social workers, food banks, and One Health clinics, and are switching to harm reduction approaches that shift animal control from punitive to supportive models to ameliorate negative consequences.[18]

A few key actions could help the public health field begin to consciously address the intersection of human and pet health. These actions would not only bring needed aid to the overburdened animal welfare movement but would also better provide for the health and welfare of families and communities:

1. Include pets in public health research;
2. Include pets in policy planning; and
3. Address barriers to animal welfare.

Pets in Public Health Research

Taking opportunities to understand the role of pets in families and including information about pets when developing interventions and evaluating public health programs are essential. Accounting for pets in lived experience expands on social determinates of health research and provides a more comprehensive picture of what barriers and challenges families face. Researchers must include pet concerns to accurately assess all barriers and facilitators affecting families and communities. For example, if measuring stressors, in addition to such things as food insecurity and lifestyle changes, researchers should also measure animal ownership and determine whether pets have challenges that contribute to overall family stress.

Pets in Policy Planning

Including pet issues in public health conversations encourages comprehensive solutions and funding for interventions and services. An informed public health response backed by research and policy that recognizes pets would allow the provision of support to pets alongside support provided to families. Public health policy planning also must include pets in key community objectives; for example, incorporating pets into the Healthy People 2030 long-term public health objectives to improve health and well-being.

Barriers to Animal Welfare

Thoughtful policy planning should include direct action to address obstacles. When instituting mandatory vaccination requirements, for example, include funding and outreach to aid families in meeting the requirements.

CONCLUSION

Most US households have pets, and people consider pets family members. Public health research and policy planning that does not consider pets cannot have maximum impact on human welfare. Our goal is for animal welfare to become well represented in public health research and policy planning for the optimal well-being of all family members. Building connections between animal welfare professionals and public health researchers and policy planners will raise awareness of how pet welfare is critical to families and communities but is not yet appropriately integrated into public health research, planning, and initiatives.

The challenges of people are challenges to their pets, and vice versa. Animal welfare has traditionally focused on the care of pets, whereas public health has focused on concern for people. However, this dichotomy is false, and we must create a strong alliance between the two related fields. To ensure that research and policies effectively include pets, animal welfare and veterinary professionals must be integrated into public health research and policy discussions at every level. By including pets as critical members of the family and community, animal welfare and public health can together address the issues that affect families. AJPH

CORRESPONDENCE

Correspondence should be sent to Emily D. Dolan, PhD, American Society for the Prevention of Cruelty to Animals, 424 East 92nd St, New York, NY 10028 (e-mail: emily.dolan@aspca.org). Reprints can be ordered at https://www.ajph.org by clicking the "Reprints" link.

PUBLICATION INFORMATION

Full Citation: Dolan ED, Wyker B, Berliner EA, Goldweber M, Hernandez A. Don't forget Fido: a call to include pets in public health research and policy to support families and communities. *Am J Public Health*. 2025;115(1):26–29.

Acceptance Date: September 19, 2024.

DOI: https://doi.org/10.2105/AJPH.2024.307879

ORCID iDs:

Emily D. Dolan https://orcid.org/0009-0008-7282-3918

Elizabeth A. Berliner https://orcid.org/0000-0001-5513-379X

CONTRIBUTORS

E. D. Dolan conceptualized the idea, contributed content, and drafted and edited the manuscript. B. Wyker, E. A. Berliner, M. Goldweber, and A. Hernandez contributed content and edited the manuscript.

ACKNOWLEDGMENTS

We thank Margaret Slater, Kevin O'Neill, Sharon Pailler, Susan Anderson, Greg Miller, Molly Sumridge, Carolyn Brown, and Christa Chadwick for lending their expertise and providing thoughtful feedback to this project.

CONFLICTS OF INTEREST

The authors have no conflicts of interest to report.

REFERENCES

1. Institute of Medicine, ed. *The Future of Public Health*. Washington, DC: National Academy Press; 1988.
2. *American Pet Products Association APPA National Pet Owners Survey 2023-2024*. American Pet Products Association; 2024.
3. Brooks HL, Rushton K, Lovell K, et al. The power of support from companion animals for people living with mental health problems: a systematic review and narrative synthesis of the evidence. *BMC Psychiatry*. 2018;18(1):31. https://doi.org/10.1186/s12888-018-1613-2
4. Irvine L, Andre C. Pet loss in an urban firestorm: grief and hope after Colorado's Marshall Fire. *Animals (Basel)*. 2023;13(3):416. https://doi.org/10.3390/ani13030416
5. Montgomery J, Liang Z, Lloyd J. A scoping review of forced separation between people and their companion animals. *Anthrozoos*. 2024;37(2):245–267. https://doi.org/10.1080/08927936.2023.2287315
6. Weiss E, Gramann S, Victor Spain C, Slater M. Goodbye to a good friend: an exploration of the re-homing of cats and dogs in the US. *Open J Anim Sci*. 2015;05(04):435–456. https://doi.org/10.4236/ojas.2015.54046
7. Lem M, Coe JB, Haley DB, Stone E, O'Grady W. The protective association between pet ownership and depression among street-involved youth: a cross-sectional study. *Anthrozoos*. 2016;29(1):123–136. https://doi.org/10.1080/08927936.2015.1082772
8. Graham TM, Rock MJ. The spillover effect of a flood on pets and their people: implications for rental housing. *J Appl Anim Welf Sci*. 2019;22(3):229–239. https://doi.org/10.1080/10888705.2018.1476863
9. Applebaum JW, Horecka K, Loney L, Graham TM. Pet-friendly for whom? An analysis of pet fees in Texas rental housing. *Front Vet Sci*. 2021;8:767149. https://doi.org/10.3389/fvets.2021.767149
10. Rose D, McMillian C, Carter O. Pet-friendly rental housing: racial and spatial inequalities. *Space Cult*. 2023;26(1):116–129. https://doi.org/10.1177/1206331220956539
11. Chadwin R. Evacuation of pets during disasters: a public health intervention to increase resilience. *Am J Public Health*. 2017;107(9):1413–1417. https://doi.org/10.2105/AJPH.2017.303877
12. Rosenkoetter MM, Covan EK, Cobb BK, Bunting S, Weinrich M. Perceptions of older adults regarding evacuation in the event of a natural

disaster. *Public Health Nurs.* 2007;24(2):160–168. https://doi.org/10.1111/j.1525-1446.2007.00620.x

13. Hallegatte S, Vogt-Schilb A, Rozenberg J, Bangalore M, Beaudet C. From poverty to disaster and back: a review of the literature. *Econ Disaster Clim Chang.* 2020;4(1):223–247. https://doi.org/10.1007/s41885-020-00060-5
14. Domingue SJ, Emrich CT. Social vulnerability and procedural equity: exploring the distribution of disaster aid across counties in the United States. *Am Rev Public Adm.* 2019;49(8):897–913. https://doi.org/10.1177/0275074019856122
15. Lem M. Serving homeless populations through a One Health approach. *Can Vet J.* 2019;60(10):1119–1120. Available at: https://pmc.ncbi.nlm.nih.gov/articles/PMC6741821. Accessed November 6, 2024.
16. McDowall S, Hazel SJ, Chittleborough C, Hamilton-Bruce A, Stuckey R, Howell TJ. The impact of the social determinants of human health on companion animal welfare. *Animals (Basel).* 2023;13(6):1113. https://doi.org/10.3390/ani13061113
17. Clancy EA. Animals as community stakeholders: inclusion of pets in social policy and practice (occasional essay). *Fam Soc.* 2014;95(4):285–289. https://doi.org/10.1606/1044-3894.2014.95.33
18. Hawes SM, Hupe T, Morris KN. Punishment to support: the need to align animal control enforcement with the human social justice movement. *Animals (Basel).* 2020;10(10):1902. https://doi.org/10.3390/ani10101902

Federal Policy Platforms and Public Health: Reinforcing the Benefits of Air Pollution Control Devices at Power Plants in the United States

Jonathan J. Buonocore, ScD, MS, Jeremy Fisher, PhD, ScM, Daniel Prull, PhD, MS, Mary D. Willis, PhD, MPH, Saravanan Arunachalam, PhD, MS, Frederica Perera, DrPH, PhD, Patrick Kinney, ScD, MS, Brian Sousa, BS, and Jonathan I. Levy, ScD

ABOUT THE AUTHORS

Jonathan J. Buonocore, Patrick L. Kinney, Brian J. Sousa, and Jonathan I. Levy are with the Department of Environmental Health, Boston University School of Public Health, Boston, MA. Jeremy Fisher and Daniel Prull are with the Sierra Club, Oakland, CA. Mary D. Willis is with the Department of Epidemiology, Boston University School of Public Health. Saravanan Arunachalam is with the Institute for the Environment, University of North Carolina, Chapel Hill. Frederica Perera is with the Department of Environmental Health, Columbia Mailman School of Public Health, New York, NY.

AJPH January 2025, Vol. 115, No. 1

Recent federal policy platforms have been proposed that include substantial changes to environmental regulation at the US Environmental Protection Agency (EPA). For instance, the 2025 Presidential Transition Project ("Project 2025")[1] has a number of proposals to change the Clean Air Act (CAA); and the America First Agenda[2] has proposals to "modernize" the CAA. If implemented, these measures may sharply reduce the future public health benefits of the CAA. These include possible harms from ceasing operation of air pollution control devices (APCDs) at power plants, which have been a bedrock of national-scale air pollution reductions for decades.

Although many policy measures proposed in Project 2025,[1] the America First Agenda,[2] and elsewhere are vaguely described, there are clear emphases on rolling back proposed and pending rules for power plants, loosening air quality standards, changing classification of air pollution sources, and reducing the EPA's enforcement powers. These changes could lead to reduced requirements to install new APCDs or to continue use of existing APCDs. Such regulatory rollbacks could undo the substantial health benefits achieved in recent years.

The CAA gives the EPA authority to develop policies to reduce emissions of major air pollutants, notably sulfur dioxide (SO_2) and nitrogen oxides (NO_x), from power plants. Under CAA authority, the EPA has developed and implemented policies that either require use of APCDs or set emissions standards at certain power plant electricity-generating units (EGUs). For plants with an emission standard, APCDs are one tool of many that can be used for compliance. The CAA has been extremely successful, with power plant SO_2 emissions decreasing by 93% and NO_x emissions decreasing by 87% from 1995 to 2022.[3] These regulations have led to large and underappreciated public health benefits; for example, the number of excess deaths attributable to coal-related $PM_{2.5}$ owing to secondary formation from SO_2 emissions declined from more than 40 000 in 2000 to 1600 in 2020.[4] Although some of these benefits resulted from declining coal use for electricity generation,[5] a substantial portion is attributable to APCDs. In 2000 only 29.2% of coal plants used flue gas desulfurization, and 1.8% used selective catalytic reduction to control SO_2 and NO_x emissions, respectively; in 2022, 82.4% and 57.9%, respectively, did so.[6]

HEALTH BENEFITS OF AIR POLLUTION CONTROL DEVICES

To understand the potential emission changes attributable to APCD use, we used reported 2023 emissions of SO_2 and NO_x from the EPA's Clean Air Markets Program Data (CAMPD)[7] and then calculated changes to power sector SO_2 and NO_x emissions under a counterfactual worst-case scenario in which existing APCDs were not operating. To develop this counterfactual scenario, we first assessed the median SO_2 and NO_x emission rates for EGUs that currently lack APCDs, differentiated by primary fuel type. We then identified all EGUs with APCDs installed as reported in CAMPD[7] and assumed that if APCDs were bypassed, they would have the median emission rates for power plants with the same primary fuel type and without APCDs. This approach allowed us to avoid data gaps and assumptions inherent in using engineering estimates or plant-specific precontrol values. Our estimate assumed that APCDs that incur operational expenses would cease operation under looser regulatory and legal oversight and that there would be no changes in fuel consumption by EGUs or power plant generation patterns.[8]

We estimated that SO_2 emissions would be 2.89 times higher and NO_x emissions 1.77 times higher without APCDs operating (1.88 million tons of SO_2 and 1.62 million tons of NO_x without APCDs vs 0.66 million tons of SO_2 and 0.658 tons of NO_x with APCDs). More than half of the SO_2 emission reductions from APCDs are currently found in just 35 power plants (or 115 EGUs of the 4089 EGUs subject to regulation and reporting to CAMPD in 2023), all of which are coal-fired power plants. More than half of NO_x emission reductions are derived from 80 power plants (or 241 EGUs), most of which (61% of power plants and 81% of EGUs) are coal fired.

We then estimated the health benefits of the emission reductions from the use of APCDs using three different reduced complexity models: peer-reviewed and publicly available social cost models for the public health impacts of $PM_{2.5}$ precursors provided in terms of per ton of pollutant emitted and differentiated by source county.[9] These reduced complexity models combine atmospheric dispersion modeling results with population data and results from two major epidemiological studies providing two point estimates of the effect of $PM_{2.5}$ on mortality risk to estimate the health benefits of air pollutant reductions.[9–11] The reduced complexity models express the results in monetary terms, using a value of statistical life (a metric commonly used in air pollution regulatory impact analysis) of $11.1 million (amounts are in 2024 US dollars).[9]

In 2023, APCDs at power plants captured approximately 1.2 million tons of SO_2 and 1.0 million tons of NO_x emissions. With the reduced complexity models, we estimated that APCDs prevented approximately 3100 to 9000 premature deaths in 2023, with an annual benefit between $35 billion and nearly $100 billion. Health benefits come from APCDs across the country, but the APCDs producing the highest benefits tend to be installed at power plants in Appalachia, the Midwest, and the Mountain West (Figure 1).

However, because secondarily formed $PM_{2.5}$ is dispersed regionally, health benefits are seen nationwide. Although pollution "hot spots" are not pronounced for secondary $PM_{2.5}$, the clustering of high-emitting sources leads to regional variability in impacts. More than 85% of these benefits are from SO_2 controls, mostly coming from coal-fired power plants. The rest come from NO_x controls installed at a mix of

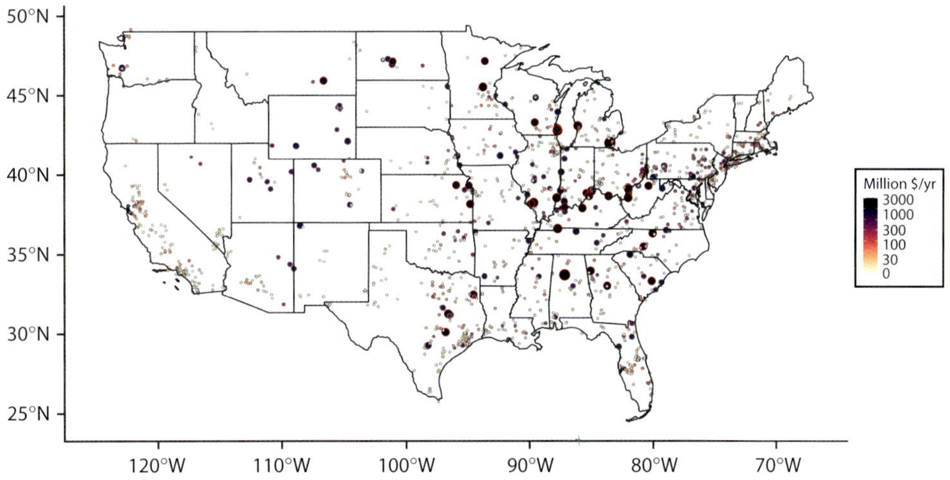

FIGURE 1— Total Health Benefits of SO_2 and NO_x Air Pollution Control Devices (APCDs) Installed on Electricity-Generating Units, at Power Plant Facility Level: United States, 2023

Note. Dollar amounts are in 2024 US dollars. Size and color of point represent the total benefits of APCDs captured at each power plant facility. Location of the points represent power plant facility locations. For facilities where latitude and longitude were not available, we assigned their locations to county centroids. Point locations were slightly adjusted to prevent overplotting. The 35 facilities with the highest benefits from SO_2 reductions are represented by points with red outlines. Results presented are from the EASIUR (Estimating Air pollution Social Impact Using Regression) model, the reduced complexity model with the middle result of the three reduced complexity models, using a concentration–response function derived from the Harvard Six Cities study.

coal, oil, diesel, and fossil (or "natural") gas power plants.

The reduced complexity models inherently underestimate the benefits of APCDs by omitting the substantial evidence for numerous morbidity outcomes associated with $PM_{2.5}$ exposure, as well as all the health effects associated with direct exposure to NO_2, SO_2, ozone (formed from NO_x emissions), and air toxics, such as mercury. These include outcomes in adults (e.g., stroke, heart attack, asthma) and in children (e.g., low birth weight, preterm birth, new cases of asthma, other respiratory illness, adverse neurodevelopmental outcomes). These models also do not incorporate potential differences in the concentration–response relationship and therefore may underestimate the effects on environmental justice communities, especially those near power plants.[12] These models may underestimate the benefits of APCDs at gas-fired power plants more than at coal-fired plants, given that health consequences from gas-fired power plants are typically driven by NO_2 and ozone exposure. Even with these omissions, the public health benefits of APCDs are substantial and disproportionately found among vulnerable individuals.

Despite the ongoing shift in the United States away from coal for electricity generation, as of 2023, coal still provided nearly 16% of electricity generation, with 43% coming from gas and the remainder from nuclear, hydroelectricity, wind, and solar energy.[5] Of the remaining coal capacity, only a small fraction of plants are planning to retire under legally enforceable commitments, with the remainder dependent in part on the future federal policy agenda. APCDs, therefore, still have an important role to play in reducing emissions from power generation, improving air quality, and protecting public health.

THE ROLE OF THE CLEAN AIR ACT IN HEALTHY DECARBONIZATION

The emission reductions associated with APCDs are predicated on regulatory requirements and enforcement; therefore, they are not guaranteed to continue if interpretation, implementation, and enforcement of the CAA or the policies developed by the EPA under authority granted by the CAA are altered. While a policy change would be unlikely to remove all APCDs, our estimates provide a sense of how large the benefits of APCDs are currently, how those benefits could be lost if interpretation of the CAA and EPA policies under authority of the CAA were weakened, and how these benefits could increase if policies were to be strengthened or if new policies were implemented.

Recently proposed federal policy agendas could create different futures for the CAA and the EPA and may affect the 2022 Inflation Reduction Act (which incentivized deployment of renewable energy resources) and other policies with connections to power plant emissions. Any discussion about the pros and cons of proposed futures for these bedrock public health policies should include the public health implications of these platforms. Our analysis suggests that policy measures that reduce APCD use would have substantial public health impacts that are likely to most heavily affect environmental justice communities near power plants with currently operating APCDs.

Moreover, the presence of APCDs influences the effectiveness of other policy measures at the federal, state, and local levels. For example, many climate action plans include electrification of buildings or transportation to reduce greenhouse gas emissions; potential health benefits of those measures will be reduced if air pollution emissions from electricity generation increases. This produces a risk of federal actions reducing the use of APCDs, which may have a cascading effect that ultimately jeopardizes our ability to address the climate crisis. Given the high stakes, especially for environmental justice communities, federal policy platforms should directly and specifically address how their policies will influence power plant air pollution emissions and the health consequences in the years ahead. AJPH

CORRESPONDENCE

Correspondence should be sent to Jonathan J. Buonocore, ScD, Assistant Professor, Boston University School of Public Health, 715 Albany St, Talbot 527 W, Boston, MA 02118-2526 (e-mail: jjbuono@bu.edu). Reprints can be ordered at https://www.ajph.org by clicking the "Reprints" link.

PUBLICATION INFORMATION

Full Citation: Buonocore JJ, Fisher J, Prull D, et al. Federal policy platforms and public health: reinforcing the benefits of air pollution control devices at power plants in the United States. *Am J Public Health*. 2025;115(1):30–33.

Acceptance Date: October 6, 2024.

DOI: https://doi.org/10.2105/AJPH.2024.307896

ORCID iDs:
Jonathan J. Buonocore https://orcid.org/0000-0001-7270-892X

Jeremy Fisher https://orcid.org/0009-0000-1792-0776

Mary D. Willis https://orcid.org/0000-0002-0247-7983

Saravanan Arunachalam https://orcid.org/0000-0002-6836-6944

Frederica Perera https://orcid.org/0000-0002-2263-7008

Brian Sousa https://orcid.org/0000-0002-5017-6990

Jonathan I. Levy https://orcid.org/0000-0002-1116-4006

CONTRIBUTORS

J. J. Buonocore performed the health impact analysis. J. J. Buonocore and J. I. Levy led the writing and editing of the editorial. D. Prull performed the power plant emission analysis. M. D. Willis and B. Sousa performed the analytical code review. B Sousa performed the data analysis. All authors contributed to study conceptualization and writing the editorial.

CONFLICTS OF INTEREST

J. J. Buonocore has received consulting fees from Avanti Group and Skeo Solutions and grants from the Environmental Defense Fund (EDF), the Wellcome Trust, Login5, the Global Methane Hub, the Liberty Mutual Foundation, the Home Energy Efficiency Team, the Massachusetts Clean Energy Center, the New York Community Trust (NYCT), and the Institute for Global Sustainability at Boston University. He also serves as a scientific adviser for HEET. M. D. Willis has received grants from the National Institutes of Health (NIH) and the Health Effects Institute (HEI). S. Arunachalam has received contracts and grants from the Environmental Protection Agency (EPA), US Department of Transportation, the Federal Aviation Administration (FAA), the Federal Highway Administration, the National Academies' Airport Cooperative Research Program, the National Aeronautics and Space Administration (NASA), the National Institute of Environmental Health Sciences, the New York State Energy Research and Development Authority, the Mid-Atlantic Regional Air Management Association, the Northeast States for Coordinates Air Use Management, the Connecticut Department of Energy and Environmental Protection, the North Carolina Department of Environmental Quality, the Texas Commission on Environmental Quality, HEI, Alberta Energy, the National Wildlife Federation, the EDF, the Wellcome Trust, the Energy Foundation, and the Barr Foundation. In addition, he has received consulting fees from the Los Angeles World Airport Authority and NYCT and expert testimony for the US Department of Justice, the North Carolina Department of Justice, and the Colorado Public Utility Commission. P. Kinney has received consulting fees from the EPA, Industrial Economics, and Abt Associates and grants from the National Oceanic and Atmospheric Administration, NIH, the Barr Foundation, HEI, and the Wellcome Trust. B. Sousa has received funds from the Boston University Institute for Global Sustainability. J. I. Levy has received consulting fees from Industrial Economics for a project funded by the California Air Resources Board and grants from the EPA, the FAA, and NIH.

REFERENCES

1. Heritage Foundation. *Mandate for Leadership: The Conservative Promise.* 2024. Available at: https://static.project2025.org/2025_MandateForLeadership_FULL.pdf. Accessed September 2, 2024.
2. America First Policy Institute. Provide clean air, clean water, and a clean environment for all Americans. Available at: https://agenda.americafirstpolicy.com/energy/provide-clean-air-clean-water-and-a-clean-environment-for-all-americans. Accessed September 1, 2024.
3. US Environmental Protection Agency. Power sector programs: progress report. October 2, 2024. Available at: https://www.epa.gov/power-sector/progress-report. Accessed October 10, 2024.
4. Henneman L, Choirat C, Dedoussi I, Dominici F, Roberts J, Zigler C. Mortality risk from United States coal electricity generation. *Science.* 2023;382(6673):941–946. https://doi.org/10.1126/science.adf4915
5. US Energy Information Administration. Electricity data browser. Available at: https://www.eia.gov/electricity/data/browser. Accessed August 29, 2024.
6. US Environmental Protection Agency. Power sector evolution. August 28, 2024. Available at: https://www.epa.gov/power-sector/power-sector-evolution. Accessed August 29, 2024.
7. US Environmental Protection Agency. Clean air markets program data. July 1, 2024. Available at: https://campd.epa.gov. Accessed July 16, 2024.
8. Schmitt T, Leptinsky S, Turner M, et al. *Cost and Performance Baseline for Fossil Energy Plants. Volume 1: Bituminous Coal and Natural Gas to Electricity.* 2022. https://doi.org/10.2172/1893822
9. Kim S-Y, Bechle M, Hankey S, Sheppard L, Szpiro AA, Marshall JD. Concentrations of criteria pollutants in the contiguous US, 1979–2015: role of prediction model parsimony in integrated empirical geographic regression. *PLoS ONE.* 2020;15(2):e0228535. https://doi.org/10.1371/journal.pone.0228535
10. Lepeule J, Laden F, Dockery D, Schwartz J. Chronic exposure to fine particles and mortality: an extended follow-up of the Harvard Six cities study from 1974 to 2009. *Environ Health Perspect.* 2012;120(7):965–970. https://doi.org/10.1289/ehp.1104660
11. Krewski D, Burnett R, Jerrett M, et al. Mortality and long-term exposure to ambient air pollution: ongoing analyses based on the American Cancer Society cohort. *J Toxicol Environ Health A.* 2005;68(13–14):1093–1109. https://doi.org/10.1080/15287390590935941
12. Wang B, Eum K-D, Kazemiparkouhi F, et al. The impact of long-term $PM_{2.5}$ exposure on specific causes of death: exposure–response curves and effect modification among 53 million US Medicare beneficiaries. *Environ Health.* 2020;19(1):20. https://doi.org/10.1186/s12940-020-00575-0

Community Health Workers as Catalysts for Mental Health Promotion in Transgender and Nonbinary Communities

Arjee Javellana Restar, PhD, MPH, Kellan Baker, PhD, MPH, Grace Wang, PhD, MPH, Karen Ashley, EdD, and April Joy Damian, PhD, MSc

ABOUT THE AUTHORS

Arjee Javellana Restar, Grace Wang, Karen Ashley, and April Joy Damian are with the Moses Weitzman Health System, Weitzman Institute, Washington, DC. Arjee Javellana Restar is also with the Department of Social and Behavioral Sciences, Yale University, New Haven, CT. Kellan Baker is with the Center for Lesbian, Gay, Bisexual, and Transgender Health and Wellbeing, Whitman-Walker Institute, Washington, DC.

AJPH January 2025, Vol. 115, No. 1

There is a significant disparity between the cisgender population and the transgender and nonbinary (trans) communities in the United States in terms of the availability and accessibility of evidence-based mental health services,[1,2] particularly given epidemiological data on elevated rates of lifetime suicide attempts (40% vs 4.6%), severe distress (39% vs 5%), and clinical depression (52% vs 8.4%) diagnoses that are well documented among this population.[3–5]

Systematically vulnerable trans communities (i.e., those who are vulnerable because of individual circumstances and broader, entrenched systems of inequality that have consistently and historically disadvantaged them)—including younger, Black, Indigenous, Latinx, Asian American, and Pacific Islander trans communities—experience pronounced stress-sensitive mental health conditions as a result of chronic stress stemming from experiences of bias, prejudice, and discrimination related to being transgender.[5] Despite recent advancements in public health's priorities and goals in the United States, trans communities continue to grapple with systemic barriers to mental health services. Community health workers (CHWs) are crucial for bridging this gap in mental health service provision.

It is well documented that trans communities have high rates of stress-sensitive mental health conditions and increased unmet mental health needs.[2] Despite these needs, access to mental health services remains a significant hurdle.[6] There are formidable deterrents to receiving help (1) at the structural level, for example, transphobia, widespread mental health stigma (e.g., viewing trans identity as a mental health illness), and lack of explicit protective policies for trans health; (2) at the social level, for example, fear of discrimination, misgendering, deadnaming, and other stigmatizing health care experiences; and (3) at the economic level, for example, the high expense of mental health services and the opportunity costs of accessing care. Additional barriers are patients' mistrust of mental health professionals, mental health providers' lack of knowledge and cultural sensitivity, and patients' shame in discussing emotional challenges.[2,6] The scarcity of resources coupled with the evolving sociopolitical contexts that undermine trans health[7] compound the limited availability of mental health services, often leaving trans community members with nowhere to turn for help and care.

As they are already embedded in the communities they serve, CHWs are uniquely positioned and well suited to address the barriers that trans communities experience in their attempts to access mental health services.[8] CHWs are key implementation agents with the potential to enhance equitable and culturally appropriate access, particularly for communities of color.[8–11] They can facilitate access to care because they are generally hired for their community expertise, understanding of the individuals they assist, and ability to foster the trust and understanding that is often missing in conventional health care settings. CHWs also often work with caregivers (e.g., neighbors, social workers, clergy members, and parents, grandparents, and other family members).

Having CHWs directly provide services—often involving outreach, education, informal counseling, social support, and advocacy—could lead to improved population health outcomes, reduced health disparities, enhanced trans-focused health intervention, and increased patient satisfaction, as well as a more efficient use of resources and alignment with the current trend toward more patient-centered, community-based, and integrated models of care. There is a potential for them to work with trans communities of color and their families to address concerns about support and acceptance. CHWs' rapport and deep community knowledge would allow them to be key facilitators in peer-led or -mentored evidence-based mental health interventions, including trans-focused interventions that use community engagement approaches.[8,9,12]

CHWs can provide health education to trans individuals and their families and caregivers about mental health issues, including the importance of seeking help, available mental health resources, and patient rights[1,8–11]; social support, which can help reduce the feelings of isolation and stigma that many trans individuals experience[1,2,11]; and links to culturally and linguistically appropriate services.[8,10] CHWs can also advocate trans needs beyond these individual-level services; for example, they can improve other health care providers' understanding of trans-specific mental health needs and promote trans-affirming practices. This could lead to improved health outcomes, increased patient satisfaction, and more efficient use of resources and alignment with the current trend toward more patient-centered, community-based, and integrated models of care.[1]

However, there are challenges to harnessing the benefits of employing CHWs. CHWs would need to be trained on community culture, language, and terminologies; best practices for affirming care (e.g., use of pronouns, names, affirming language); best practices on how to ask sensitive questions about gender goals (e.g., desire for hormones and surgeries); and mental health concerns.[1,3] Developing accessible (e.g., virtual[10]) gender-affirming care training as part of upskilling or specialty-focused training for CHWs could be a feasible solution. These challenges also apply to caregivers, and CHWs, once trained, could educate caregivers and families, particularly of trans youths, on navigating services.

Although the high expense of accessing mental health services cannot be changed by training CHWs, their training could include how to help trans youths and their families access cost-saving financial services and programs that can help lower economic strains. This could also include education on insurance coverage, medical gender affirmation (e.g., hormone or surgical interventions), social and legal transition steps (e.g., updating gender marker and legal name), and communication strategies in families and peer networks. This support is particularly critical for trans community members in the current political environment, in which numerous US states are targeting trans people with legislation to ban best-practice medical care and restrict the ability of trans people to access restrooms, participate in sports, and navigate other foundational elements of daily life.[7]

There is also the potential to invest in and train CHWs, particularly those who are trans community members from racially marginalized groups with lived experiences, in evidence-based treatment, such as cognitive behavioral therapy, and in trans-affirmative evidence-based mental health intervention[1,9]; this is particularly important given hurdles to hiring CHWs who can be deemed trustworthy, are vetted, and are culturally competent. As with most programs experiencing limited access to resources, including time and funding, sustainable investments in CHW programs are essential to ensure continuity and success.[1] Lastly, given that most research on the impact of CHW on mental health has, to our knowledge, been conducted in the context of the larger LGBTQ (lesbian, gay, bisexual, transgender/-sexual, queer or questioning) communities,[1,8] robust gender-specific research on the effectiveness of CHWs in improving mental health outcomes in trans populations is crucial to inform practice and policy.

Integrating CHWs across varied health care settings could provide a cost-effective approach to delivering evidence-based trans-affirming mental health services. Trans communities often seek mental health care services from a variety of settings, including private practices, federally qualified health centers, virtual medical clinics, community health centers, and general mental health care settings in local communities.[2,3] CHWs' integration into broad mental health and trans health services in these settings would be a significant health equity goal.[3]

It is important for community-based health care systems to delineate formative programming to tailor CHWs' training in gender-affirming care; this should involve engaging trans-focused community-based service organizations as partners. Additionally, investing in studies to evaluate the effectiveness of peer-led CHWs in delivering evidence-based mental health treatment is crucial for further informing best practices. Although CHW's are not immune to experiencing or perpetuating barriers, serious efforts are needed to address social and structural transphobia in mental health service system settings directly and more broadly across all providers. Ensuring that mental health services are accessible to and available for all requires that the health care workforce unlearn stigma and reflect and engage with communities, including trans communities.

CHWs equipped with knowledge and competence in affirming evidence-based mental health services could help bring evidence-based mental health research into practice ubiquitously and contribute to this public health goal. AJPH

CORRESPONDENCE

Correspondence should be sent to Dr. Arjee Javellana Restar, PhD, MPH, Weitzman Institute, Moses Weitzman Health System, Washington, DC 20011 (e-mail: restara@mwhs1.com). Reprints can be ordered at https://www.ajph.org by clicking the "Reprints" link.

PUBLICATION INFORMATION

Full Citation: Restar AJ, Baker K, Wang G, Ashley K, Damian AJ. Community health workers as catalysts for mental health promotion in transgender and nonbinary communities. *Am J Public Health*. 2025;115(1):34–36.

Acceptance Date: October 6, 2024.

DOI: https://doi.org/10.2105/AJPH.2024.307898

ORCID iDs:

Arjee Javellana Restar https://orcid.org/0000-0003-2992-8198

Grace Wang https://orcid.org/0000-0002-1392-1218

Karen Ashley https://orcid.org/0000-0001-5525-2377

CONTRIBUTORS

A. J. Restar conceptualized, developed, and wrote the editorial. K. Baker, G. Wang, K. Ashley, and A. J. Damian contributed edits and vital insights to the final version of the editorial.

ACKNOWLEDGMENTS

A. J. Restar is supported by the Research Education Institute for Diverse Scholars Program at Yale University School of Public Health, funded by the National Institute of Mental Health (grant R25MH087217), American Foundation for AIDS Research, the Foundation of AIDS Research, and the Weitzman Institute of the Moses Weitzman Health System.

Note. The content of this editorial is solely the responsibility of the authors and does not necessarily represent the official views of the funders.

CONFLICTS OF INTEREST

The authors have no conflicts of interest to declare.

REFERENCES

1. Pachankis JE, Clark KA, Jackson SD, Pereira K, Levine D. Current capacity and future implementation of mental health services in US LGBTQ community centers. *Psychiatr Serv*. 2021;72(6): 669–676. https://doi.org/10.1176/appi.ps.202000575
2. Scheim AI, Baker KE, Restar AJ, Sell RL. Health and health care among transgender adults in the United States. *Annu Rev Public Health*. 2022;43:503–523. https://doi.org/10.1146/annurev-publhealth-052620-100313
3. Restar AJ. Gender-affirming care is preventative care. *Lancet Reg Health Am*. 2023;24:100544. https://doi.org/10.1016/j.lana.2023.100544
4. James SE, Herman JL, Rankin S, Keisling M, Mottet L, Anafi M. *The Report of the 2015 US Transgender Survey*. 2016. Available at: https://transequality.org/sites/default/files/docs/usts/USTS-Full-Report-Dec17.pdf. Accessed October 22, 2024.
5. Pinna F, Paribello P, Somaini G, et al. Mental health in transgender individuals: a systematic review. *Int Rev Psychiatry*. 2022;34(3–4):292–359. https://doi.org/10.1080/09540261.2022.2093629
6. Snow A, Cerel J, Loeffler DN, Flaherty C. Barriers to mental health care for transgender and gender-nonconforming adults: a systematic literature review. *Health Soc Work*. 2019;44(3):149–155. https://doi.org/10.1093/hsw/hlz016
7. Restar AJ, Layland EK, Davis B, Thompson H, Streed C. The public health crisis state of transgender health care and policy. *Am J Public Health*. 2024;114(2):161–163. https://doi.org/10.2105/AJPH.2023.307523
8. Barnett ML, Salem H, Rosas YG, et al. Adapting community health worker care models to advance mental health services among LGBTQ youth. *Adm Policy Ment Health*. 2023;50(4):658–672. https://doi.org/10.1007/s10488-023-01268-9
9. Barnett ML, Lau AS, Miranda J. Lay health worker involvement in evidence-based treatment delivery: a conceptual model to address disparities in care. *Annu Rev Clin Psychol*. 2018;14:185–208. https://doi.org/10.1146/annurev-clinpsy-050817-084825
10. Damian AJ, Robinson S, Manzoor F, et al. A mixed methods evaluation of the feasibility, acceptability, and impact of a pilot project ECHO for community health workers (CHWs). *Pilot Feasibility Stud*. 2020; 6:132. https://doi.org/10.1186/s40814-020-00678-y
11. Chang W, Oo M, Rojas A, Damian AJ. Patients' perspectives on the feasibility, acceptability, and impact of a community health worker program: a qualitative study. *Health Equity*. 2021;5(1):160–168. https://doi.org/10.1089/heq.2020.0159
12. Restar A, Minalga BJ, Quilantang MI, et al. Mapping community-engaged implementation strategies with transgender scientists, stakeholders, and trans-led community organizations. *Curr HIV/AIDS Rep*. 2023;20(3):160–169. https://doi.org/10.1007/s11904-023-00656-y

Safeguarding SNAP as an Effective Antihunger Program: Myths and Potential Harms of Adding Diet Quality as a Core Objective

Danielle M. Krobath, PhD, Jourdyn A. Lawrence, PhD, MSPH, Benjamin W. Chrisinger, PhD, MUEP, and Adolfo G. Cuevas, PhD

ABOUT THE AUTHORS

Danielle M. Krobath is with the Arnold School of Public Health, University of South Carolina, Columbia, and the Friedman School of Nutrition Science and Policy, Tufts University, Boston, MA. Jourdyn A. Lawrence is with the Dornsife School of Public Health, Drexel University, Philadelphia, PA. Benjamin W. Chrisinger is with the Department of Community Health, Tufts University, Medford, MA. Adolfo G. Cuevas is with the School of Global Public Health and the Center for Anti-Racism, Social Justice, and Public Health, New York University, New York, NY.

Food insecurity is a critical threat to the health and well-being of the US population.[1] The US Department of Agriculture (USDA) defines food insecurity as "limited or uncertain access to adequate food." An estimated 12.8% (17.0 million) of US households experienced food insecurity in 2022.[2] Food insecurity risk is unequally distributed across racial and ethnic groups; structural racism and other forms of economic and social disenfranchisement place Black, Hispanic, Indigenous, and immigrant individuals at the highest risk of poverty and low or very low food security.[3,4] Food insecurity, a source of toxic stress,[5] is associated with adverse psychological health outcomes (e.g., depression and anxiety) and a greater risk of obesity, hypertension, and other cardiometabolic diseases.[6,7]

Among the largest and most effective federal tools for addressing food insecurity is the Supplemental Nutrition Assistance Program (SNAP). The Food and Nutrition Act of 2008, commonly called the Farm Bill, reinaugurated earlier versions of the federal Food Stamps Program as SNAP, stating that "to alleviate such hunger and malnutrition, a supplemental nutrition assistance program is herein authorized which will permit low-income households to obtain a more nutritious diet through normal channels of trade by increasing food purchasing power for all eligible households who apply for participation." In 2022, government spending on SNAP totaled $119.4 billion, assisting 41.2 million Americans each month (more than 40% of whom were children).[2] Because the harms of food insecurity have devastating lifelong effects, prevention must remain a central goal of public health.

SNAP is the subject of frequent debate in both media and politics, often along broad partisan ideologies.[8] Yet, policymakers and public health advocates across the aisle are currently discussing significant changes to the goals and structure of SNAP by advocating for a new core program objective of improving diet quality. If successful, this would shift SNAP from an antihunger income support program to a dietary health intervention through new nutrition standards limiting the foods and beverages covered by benefits.

Although proponents point to predicted health benefits from SNAP restrictions, these nutritionally focused outcomes threaten the dignity and autonomy of participants and do not fully account for impacts beyond purchasing "junk" foods.[9] Imposing nutritional restrictions will interfere with the primary function of SNAP—reducing hunger by increasing purchasing power—without addressing the root causes of chronic disease disparities. In the following sections, we elaborate on three misconceptions underlying the rationale for making diet quality a core objective and restricting purchases along nutritional lines in SNAP. We then discuss hypothesized pathways through which restrictions may exacerbate health disparities. We conclude by highlighting how restrictions fit into a broader historical embodiment of systemic racism in US social welfare policy.[10]

MISCONCEPTIONS

We focus on the following three misconceptions associated with the rationale for making diet quality a core

AJPH January 2025, Vol. 115, No. 1

objective and restricting purchases along nutritional lines:

1. SNAP contributes to unhealthy dietary intake and causes health disparities.
2. Nutritional restrictions in SNAP will improve health and prevent disease among low-income Americans.
3. SNAP can be improved if it is more like the Special Supplemental Nutrition Program for Women, Infants, and Children (WIC).

Misconception 1

Advocates for restrictions believe that participants use SNAP to purchase unhealthy foods, yet the overall nutritional quality of their food purchases does not substantially differ from that among other Americans.[11] Diet quality is also similar between SNAP participants and the general population. A 2021 USDA study examined differences in diet quality between SNAP participants, income-eligible nonparticipants, and higher income Americans using National Health and Nutrition Examination Survey data from 2011 to 2016.[12] Diet quality, assessed with the Healthy Eating Index-2015 (HEI), was quantified as adherence to the Dietary Guidelines for Americans.

The mean Healthy Eating Index score for SNAP participants was 55 (out of 100), as compared with 57 for income-eligible nonparticipants and 60 for ineligible nonparticipants. The five-point score variance indicates that most Americans fail to meet federal dietary recommendations and does not justify imposing restrictions that limit autonomy solely among SNAP participants. In fact, SNAP participants purchase and consume healthier foods immediately after receiving monthly benefits than later in the same cycle, indicating that increased frequency and value of benefits could improve diet quality more ethically and efficiently than item restrictions.[13]

Supporters of adding diet quality as a core objective and restricting purchases in SNAP may also suggest that the lack of nutritional standards in the program causes obesity disparities among children and adults. After controlling for nonrandom selection into the program, most previous research has shown that SNAP participants are (at worst) no less cardiometabolically healthy than nonparticipants and (at best) healthier than eligible nonparticipants, particularly with respect to obesity risk. The aforementioned 2021 USDA study compared the cardiometabolic health of SNAP participants, eligible nonparticipants, and ineligible individuals. The results showed that women in SNAP had a slightly higher obesity prevalence than other women; overall, however, there were no significant differences in adult and child obesity rates.[12] Thus, although health and obesity disparities persist along income lines in the United States, the evidence suggests that the design of SNAP is not to blame.

Some proponents of restrictions purport that high rates of obesity and other chronic diseases among SNAP participants impose significant financial burdens on the economy and contribute to rising health care costs. Actually, SNAP reduces medical spending and increases health care access. In comparison with low-income nonparticipating adults, SNAP participants incur roughly 25% lower health care costs per year ($1400 less yearly). Medical cost savings are even stronger for members of low-income populations with chronic diseases; hypertensive adults in SNAP save nearly $2700 more per year than their counterparts.[14]

Misconception 2

There is scant evidence to support the belief that restrictions would achieve their stated outcomes, and rigorously testing potential causal effects is challenged by nonrandom self-selection into the program. Specifically, relative to income-eligible nonparticipants, individuals who take the time to navigate various administrative hurdles and enroll in SNAP have a greater prevalence of risk factors for nutrition-related chronic diseases, such as more severe food insecurity and deeper poverty.[15] However, one recent quasi-experimental study estimated that SNAP restrictions were associated with slight reductions in "junk food" spending but no significant changes in diet quality or body weight.[16] Overall, the evidence suggests that SNAP restrictions may not be an effective way of improving proximal (i.e., diet) or distal (i.e., obesity) outcomes.

Public health has long emphasized the causal effects of diet on obesity and other nutrition-related disease risks. Although crucial for health and longevity, diet is not the sole determinant of chronic disease risk or progression. These conditions are driven by overlapping biological, psychological, and social factors, including genetics, social determinants (e.g., food insecurity, housing, health care), and numerous nondietary health behaviors (e.g., sleep, physical activity). Even if SNAP restrictions were able to achieve dietary change equitably, diet is but one of many chronic disease risk factors disproportionately faced by low-income populations.

Misconception 3

SNAP effectively reduces food insecurity and prevents hunger, particularly among households with children and those facing extreme disadvantage. Previous research has shown that households with children that participated in SNAP for 6 months experienced a one-third reduction in food insecurity risk.[17] "Very low" food security—the most severe form—indicates that household members skipped meals and that their food intake was reduced because they could not afford food. Adults with very low food security are more than 40% as likely as others to develop hypertension, coronary heart disease, and other cardiovascular diseases.[18] SNAP reduces the risk of very low food security by roughly 20% and is one of the only safeguards against poverty in the United States; only approximately 4% of SNAP households without children and 10% of SNAP households with children receive cash welfare benefits from the government.[19] By successfully improving food security, the structure of SNAP buffers against the harmful effects of poverty and hunger on health.[17]

Proponents of restrictions argue that SNAP should be modeled after WIC to improve population health. This assumes that the item-restricted WIC program could be successfully scaled to the size and scope of SNAP. However, there are critical differences in program goals and structure. WIC is designed as a health intervention that prevents diet-related diseases among nutritionally at-risk populations (e.g., people with anemia or previous pregnancy complications) by providing food packages with the specific nutrients needed during pregnancy, breastfeeding, infancy, and early childhood. Meanwhile, SNAP is an antihunger program that serves about 6.5 times more Americans than WIC and is designed to empower families through financial assistance for groceries of choice. The differences in administrative burdens on retailers are also nontrivial, given the known difficulties in redeeming WIC benefits in some places.[20] Finally, participation rates in WIC drastically decline between the periods of infancy and two to five years of age, partially because of lowered perceived value once formula is no longer needed.

Another assumption is that WIC is more politically palatable than SNAP because of its nutritional restrictions. Proponents may hope that moving SNAP toward a more nutritionally focused, item-restricted program will insulate it from future cuts, although recent funding threats to WIC suggest otherwise. The federal government must ensure that, as an entitlement program, SNAP has sufficient funding to serve all eligible and enrolled participants at any given time.[17] Unlike SNAP, WIC is a discretionary program that requires agreement from the House of Representatives and Senate appropriations committees for annual funding, so there is always a chance that eligible WIC participants may experience benefit loss or the inability to enroll. The looming uncertainties surrounding funding of WIC, which is both smaller and more underused than SNAP, cast doubt on whether its design makes it impervious to partisan budget cuts.

CONSEQUENCES OF NUTRITIONAL RESTRICTIONS

Evidence does not support the assertion that setting nutrition standards for eligible SNAP purchases will improve diet quality or health. On the contrary, evidence suggests that should restrictions be implemented, they may instead produce a paradoxical effect through accumulation of new stressors that exacerbate preventable health disparities.

Restrictions could reduce household purchasing power for food (by households either exiting the program or receiving lower benefit amounts each month), which may increase stress through additional financial strain.[21] Often, SNAP allotments are already insufficient in meeting monthly food costs, and restrictions—especially if insensitive to relative food costs—could upset delicate budgeting strategies employed by households with the greatest economic barriers. Financial strain ripples through relationships and increases food insecurity risk as well as intrafamilial tensions caused by the stress imposed by insufficient resources.[5] Finally, the top-down approach embedded in restriction proposals would foster an increasingly stigmatizing and hostile social environment against low-income people, increasing their exposure to discrimination and, in turn, stress levels.[22]

Research by Herd and Moynihan underscores that introducing new item restrictions in SNAP would raise the administrative burden (psychological, time, and financial) for both retailers and consumers, reducing SNAP participation rates and creating additional racial health disparities.[23] Since 2004, all states have distributed SNAP benefits via electronic benefit transfer cards to reduce recipient stigma and encourage retailer participation by streamlining the redemption process. However, the stigma carried by electronic benefit transfer cards persists and would be exacerbated by new restrictions through the burden of split payments at the point of sale. Restrictions would also affect the retail side, particularly for small businesses that may face difficulty complying with new rules.

Overall, SNAP restrictions may increase health disparities by reinforcing stress through greater administrative burdens. Stress is particularly relevant given its impacts on energy balance and numerous diet-related chronic diseases. Stress can influence cardiometabolic health directly through biological mechanisms (i.e., elevated C-reactive protein levels and cortisol, which can contribute to excess inflammation and adiposity)[24] and indirectly through behavioral coping mechanisms, such as excess energy intake and suboptimal physical activity levels, and elevated risk of depression and anxiety. Thus, one might expect SNAP restrictions to worsen, not alleviate, physical and mental health disparities in the United States.

SUSPICION AND SYSTEMIC RACISM IN THE US SOCIAL SAFETY NET

We must acknowledge the ways in which proposed reforms to SNAP fit into larger histories of systemic racism. As with other aspects of the social safety net in the United States, the context in which SNAP was implemented reflected entrenched racial biases and beliefs about the "undeserving poor."[25] The origins of the racist and classist rhetoric against social welfare programs partially stem from the Reagan administration's public campaigning against the "welfare queen," an ongoing stereotype insinuating that low-income Black mothers are too lazy to work, misuse public welfare programs, are incapable of making rational or honest decisions, and have children only to receive government assistance. This odious stereotype is rooted in beliefs about the "deservingness" of the poor for public assistance, seeking to delineate groups who merit aid based on moral, biological, or cultural factors rather than acknowledge poverty as an intentional outcome stemming from specific policy decisions and priorities.[25]

These framings reify racist stereotypes; reinforce a linkage of poverty to marginalized racial identities, especially Blackness; and are increasingly evident in research examining the realized implications of such biases. For instance, Snowden found significantly lower SNAP coverage rates among adults in states where White residents had higher levels of anti-Black biases.[26]

Discriminatory rhetoric determines who has access to and can use social safety net programs. Implicit in SNAP restriction ideology is a belief that low-income individuals are unable or unwilling to use benefits "correctly." This narrative may suggest that people deserve federal food assistance only if benefits are used to purchase and consume a set of foods approved by the government, ignoring the complex determinants of food choice. Evaluations of congressional transcripts from 2000 to 2018 revealed increasingly punitive approaches to antihunger policies and a growing legislative discourse that shapes SNAP participants as dependent, criminal, and obese, presenting both weight and poverty in a moral framework.[27] It is no coincidence that stereotypes (e.g., "welfare queen") and questions of ability (e.g., making healthy purchases) manifest and affect social policies today given the historical contexts of anti-Blackness and other forms of racism in which antipoverty programs such as food stamps were introduced.[3]

Introducing additional restrictions into SNAP would have an impact on all recipients but would disproportionately affect those holding marginalized identities, primarily Black individuals and other people of color. Within discussions of proposed nutritional restrictions, there remains undue scrutiny of where, how, and on what items SNAP participants spend funds intended to lessen hunger and alleviate financial strain. In comparison with other racialized individuals, Black shoppers experience more surveillance, suspicion, and mistreatment in many aspects of their daily life, including in retail settings. Thus, restrictions may further drive racial disparities in stress as populations are differentially scrutinized while attempting to shop for groceries. Restrictions reinforce an ideology of personal responsibility and ignore structural determinants giving rise to US food environments, such as the consistently fewer supermarkets (a primary redemption site for SNAP benefits) in low-income Black neighborhoods.[28]

CONCLUSION

US social welfare programming sometimes focuses on inflicting paternalistic ideals on individuals experiencing poverty rather than addressing the interconnected social, political, and economic determinants of health. SNAP restrictions reduce autonomy and ignore the root causes of health disparities while critiquing the purchasing and dietary decisions of low-income individuals seeking support for hunger. The proposal to create nutritional criteria for SNAP-eligible items—which on its face may appear race neutral and aimed toward preventing disease—could exacerbate racial inequities in health and SNAP utilization. Rather than singling out the behaviors of low-income individuals, nutrition policies and interventions should strive to address the existing racialized and gendered oppression embedded throughout the social safety net while improving the diet quality of the entire population. AJPH

CORRESPONDENCE

Correspondence should be sent to Danielle M. Krobath, Department of Epidemiology and Biostatistics, Arnold School of Public Health, University of South Carolina, 915 Greene St, Columbia, SC 29208 (e-mail: dkrobath@mailbox.sc.edu). Reprints can be ordered at https://www.ajph.org by clicking the "Reprints" link.

PUBLICATION INFORMATION

Full Citation: Krobath DM, Lawrence JA, Chrisinger BW, Cuevas AG. Safeguarding SNAP as an effective antihunger program: myths and potential harms of adding diet quality as a core objective. *Am J Public Health*. 2025;115(1):37–41.

Acceptance Date: August 30, 2024.

DOI: https://doi.org/10.2105/AJPH.2024.307863

ORCID iDs:

Danielle M. Krobath https://orcid.org/0000-0003-2607-5302

Benjamin W. Chrisinger https://orcid.org/0000-0002-1480-6481

CONTRIBUTORS

All of the authors contributed to the conceptualization, drafting, and revising of the article.

CONFLICTS OF INTEREST

The authors have no conflicts of interest to report.

REFERENCES

1. Coleman-Jensen A, Gregory C, Singh A. Household food security in the United States in 2013. Available at: https://www.ers.usda.gov/webdocs/publications/45265/48787_err173.pdf. Accessed June 11, 2024.
2. Rabbitt MP, Hales LJ, Burke MP, Coleman-Jensen A. Household food security in the United States in 2022. Available at: http://www.ers.usda.gov/publications/pub-details/?pubid=107702. Accessed June 11, 2024.
3. Bowen S, Elliott S, Hardison-Moody A. The structural roots of food insecurity: how racism is a fundamental cause of food insecurity. *Sociol Compass*. 2021;15(7):e12846. https://doi.org/10.1111/soc4.12846
4. Flores-Lagunes A, Jales HB, Liu J, Wilson NL. The differential incidence and severity of food insecurity by racial, ethnic, and immigrant groups over the great recession in the United States. *AEA Pap Proc*. 2018;108:379–383. https://doi.org/10.1257/pandp.20181106
5. Leung CW, Odoms-Young A, Essel K. Food insecurity is a source of toxic stress. *JAMA Pediatr*. 2024;178(4):327. https://doi.org/10.1001/jamapediatrics.2023.6400
6. Chang R, Javed Z, Taha M, et al. Food insecurity and cardiovascular disease: current trends and future directions. *Am J Prev Cardiol*. 2021;9:100303. https://doi.org/10.1016/j.ajpc.2021.100303
7. Bruening M, Dinour LM, Chavez JBR. Food insecurity and emotional health in the USA: a systematic narrative review of longitudinal research. *Public Health Nutr*. 2017;20(17):3200–3208. https://doi.org/10.1017/S1368980017002221
8. Chrisinger BW, Kinsey EW, Pavlick E, Callison-Burch C. SNAP judgments into the digital age: reporting on food stamps varies significantly with time, publication type, and political leaning. *PLoS One*. 2020;15(2):e0229180. https://doi.org/10.1371/journal.pone.0229180
9. Gundersen C. Ensuring the dignity and autonomy of SNAP recipients. *Physiol Behav*. 2020;221:112909. https://doi.org/10.1016/j.physbeh.2020.112909
10. Bailey ZD, Feldman JM, Bassett MT. How structural racism works—racist policies as a root cause of US racial health inequities. *N Engl J Med*. 2021;384(8):768–773. https://doi.org/10.1056/NEJMms2025396
11. Food and Nutrition Service. Foods typically purchased by Supplemental Nutrition Assistance Program (SNAP) households. Available at: https://www.fns.usda.gov/snap/foods-typically-purchased-supplemental-nutrition-assistance-program-snap-households. Accessed December 5, 2023.
12. Food and Nutrition Service. Indicators of diet quality, nutrition, and health for Americans by program participation status, 2011–2016: the SNAP report. Available at: https://www.fns.usda.gov/snap/indicators-diet-quality-nutrition-and-health-americans-program-participation-status-2011. Accessed December 5, 2023.
13. Whiteman ED, Chrisinger BW, Hillier A. Diet quality over the monthly Supplemental Nutrition Assistance Program cycle. *Am J Prev Med*. 2018;55(2):205–212. https://doi.org/10.1016/j.amepre.2018.04.027
14. Berkowitz SA, Seligman HK, Rigdon J, Meigs JB, Basu S. Supplemental Nutrition Assistance Program (SNAP) participation and health care expenditures among low-income adults. *JAMA Intern Med*. 2017;177(11):1642–1649. https://doi.org/10.1001/jamainternmed.2017.4841
15. Nord M, Golla M. Does SNAP decrease food insecurity? Untangling the self-selection effect. Available at: http://www.ers.usda.gov/publications/pub-details/?pubid=46297. Accessed June 11, 2024.
16. Harnack LJ, Oakes JM, Elbel B, et al. Effects of inclusion of food purchase restrictions and incentives in a food benefit program on diet quality and food purchasing: results from a randomized trial. *J Acad Nutr Diet*. 2024;124(5):569–582.e3. https://doi.org/10.1016/j.jand.2023.11.024
17. Keith-Jennings B, Llobrera J, Dean S. Links of the Supplemental Nutrition Assistance Program with food insecurity, poverty, and health: evidence and potential. *Am J Public Health*. 2019;109(12):1636–1640. https://doi.org/10.2105/AJPH.2019.305325
18. Gregory CA, Coleman-Jensen A. Food insecurity, chronic disease, and health among working-age adults. Available at: http://199.135.94.241/publications/pub-details/?pubid=84466. Accessed December 5, 2023.
19. Cronquist K. Characteristics of Supplemental Nutrition Assistance Program households: fiscal year 2019. Available at: https://www.fns.usda.gov/research/snap/characteristics-snap-households-fy-2019. Accessed June 11, 2024.
20. Barnes CY. "It takes a while to get used to": the costs of redeeming public benefits. *J Public Adm Res Theory*. 2021;31(2):295–310. https://doi.org/10.1093/jopart/muaa042
21. Pearlin LI, Schieman S, Fazio EM, Meersman SC. Stress, health, and the life course: some conceptual perspectives. *J Health Soc Behav*. 2005;46(2):205–219. https://doi.org/10.1177/002214650504600206
22. Gaines-Turner T, Simmons JC, Chilton M. Recommendations from SNAP participants to improve wages and end stigma. *Am J Public Health*. 2019;109(12):1664–1667. https://doi.org/10.2105/AJPH.2019.305362
23. Herd P, Moynihan DP. *Administrative Burden: Policymaking by Other Means*. New York, NY: Russell Sage Foundation; 2018. https://doi.org/10.7758/9781610448789
24. Lawrence JA, Kawachi I, White K, et al. A systematic review and meta-analysis of the Everyday Discrimination Scale and biomarker outcomes. *Psychoneuroendocrinology*. 2022;142:105772. https://doi.org/10.1016/j.psyneuen.2022.105772
25. Katz MB. *The Undeserving Poor: America's Enduring Confrontation with Poverty: Fully Updated and Revised*. 2nd ed. New York, NY: Oxford University Press; 2013.
26. Snowden LR. US states' racial bias correlates with less SNAP participation by "undeserving poor" adults and lower unemployment benefit maximums. *Poverty Public Policy*. 2023;15(2):133–149. https://doi.org/10.1002/pop4.371
27. Scampini R. The food police: food stamps, surveillance, and the construction of the undeserving hungry. Available at: https://dc.uwm.edu/etd/2832. Accessed December 5, 2023.
28. Bower KM, Thorpe RJ, Rohde C, Gaskin DJ. The intersection of neighborhood racial segregation, poverty, and urbanicity and its impact on food store availability in the United States. *Prev Med*. 2014;58:33–39. https://doi.org/10.1016/j.ypmed.2013.10.010

Prior Authorization Requirements and Medicaid Enrollees' Use of Tobacco Cessation Medications, Colorado, 2023

Marcus Dillender, PhD, and Robin Mermelstein, PhD

Despite tobacco cessation medications being a first-line treatment for quitting smoking, a majority of Medicaid programs require health care providers to obtain prior authorization before prescribing them. We examined the impact of Colorado's Medicaid program removing its prior authorization requirement for these drugs on their use and estimated the additional number of Coloradoans who used these therapies in 2023 because of the policy change. The findings indicate that these requirements decrease low-income people's use of these medications. (*Am J Public Health*. 2025;115(1):42–46. https://doi.org/10.2105/AJPH.2024.307868)

AJPH January 2025, Vol. 115, No. 1

Smoking is the leading cause of preventable disease in the United States, and reducing smoking rates is a public health priority.[1] Tobacco cessation medications are recommended as a first-line treatment for people trying to quit smoking.[2] However, less than one third of smokers use these medications when trying to quit.[2] Relative to people with high incomes, people with low incomes are more likely to smoke and less likely to use tobacco cessation medications when trying to quit smoking.[2] Many low-income people are insured by Medicaid, and a potential reason for the limited use of tobacco cessation medications among low-income smokers is that Medicaid programs restrict the use of these medications through various managed care practices. One practice in particular that is widely used in Medicaid programs and has the potential to reduce the use of tobacco cessation medications is requiring doctors to obtain prior authorization (PA) from Medicaid administrators before prescribing tobacco cessation medications to Medicaid enrollees. As of 2018, more than two thirds of state Medicaid programs had prior authorization requirements (PARs) in place for tobacco cessation medications.[3]

Proponents of PARs argue that they can improve prescribing practices by leading to safer and more cost-effective prescribing while still maintaining patients' access to treatment.[4,5] In Medicaid programs, in particular, PA requests are nearly always approved.[6,7] PA's detractors argue that PARs are burdensome for health care providers and have the potential to reduce access to beneficial care.[8–10] Even in settings where PA requests are nearly universally approved, PARs can reduce access to medications by affecting providers' prescribing patterns. Though the hurdles for obtaining PA are typically small in Medicaid programs,[6,11] research has shown that even low-burden PARs can have large impacts on prescribing patterns.[12]

INTERVENTION AND IMPLEMENTATION

In this study, we used quasi-experimental research methods to examine the effect of Colorado's Medicaid program removing its PAR for two types of tobacco cessation medications—nicotine-replacement medications and varenicline—on the use of these medications. Before November 1, 2018, Colorado health care providers had to obtain PA from Medicaid administrators before they could prescribe nicotine-replacement medications or varenicline to Medicaid enrollees. Beginning on November 1, 2018, providers could prescribe up to 180 days of these targeted tobacco cessation medications without first obtaining PA. The medications could be obtained at pharmacies with no out-of-pocket costs for Medicaid enrollees.

PLACE, TIME, AND PERSONS

The treatment sample consists of Colorado Medicaid enrollees aged 18 to 64 years within five quarters of the PAR being removed. We included five quarters before and after the removal of the PAR to facilitate assessing how outcomes trended before and after the PAR was removed. We estimated the impact of removing the PAR using a difference-in-differences research design that compared how differences in prescription utilization between Medicaid enrollees and a control group of people not enrolled in Medicaid changed after Colorado Medicaid removed its PAR. For the control group, we identified individuals aged 18 to 64 years with health insurance purchased through the individual market exchanges during the same period because Medicaid PA rules would be unlikely to have major effects on their use of these medications. The treatment group of people covered by Medicaid includes 3 392 610 quarterly observations from 339 261 individuals. The control group of people covered by private insurance includes 4 567 410 observations from 456 741 individuals.

PURPOSE

Despite the importance of access to tobacco cessation medications and the widespread use of PARs in Medicaid programs, little has been known about the impact of PARs on tobacco cessation medication use. Prominent public health leaders have called for additional research into the impact of public policies and insurance design on the use of tobacco cessation treatments.[2,13] The purpose of this study was to examine the impact of removing PARs for tobacco cessation medications in Medicaid programs.

EVALUATION AND ADVERSE EFFECTS

We used data from the Colorado All Payer Claims Database on prescription drugs and created measures that summarized each person's use of tobacco cessation medication in each quarter. In addition, we used the database's eligibility file with information on when people were covered by specific insurance plans and the database's enrollee-level file with basic information on enrollees, including their gender, age, and zip code.

To implement the difference-in-differences approach, we estimated linear probability models that include indicator variables for being enrolled in Medicaid and for being male, fixed effects for quarters relative to the policy change, zip-code-of-residence fixed effects, age, and an indicator variable for being a Medicaid enrollee interacted with an indicator variable for the PAR having been removed. The quarter fixed effects capture statewide time trends in the use of tobacco cessation medications shared by Medicaid and private enrollees, while the Medicaid indicator variable accounts for baseline differences between Medicaid and private enrollees. The coefficient on the indicator variable for Medicaid enrollees after the PAR was removed was the estimated impact of removing the PAR on Medicaid enrollees. We estimated three models, one for each of the following outcomes: (1) receiving either varenicline or nicotine-replacement therapy in a quarter, (2) receiving varenicline in a quarter, and (3) receiving nicotine-replacement therapy in a quarter.

Figure 1 plots percentage point differences in the shares of Medicaid and private enrollees using tobacco cessation medications in each quarter relative to the shares of the respective samples using these medications in the first quarter of the analysis period. Specifically, for each quarter of the data, Figure 1 plots the share of each sample receiving either varenicline or nicotine replacement therapy in that quarter minus the share of the sample receiving either of these medications in the first quarter of the analysis period. The use of tobacco cessation medications trended in parallel for the treatment and control groups until Colorado's Medicaid program removed the PAR for tobacco cessation medications. After the PAR was removed, the use of tobacco cessation medications for the private control group did not change, while Medicaid enrollees' use of tobacco cessation medications immediately increased in the following quarter.

Table 1 displays the estimated effects of removing the PAR from the difference-in-differences models. Consistent with Figure 1, the estimate in column 1 indicates that removing the PAR increased the likelihood that Medicaid enrollees received a prescription for varenicline or nicotine-replacement therapy by 0.32 percentage points, which is a 68% increase in prescriptions for one of these medications relative to the baseline share of Medicaid enrollees who received them when prescribers had to receive PA before prescribing them of 0.46%. Columns 2 and 3 display separate estimates of the impact of removing the PAR on prescriptions for varenicline and prescriptions for nicotine-replacement therapy. Removing the PAR

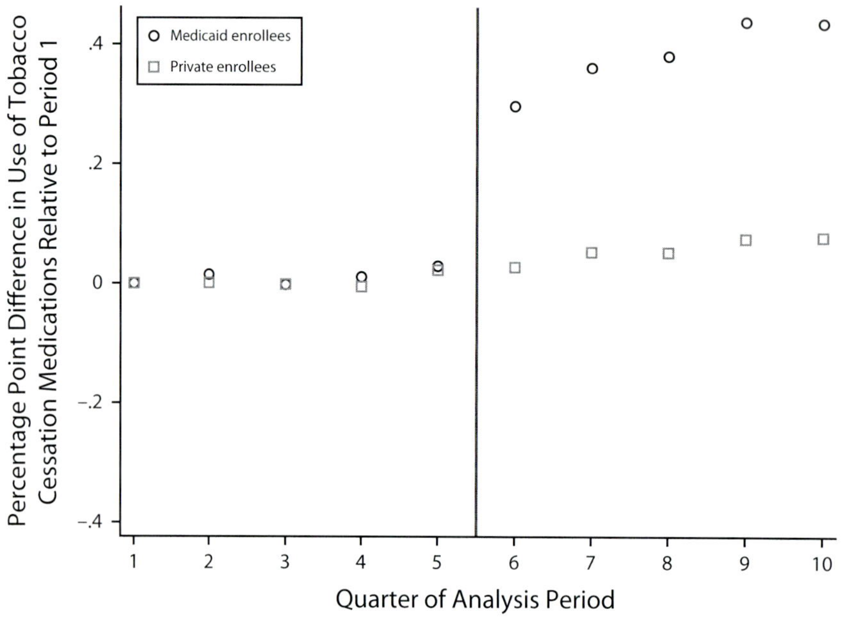

FIGURE 1— Changes in the Use of Tobacco Cessation Medications Over the Analysis Period for Medicaid and Private Enrollees: Colorado, 2017–2020

Note. The vertical line indicates when the prior authorization requirement (PAR) for tobacco cessation medications for Medicaid enrollees was removed.

increased the likelihood that a Medicaid patient received varenicline in a quarter by 55% and nicotine-replacement therapy in a quarter by 92% relative to the baseline shares of 0.29% and 0.18%.

We next used the March 2023 Current Population Survey[14] to estimate the additional number of Colorodoans who used these medications in 2023 because of the Colorado Medicaid program's removal of the PAR for tobacco cessation medications. A quarterly increase in the share of people using tobacco cessation medications of 0.32 translates to an annual increase in the number of quarters of use of tobacco cessation medications of 1.28 per 100 Medicaid enrollees (a 0.32 per-quarter increase multiplied by four quarters in a year). Assuming all enrollees received the two quarters of these medications

TABLE 1— The Effect of Removing the Prior Authorization Requirement (PAR) on the Use of Tobacco Cessation Medications: Colorado, 2017–2020

	Outcomes: Receives a Prescription for the Following		
	Model 1: Varenicline or Nicotine-Replacement Therapy[a]	Model 2: Varenicline	Model 3: Nicotine-Replacement Therapy
Effect of removing PAR, B (SE)	0.32* (0.01)	0.16* (0.01)	0.17* (0.01)
Mean of outcome for Medicaid enrollees before policy change[b]	0.46	0.29	0.18

Note. This table displays difference-in-differences estimates of the percentage point effect of Colorado's Medicaid program removing its PAR for prescriptions for targeted tobacco cessation medications from linear probability models. The sample for each regression had 7 960 020 individuals. The regression models control for an indicator variable for being enrolled in Medicaid, fixed effects for quarters relative to the policy change, zip-code-of-residence fixed effects, an indicator variable for being male, and age.
[a]The first entry next to "Effect of removing PAR" is the estimated effect from the difference-in-differences model, B, while the SE clustered at the individual level is next to the estimated effect in parentheses.
[b]The values in this row are raw percentages and are not outputs from the regression models.
*P < .01.

allowed by the Colorado Medicaid program, the estimate indicates that removing the PAR for these medications led to a 0.64-percentage-point increase in the share of the Medicaid population receiving this treatment within the first year of the PAR being removed (1.28/2 = 0.64). Multiplying this number by the 2023 number of Medicaid enrollees in Colorado aged 18 to 64 years estimated from the Current Population Survey of approximately 460 000 indicates that removing the PAR led to roughly 2900 additional Coloradoans receiving tobacco cessation medications in 2023. Thus, we estimate that Colorado removing the PAR raised the total number of Colorado's Medicaid enrollees using tobacco cessation medications from roughly 4200 to more than 7000. For context, the estimated number of Colorado Medicare enrollees using tobacco cessation medications in 2023 was 2700, which we obtained by multiplying the share of Medicare enrollees using tobacco cessation medications in the claims data by the number of Medicare enrollees estimated from the Current Population Survey.

SUSTAINABILITY

The increased use of tobacco cessation medications from removing PARs will increase costs for Medicaid programs by increasing spending on these drugs. However, the increased costs from spending on tobacco cessation medications must be weighed against cost savings from potential reductions in smoking. Research indicates that tobacco cessation medications can reduce overall costs in the long term.[15]

PUBLIC HEALTH SIGNIFICANCE

Despite the widespread use of PARs for tobacco cessation medications in Medicaid, there has been a relatively limited understanding of their impacts. Our findings indicate that PARs reduce people's use of tobacco cessation medications and that removing these requirements can greatly increase the number of people using tobacco cessation medications. As Medicaid covers people with low incomes, this increase in the use of targeted tobacco cessation medications would reduce socioeconomic disparities in who accesses them. AJPH

ABOUT THE AUTHORS

Marcus Dillender is with the Department of Economics, Vanderbilt University, Nashville, TN. Robin Mermelstein is with the Department of Psychology and the Institute for Health Research and Policy, University of Illinois at Chicago.

CORRESPONDENCE

Correspondence should be sent to Marcus Dillender, 2301 Vanderbilt Place PMB 1819, Nashville, TN 37235 (e-mail: marcus.o.dillender@vanderbilt.edu). Reprints can be ordered at https://www.ajph.org by clicking the "Reprints" link.

PUBLICATION INFORMATION

Full Citation: Dillender M, Mermelstein R. Prior authorization requirements and Medicaid enrollees' use of tobacco cessation medications, Colorado, 2023. *Am J Public Health*. 2025;115(1):42–46.

Acceptance Date: August 31, 2024.

DOI: https://doi.org/10.2105/AJPH.2024.307868

ORCID iDs:

Marcus Dillender https://orcid.org/0000-0003-3838-2465

Robin Mermelstein https://orcid.org/0000-0002-8690-1074

CONTRIBUTORS

M. Dillender contributed to all aspects of the study, including developing hypotheses, performing data analysis, interpreting and framing the results, and writing and editing the article. R. Mermelstein contributed to the study by interpreting and framing the results and writing and editing the article.

ACKNOWLEDGMENTS

This work was funded by the National Cancer Institute (R03CA270451).

Note. Results do not imply the endorsement of the National Cancer Institute.

CONFLICTS OF INTEREST

The authors have no conflicts of interest to disclose.

HUMAN PARTICIPANT PROTECTION

This study was reviewed and approved by Vanderbilt's institutional review board (application 222095).

REFERENCES

1. US Department of Health and Human Services. *The Health Consequences of Smoking—50 Years of Progress: A Report of the Surgeon General*. Atlanta, GA: Centers for Disease Control and Prevention, National Center for Chronic Disease Prevention and Health Promotion, Office on Smoking and Health; 2014.
2. Office of the Surgeon General. *Smoking Cessation: A Report of the Surgeon General*. Washington, DC: US Department of Health and Human Services; 2020.
3. DiGiulio A, Jump Z, Babb S, et al. State Medicaid coverage for tobacco cessation treatments and barriers to accessing treatments—United States, 2008–2018. *MMWR Morb Mortal Wkly Rep*. 2020;69(6):155–160. https://doi.org/10.15585/mmwr.mm6906a2
4. Council for Affordable Quality Healthcare. CAQH CORE releases operating rules to promote automation for prior authorization. May 15, 2019. Available at: https://www.prnewswire.com/news-releases/caqh-core-releases-operating-rules-to-promote-automation-for-prior-authorization-300850964.html. Accessed October 10, 2024.
5. America's Health Insurance Plans and the Blue Cross Blue Shield Association. *Utilization Management: Barriers to Care and Burdens on Small Medical Practices*. Washington, DC: Committee on Small Business; 2019.
6. Andersen M. Constraints on formulary design under the Affordable Care Act. *Health Econ*. 2017;26(12):e160–e178. https://doi.org/10.1002/hec.3491
7. Delate T, Mager DE, Sheth J, Motheral BR. Clinical and financial outcomes associated with a proton pump inhibitor prior-authorization program in a Medicaid population. *Am J Manag Care*. 2005;11(1):29–36.
8. Casalino LP, Nicholson S, Gans DN, et al. What does it cost physician practices to interact with health insurance plans? *Health Aff (Millwood)*. 2009;28(4, suppl 1):w533–w543. https://doi.org/10.1377/hlthaff.28.4.w533

9. Huskamp HA, Deverka PA, Epstein AM, Epstein RS, Mcguigan KA, Frank RG. The effect of incentive-based formularies on prescription-drug utilization and spending. *N Engl J Med.* 2003;349(23):2224–2232. https://doi.org/10.1056/NEJMsa030954
10. 2020 AMA Prior Authorization (PA) Physician Survey. Chicago, IL: American Medical Association; 2021.
11. Hargrave E. Trends in US Prescription Drug Benefits, 2006–2015. Chicago, IL: NORC at the University of Chicago; 2017.
12. Dillender M. What happens when the insurer can say no? Assessing prior authorization as a tool to prevent high-risk prescriptions and to lower costs. *J Public Econ.* 2018;165:170–200. https://doi.org/10.1016/j.jpubeco.2018.07.006
13. *Tobacco Control Research Priorities for the Next Decade: Working Group Recommendations for 2016–2025.* Bethesda, MD: National Cancer Institute; 2016.
14. Flood S, King M, Rodgers R, Ruggles S, Warren JR. Integrated Public Use Microdata Series, Current Population Survey: Version 8.0. Minneapolis, MN: IPUMS; 2020. https://doi.org/10.18128/D030.V8.0
15. Baker CL, Ding Y, Ferrufino CP, Kowal S, Tan J, Subedi P. A cost–benefit analysis of smoking cessation prescription coverage from a US payer perspective. *Clinicoecon Outcomes Res.* 2018;10:359–370. https://doi.org/10.2147/CEOR.S165576

Equity Zones: Building the Bridge to Transformation

Christopher Ausura, BS, Genese Turner, MIPS, Jennifer Latham, MPH, Nicole Marcus, BS, Susanne Schnell, MA, and Brian Edmiston, MPH

This article is a call to action for transformative health equity initiatives empowering communities to address systemic health inequities through expanded implementation and enhanced evaluation of health equity zone models. These models prioritize community capacity building and power sharing for upstream, transformative change, urging increased investment in transformative public health practice. Lessons from Rhode Island and Chicago, Illinois, highlight strategies for preventing health inequities and reducing downstream needs among vulnerable populations, underscoring the need for developing innovative evaluation practices measuring transformative change. (*Am J Public Health*. 2025;115(1):47–51. https://doi.org/10.2105/AJPH.2024.307872)

AJPH January 2025, Vol. 115, No. 1

Public health can learn from two equity zone initiatives that prioritize preventing health inequities and reducing treatment needs among underserved populations. Recognizing social determinants of health (SDOH) and systemic racism[1] as primary drivers of health inequity and outcomes largely preventable,[2] it is clear that equity requires understanding differing needs and investing accordingly.

The COVID-19 pandemic highlighted the impact of these inequities, with higher transmission rates and deaths in populations more negatively affected by SDOH. While responses eventually aimed to address inequities,[3] they were often temporary and failed to improve social, environmental, and economic conditions. Efforts to make health care and social services more accessible did not resolve underlying structural drivers[4] of health inequity.

Rhode Island Department of Health's (RIDOH's) Health Equity Zones (HEZs) and the Chicago Department of Public Health's (CDPH's) Healthy Chicago Equity Zones (HCEZs) are models for transformative changes to social, environmental, and economic determinants. These community co-owned approaches build collaboratives, conduct assessments, and implement data-driven SDOH action plans.

INTERVENTION AND IMPLEMENTATION

Traditional interventions improve short-term outcomes but do not achieve systemic changes. The equity zone model supports systemic change along a continuum (Figure 1) that involves time-intensive, community co-led interventions addressing structural inequities, requiring intentional resource investment and equitable response to community needs.

The equity zone continuum starts with building relationships and trust to create a shared vision. It culminates with community co-owned systems-level change strategies. During the time-intensive transition to long-term outcomes, community-led interventions address structural inequities, supporting transformational work and upstream change. This requires intentional resource investment, initially by leveraging and braiding programmatic resources to equitably meet community needs. However, progress stalls if resources remain tied solely to programmatic outcomes; true transformation requires transformational resources.

Authentic trust building and power sharing[5] with communities, in all aspects of design, is critical for operationalizing equity. Both CDPH and RI, with their community partners, consistently reflect on institutional power dynamics, fostering community ownership, capacity, and skills for local change. This collective commitment has empowered community members to lead systems-level changes, reinforcing the equity-centered model as community ownership evolves. The equity-centered approach builds new frameworks (Figure 2) for community-owned transformational change.

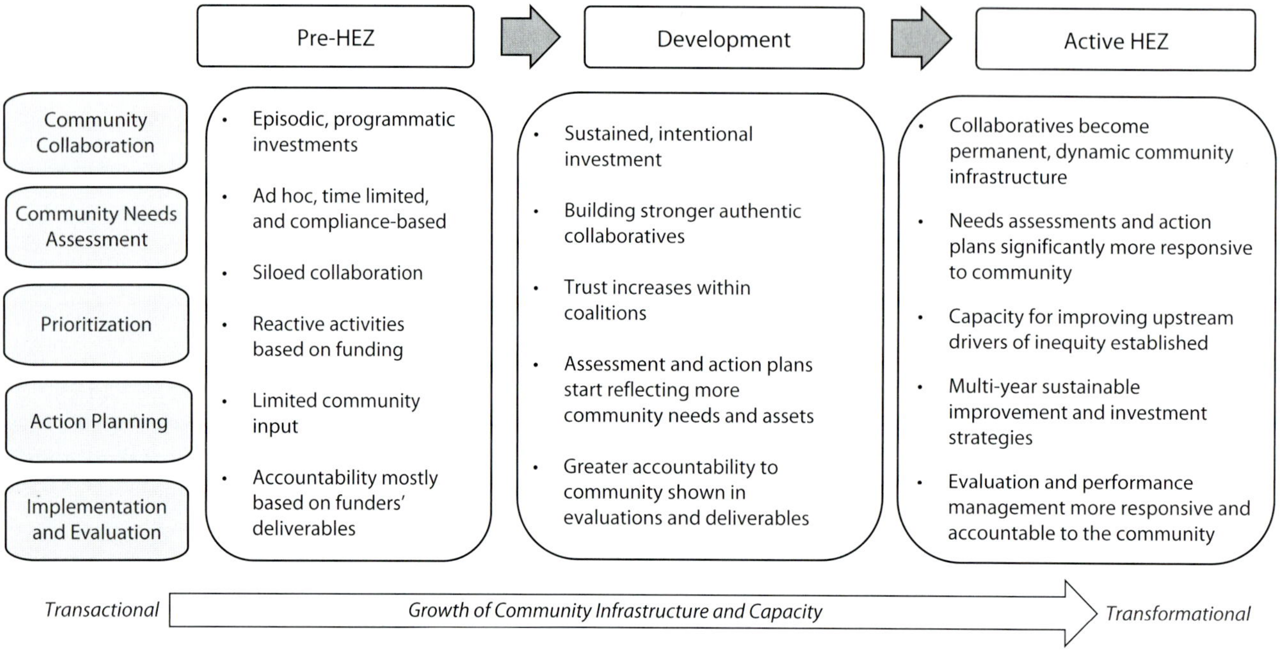

FIGURE 1— **Rhode Island Health Equity Zone (HEZ) Continuum, From Pre-HEZ to Established HEZ**

Note. Modified version of the continuum adapted for publication.

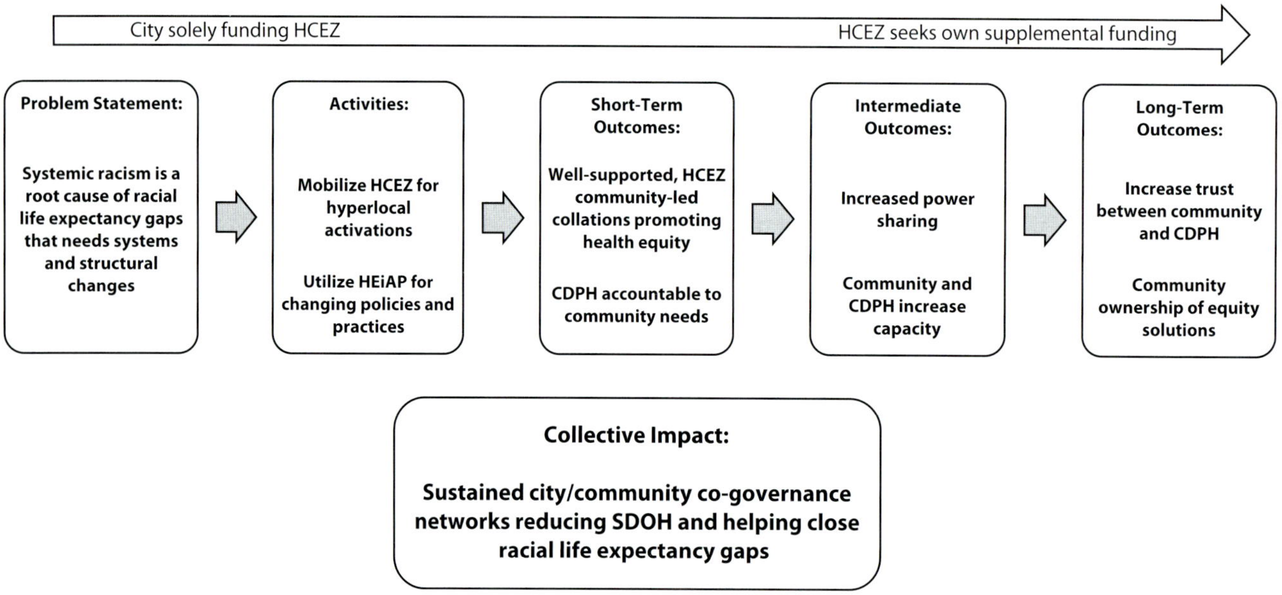

FIGURE 2— **Healthy Chicago Equity Zones (HCEZ) High-Level Change Model Process With Health Equity in All Policies (HEiAP) to Reduce Negative Impact of Social Determinants of Health (SDOH)**

Note. Modified version for publication adapted from University of Illinois Chicago (UIC), School of Public Health, Chicago Department of Public Health–UIC draft Health Disparities Grant Evaluation.

PLACE, TIME, AND PERSONS

RIDOH's statewide HEZ model[6,7] (2009–present) leverages braided funding to support 14 communities, covering approximately 75% of RI's population. Each RI HEZ codevelops community-specific strategies for achieving sustained community health and economic well-being. Using the RI model as a starting point, CDPH's HCEZ[8] (2021–present) built a citywide, 6-region approach of hyperlocal partnerships to support the community-codeveloped Healthy Chicago movement of equitable opportunities for optimal health and well-being for all Chicagoans. Both initiatives are primarily resourced through federal funds and prioritize communities that meet the following criteria:

- racially and ethnically diverse,
- high levels of health disparities,
- low-income households,
- higher chronic disease rates, and
- persistent SDOH inequities.

Interventions focus on creating environments that support healthy living, equitable health outcomes, and addressing the root causes of health disparities.

PURPOSE

Both RI and Chicago programs recognize that equity is not achievable without replicable operational frameworks supporting structural, system-level changes in partnerships across sectors, including individuals and communities impacted by inequity. They demonstrate that investments in community-driven change reduce inequities.[4] Across the nation, jurisdictions are replicating equity zones and building community capacity to drive upstream, transformational change.

Operational equity—putting a plan to embed equity and power-sharing into all processes and activities of an organization through codesign and sustained community-level investment—is essential for transformational, upstream change. Operational equity creates foundations for innovative transformational models whose structure differs from existing models, typically originating and driven from the top down. In developing equity zones, both health departments focused on the following operational considerations:

- Community capacity acts as both a facilitator and barrier to equitable SDOH improvement. Sustained strategic focus (time and intent) on improving SDOH conditions within a specific locale is crucial. However, equitable change depends on local capacity to lead these efforts. Without this capacity, changes to SDOH conditions remain inequitable as community members lack the agency to direct responsive efforts. Developing equitable community capacity requires dedicated time and funding.
- Similar demographic populations in different geographic areas can experience vastly different SDOH conditions because of their proximity to SDOH triggers. For instance, one community might face inadequate public transportation to a grocery store while another has no grocery store at all, leading to significantly different needs, impacts, barriers, and conditions for change.
- Existing resources for programs and interventions are misaligned with transformational change goals. Community needs assessments measure inequities without providing resources or operational frameworks for improvements. Programmatic interventions are episodic, with short-term timelines failing to provide adequate time or intent to achieve upstream systems and policies that perpetuate inequitable conditions. While they address SDOH symptoms, they do not improve underlying conditions without more equity-centered program decision-making.[9]

EVALUATION AND ADVERSE EFFECTS

The lack of transformational evaluation models limits our ability to assess upstream factors impacting systemic inequities in the shorter term while also limiting sustainable resources for transformational change efforts. Evaluation of specific factors contributing to advancing health equity is critical to demonstrating efficacy of transformational change models like equity zones and driving sustainable investment in community transformation efforts. In addition to traditional downstream health outcomes, our updated evaluation frameworks utilize leading midstream and upstream measures of SDOH alongside community narratives to more appropriately represent transformational change. These approaches combine foundational theory and evaluation practices including systems theory,[10] participatory evaluation,[11] empowerment evaluation,[12] transformational evaluation,[13] and contribution analysis[14] with causal diagramming methods.

Current evaluation efforts for equity zones point to powerful benefits supporting improved long-term health outcomes, decreased disparities, and community resilience. RIDOH recently conducted a third-party outcome analysis of social vulnerability and found that through engaging differentially vulnerable populations, the HEZ model has meaningfully decreased social vulnerability attributable to SDOH in HEZ communities. Using a weighted and standardized composite social vulnerability score ("HEZ Composite Score") calculated from data on RI's 15 Health Equity Measures of SDOH,[15] the data confirmed that RI HEZ communities had significantly higher composite social vulnerability scores compared with the non-HEZ reference group. Yet, significantly, RI HEZ communities had an overall 21% decrease in the weighted composite social vulnerability score, comparing 2018 to 2022, in contrast to a 0.4% change among non-HEZ communities (Figure A, available as a supplement to the online version of this article at http://www.ajph.org.). This is indicative of significant positive improvements in SDOH in the RI HEZ communities. In addition, the data show only a slight (2%) increase in the social vulnerability in RI HEZ communities from 2019 to the first year of COVID-19 in 2020; in comparison, the non-HEZ reference group showed a 15% increase in social vulnerability during that same time (Figure A). These data support the resilience of RI HEZ communities in an emergent crisis, likely arising from the increased capacity and trust required to identify and effectively address the changing needs of the community.

Early HCEZ evaluations show indicators pointing to similar factors such as trust-building and skill development as important in reducing SDOH (Figure B, available as a supplement to the online version of this article at http://www.ajph.org.). Transformational change measures, such as trust, capacity-building, empowerment, and collaboration, are critical to better understanding the impact on equity in the shorter term.

Upstream-focused, transformative factors need additional exploration to be widely accepted as valid reporting measures demonstrating true system-level impact of transformational change efforts. As such, investment in sustainability of ongoing implementation efforts like equity zones, and development of valid, accepted metrics of change are urgently needed to drive scaled investment in transformational change models.

SUSTAINABILITY

Rhode Island's and Chicago's transformational equity zones are ongoing, scaled frameworks transforming community conditions by addressing structural drivers of inequity. Both models are primarily funded with programmatic, federal resources and have benefitted from scaled investment of COVID-19 response and recovery funding. Despite commitment of leadership to transformational change and equity, competing public health priorities in an environment of shrinking public health funding continues to present barriers to sustainably funding these innovative approaches.

Adequately funding and continuing to improve evaluation of transformational health equity initiatives like equity zones to build momentum and achieve systemic, structural changes to drivers of inequities in communities is critical for transitioning from transactional treatment of ongoing inequities to equitable, transformational change.

Enacting changes and making investments now will empower jurisdictions across the nation to begin transitioning from normative, transactional public health practices to new methods and frameworks that will improve SDOH and advance health equity in the future.

PUBLIC HEALTH SIGNIFICANCE

To tackle SDOH and advance health equity, we must invest strategically in transformative community initiatives. Prioritizing affordable housing, local food systems, education, workforce development, civic engagement, and neighborhood cohesion not only eases health care burdens but also improves outcomes and extends lives.[4] Achieving such change requires rethinking implementation and evaluation methods. Equity zones represent a crucial step forward, empowering public health to operationalize equity. This is a call to action for further support of these and other innovative models across the nation as they are essential to ensuring gains are scaled and sustained. AJPH

ABOUT THE AUTHORS

Christopher Ausura and Jennifer Latham are with the State of Rhode Island Department of Health, Providence. Genese Turner, Nicole Marcus, and Brian Edmiston are with the Chicago Department of Public Health, Chicago, IL. Susanne Schnell is with the Public Health Institute of Metropolitan Chicago, Chicago.

CORRESPONDENCE

Correspondence should be sent to Genese Turner, Chicago Department of Public Health, 111 W Washington St, Floor 4, Chicago, IL 60602 (e-mail: genese.turner@cityofchicago.org). Reprints can be ordered at https://www.ajph.org by clicking the "Reprints" link.

PUBLICATION INFORMATION

Full Citation: Ausura C, Turner G, Latham J, Marcus N, Schnell S, Edmiston B. Equity zones: building the bridge to transformation. *Am J Public Health*. 2025;115(1):47–51.
Acceptance Date: September 15, 2024.

DOI: https://doi.org/10.2105/AJPH.2024.307872

ORCID iDs:
Genese Turner https://orcid.org/0009-0008-6887-0519

Jennifer Latham https://orcid.org/0009-0002-5435-3613

CONTRIBUTORS

All authors have contributed equally to this work and are considered joint first authors.

ACKNOWLEDGMENTS

The authors would like to highlight the transformational impact of the Centers for Disease Control and Prevention (CDC) COVID Disparities grant, OT21-2103: National Initiative to Address COVID-19 Health Disparities Among Populations at High-Risk and Underserved, Including Racial and Ethnic Minority Populations and Rural Communities, and thank the CDC for their support of this work.

The Chicago authors would like to thank the Healthy Chicago Equity Zone (HCEZ) Regional Lead partners: Greater Auburn-Gresham Development Corporation, Northwest Center, Phalanx Family Services, Sinai Community Institute, Southwest Organizing Project, Swedish Covenant Hospital, West Side United/Rush Medical University, the Community Lead organizations, and all HCEZ partners for their co-leadership and support of the HCEZ initiative. The authors would also like to thank the City of Chicago and Chicago Department of Public Health (CDPH) staff and leadership, CDPH Offices of Community Planning and Equity Zones and Health Equity in All Policies, Public Health Institute of Metropolitan Chicago, Illinois Public Health Institute, the Chicago Mayor's Office of Equity and Racial Justice, and the University of Illinois at Chicago–School of Public Health for their support of this initiative. A special thank you to Paula Crose, CDC Public Health Associate Program, for her contributions to the HCEZ initiative and collaboration on this article. The Rhode Island authors would like to acknowledge and thank the Rhode Island Health Equity Zone collaboratives and their leaders, who work tirelessly with residents in our communities to advance health equity. The authors would also like to acknowledge the actions and support of leadership within the RI Legislature, Governor, Executive Office of Health and Human Services, and Department of Health for the vision and commitment to continue to support the Health Equity Zone initiative, and through this initiative, the health and well-being of all Rhode Islanders. The Rhode Island authors also would like to acknowledge their partnership with Social Contract LLC in the analysis of social determinants of health and health outcomes in RI communities.

This article was originally submitted as part of the *AJPH* special supplement on "CDC's Initiative to Address COVID-19 Health Disparities: Lessons Learned," from the National Network of Public Health Institutes (https://ajph.aphapublications.org/toc/ajph/114/S7).

CONFLICTS OF INTEREST

There are no potential or actual conflicts of interest from funding or affiliation-related activities.

HUMAN PARTICIPANT PROTECTION

Institutional review board approval not required as this study did not involve human participants, identifiable private information, or interventions.

REFERENCES

1. Braveman P, Gottlieb L. The social determinants of health: it's time to consider the causes of the causes. *Public Health Rep.* 2014;129(suppl 2):19–31. https://doi.org/10.1177/00333549141291S206
2. Institute of Medicine. *Unequal Treatment: Confronting Racial and Ethnic Disparities in Health Care.* Washington, DC: National Academies Press; 2003.
3. Chicago Department of Public Health. Healthy Chicago 2025: Community Health Improvement Plan. 2020. Available at: https://www.chicago.gov/content/dam/city/depts/cdph/statistics_and_reports/HC2025_917_FINAL.pdf. Accessed May 24, 2024.
4. A Conceptual Framework for Action on the Social Determinants of Health. Social Determinants of Health Discussion Paper 2. Geneva, Switzerland: World Health Organization; 2010.
5. Arnstein SR. Arnstein's Ladder of Citizen Participation. The Citizen's Handbook. Available at: https://citizenshandbook.org/arnsteinsladder.html. Accessed May 24, 2024.
6. ChangeLab Solutions and Rhode Island Department of Health. Health Equity Zones: A Toolkit for Building Healthy and Resilient Communities. 2021. Available at: https://health.ri.gov/publications/toolkits/health-equity-zones.pdf. Accessed December 12, 2023.
7. Patriarca M, Ausura CJ. Introducing Rhode Island's Health Equity Zones. *R I Med J (2013).* 2016;99(11):47–48.
8. City of Chicago. Healthy Chicago Equity Zones. Available at: https://www.chicago.gov/city/en/depts/cdph/supp_info/healthy-communities/healthy-chicago-equity-zones.html. Accessed May 24, 2024.
9. City of Chicago. Health Equity in All Policies. Available at: https://www.chicago.gov/city/en/depts/cdph/provdrs/healthy_communities/supp_info/heiap-chicago.html. Accessed May 24, 2024.
10. Trochim WM, Urban JB. Theoretical foundations and philosophical orientation of Relational Systems Evaluation. *New Dir Eval.* 2021;169(169):19–30. https://doi.org/10.1002/ev.20449
11. Cousins JB, Earl LM. The case for participatory evaluation. *Educ Eval Policy Anal.* 1992;14(4):397–418. https://doi.org/10.3102/01623737014004397
12. Fetterman DM. *Foundations of Empowerment Evaluation.* Thousand Oaks, CA: Sage; 2021.
13. Mertens DM. Transformative evaluation for equitable and inclusive public policy. In: Varone F, Jacob S, Bundi P, eds. *Handbook of Public Policy Evaluation.* Northampton, MA: Edward Elgar Publishing; 2023:169–185. https://doi.org/10.4337/9781800884892.00019
14. Mayne J. Addressing cause and effect in simple and complex settings through contribution analysis. In: Schwartz R, Forss K, Marra M, eds. *Evaluating the Complex.* Philadelphia, PA: Routledge; 2011.
15. State of Rhode Island Department of Health. Rhode Island Health Equity Measures. Available at: https://health.ri.gov/data/healthequity. Accessed May 14, 2024.

Escaping Disaster: Understanding the Drivers and Disparities in Disaster Displacement in the United States

Kristina W. Kintziger, PhD, MPH, and Sarah Elizabeth Scales, PhD, MPH

ABOUT THE AUTHORS

Kristina W. Kintziger and Sarah Elizabeth Scales are with the Department of Environmental, Agricultural, and Occupational Health, College of Public Health, University of Nebraska Medical Center (UNMC), Omaha, and the Water, Climate and Health Program at UNMC.

See also Aung and Sehgal, p. 55.

AJPH January 2025, Vol. 115, No. 1

Extreme weather events are becoming more frequent and having a greater impact on our communities. In the 1980s, the United States experienced an average of 3.3 climate- and weather-related disasters annually that resulted in at least $1 billion in damages (one every 17 weeks). These events caused an average of $21.9 billion in damages and resulted in 299 deaths per year. In 2023, the United States experienced 28 events (one every two weeks), resulting in $95.1 billion in damages and 492 deaths.[1]

Disasters arise from a complex interaction between the hazards themselves, the exposure of people and their communities to these hazards, and the vulnerabilities that stem from social, economic, cultural, and political factors.[2] Although human-caused climate change is increasing the frequency and often the intensity of extreme weather events,[3] human costs are also rising through a combination of population growth and development. Expansion often occurs in areas at high risk for these disasters (e.g., coastal areas, river floodplains). The increasing frequency and severity of these disasters increase the likelihood of population displacement.

DISASTER DISPLACEMENT

Globally, three times as many people experience internal displacement from disasters than from conflict (31 million vs 10 million, respectively, in 2020).[2] In the United States, approximately 2.5 million people were displaced through disasters in 2023.[4] These figures become more stark when considering growing climate migration, which includes immigrants, refugees, and asylum seekers who cross international borders in response to climate-related drivers.[5,6] Displacement can be affected by individual-level vulnerabilities and have both short- and long-term impacts on the health and well-being of the displaced person. Displacement can lead to increased risk of illness (e.g., because of disruptions in access to health care, clean water, adequate food, and exacerbating existing conditions) and injury (e.g., because of evacuation or recovery efforts). Unemployment and economic losses associated with disasters and displacement can increase stress, depression, and anxiety. Other impacts include disruption in education, increased risk of gender-based violence, and increased vulnerability to future disasters.[7]

CHALLENGES IN ADDRESSING RISK

To effectively reduce the risk of disaster displacement in the United States, we must better understand the underlying factors contributing to displacement. Postdisaster rapid needs assessments and observational studies provide some insights into individual-level vulnerabilities and disaster-related outcomes. However, these are limited in scope to immediate needs or specific events, which restricts our ability to understand disparities in disaster outcomes across multiple vulnerabilities, disaster types, and regions and from a long-term perspective. Currently, the only nationally representative source of disaggregated data on disaster displacements is the US Census Bureau's Household Pulse Survey (HPS), which added questions on disaster displacement to the 2023 cycle.[4] The article by Aung and Sehgal in this issue of *AJPH* (p. 55) uses HPS data to understand associations between individual-level characteristics and displacement and to examine specific disaster impacts related to these characteristics and disaster type, among people who reported displacement.

EXAMINING VULNERABILITIES: A STARTING POINT

According to Aung and Sehgal, more than 3.1 million Americans were displaced from their homes in the previous year because of a "natural disaster" (HPS terminology), with most related to hurricanes (36.5%). Older people; racial and ethnic minorities; people with lesbian, gay, bisexual, transgender, queer, non-straight, or non-cisgender identities (LGBTQ+); and lower-income or widowed, divorced, or separated individuals were more likely to be displaced. This report also explored less commonly studied characteristics, including social determinants of health (e.g., food and energy insecurity) and functional disabilities. Food or energy insecurity, having one or more functional disability, living in a home categorized as "other" (e.g., mobile home, boat), being behind on rent or mortgage payments, having children, and living in the South or West were also associated with displacement. Disparities in impacts from these disasters among those displaced were noted. Older age increased the odds of long-term displacement (i.e., six months or more) and property damage. Identifying as LGBTQ+ increased the odds of long-term displacement, unsanitary conditions, and fear of crime. Identifying as Black or Hispanic was associated with food and water shortages, unsanitary conditions, electricity loss, and fear of crime. Feelings of isolation were associated with being widowed, divorced, separated, or never married and with lower incomes.

FROM RESEARCH TO ACTION: REDUCING DISPARITIES

The HPS and the Aung and Sehgal study offer us a foundation for examining social determinants of health and other individual characteristics that increase risk for disaster displacement on the national scale. Their findings corroborate other research and generally accepted realities in public health emergency preparedness and emergency management. However, we need to bolster the near-real-time collection of displacement data in disaster contexts. Building robust national surveillance and reporting mechanisms for internal displacement during and following disasters is a key step toward reducing disparities.

In global contexts, internally displaced persons are the proverbial "canary in the coal mine" for health system functionality; these populations often face the most barriers to accessing care and have poorer health outcomes than either host or refugee populations. This observation is not dissimilar to the disparities seen in health care access and outcomes for racial and ethnic minorities. To effectively address health inequities in disasters, research must more prominently consider the compounding and cascading effects of individual- and household-level vulnerability. This is evidenced by the disproportionate displacement of minorities, those with lower socioeconomic status, and those with other social vulnerabilities as demonstrated by Aung and Sehgal.

For example, Hurricane Katrina's devastating impact in 2005, which displaced more than a million people across the Gulf Coast, highlighted the critical need for robust internal displacement tracking protocols to ensure continuity of care for vulnerable populations, particularly for large-scale evacuations that cross state lines. In the greater New Orleans area, 130 tuberculosis (TB) patients were receiving direct observed therapy under the Louisiana TB Control Program. Although all patients were eventually located and reconnected with care, the process took significant time (two months).[8] Delays in TB treatment can pose serious risks to both individuals and the broader community, including increased drug resistance. Furthermore, in the United States, the incidence of TB is higher for racial and ethnic minorities, including documented and undocumented recent arrivals, refugees, asylum seekers, and immigrants.[9] The effects of displacement—especially secondary or tertiary displacement—and further disruptions to care exacerbate preexisting socioeconomic vulnerabilities. Culturally and linguistically appropriate messaging and proactive designation of safe spaces for accessing shelter, services, and care can improve the capture of displacement data and contribute to improved public health policy and practice in complex emergencies.

CONCLUSIONS

Internal displacement is a term used far more frequently in global health and geopolitics than in the United States. However, the global agenda for disaster risk reduction and domestic priorities for creating a more climate-resilient nation are complementary. The Sendai Framework for Disaster Risk Reduction[10] highlights the importance of the development and reporting of age, gender, and disability disaggregated data and preparedness policies and trainings that consider the needs of displaced populations before, during, and after disasters. In the United States, the National Academies of Science, Engineering, and Medicine has placed similar emphasis on developing a robust evidence base for public health action in disaster contexts.[11] Together, these initiatives underscore the persistent need to improve disaster data ecosystems, including displacement surveillance, and reporting. As disasters caused by extreme weather become more frequent and severe, it is crucial to include displacement as a fundamental consideration in all public health planning, policy, and action. AJPH

CORRESPONDENCE

Correspondence should be sent to Kristina W. Kintziger, 984388 Nebraska Medical Center, Omaha, NE 68198-4388 (e-mail: kkintziger@unmc.edu). Reprints can be ordered at https://www.ajph.org by clicking the "Reprints" link.

PUBLICATION INFORMATION

Full Citation: Kintziger KW, Scales SE. Escaping disaster: understanding the drivers and disparities in disaster displacement in the United States. *Am J Public Health*. 2025;115(1):52–54.

Acceptance Date: September 27, 2024.

DOI: https://doi.org/10.2105/AJPH.2024.307889

ORCID iDs:
Kristina W. Kintziger https://orcid.org/0000-0003-3555-7805

Sarah Elizabeth Scales https://orcid.org/0000-0001-9983-5304

CONTRIBUTORS

K. W. Kintziger conceptualized and led the drafting of the editorial. S. E. Scales contributed to the writing and editing. Both authors performed the literature search and reviewed the editorial.

CONFLICTS OF INTEREST

The authors report no potential or actual conflicts of interest from funding or affiliation-related activities pertinent to this editorial.

REFERENCES

1. National Oceanic and Atmospheric Association. US billion-dollar weather and climate disasters. 2024. Available at: https://www.ncei.noaa.gov/access/billions. Accessed June 15, 2024.
2. *Global Assessment Report on Disaster Risk Reduction 2022: Our World at Risk: Transforming Governance for a Resilient Future.* Geneva, Switzerland: United Nations Office for Disaster Risk Reduction; 2022.
3. *Fifth National Climate Assessment.* Washington, DC: US Global Change Research Program; 2023.
4. Household Pulse Survey. 2024. Available at: https://www.census.gov/programs-surveys/household-pulse-survey.html. Accessed September 1, 2024.
5. United Nations. With conflicts, climate change pushing displacement to record levels, third committee highlights need to ramp up refugee funding, address root causes. 2023. Available at: https://press.un.org/en/2023/gashc4395.doc.htm. Accessed September 21, 2024.
6. Greenfield N. Climate migration and equity. 2022. Available at: https://www.nrdc.org/stories/climate-migration-equity?gad_source=1&gclid=Cj0KCQjwgL-3BhDnARIsAL6KZ685URvosxh9t4oBUi73rWwzfi9oxRfLRUZPH9q5SSnzLEEVulaNit0aAiYFEALw_wcB. Accessed September 21, 2024.
7. *Disaster Displacement: How to Reduce Risk, Address Impacts and Strengthen Resilience: A Companion for Implementing the Sendai Framework Target (E).* Geneva, Switzerland: United Nations Office for Disaster Risk Reduction; 2019.
8. Centers for Disease Control and Prevention. Tuberculosis control activities after Hurricane Katrina—New Orleans, Louisiana, 2005. *MMWR Morb Mortal Wkly Rep.* 2006;55(12):332–335. Available at: https://www.cdc.gov/mmwr/preview/mmwrhtml/mm5512a2.htm. Accessed September 21, 2024.
9. Centers for Disease Control and Prevention. *Reported Tuberculosis in the United States, 2022.* Atlanta, GA: Division of Tuberculosis Elimination, National Center for HIV, Viral Hepatitis, STD, and TB Prevention; 2023.
10. *Sendai Framework for Disaster Risk Reduction 2015–2030.* Geneva, Switzerland: United Nations Office for Disaster Risk Reduction; 2015.
11. *Evidence-Based Practice for Public Health Emergency Preparedness and Response.* Washington, DC: National Academies of Sciences, Engineering, and Medicine; 2020.

Prevalence, Correlates, and Impacts of Displacement Because of Natural Disasters in the United States From 2022 to 2023

Ther W. Aung, PhD, and Ashwini R. Sehgal, MD

See also Kintziger and Scales, p. 52.

Objectives. To quantify the prevalence, correlates, and impacts of displacement because of natural disasters in the United States.

Methods. We pooled data across 10 independent survey samples from the Census Bureau Household Pulse Survey from December 2022 to September 2023. Survey questions asked about displacement from home because of natural disasters, duration of displacement, and impacts of disasters.

Results. In our weighted sample of 213 234 003 adults, 3 166 500 (1.5%) reported displacement in the past year because of a natural disaster. People of color, sexual and gender minority populations, and those with lower incomes, disabilities, or unfavorable social determinants of health (SDOH) such as food insecurity were more likely to report displacement. Long-term displacement was more common with fires compared with other disasters. Disaster impacts, including food and water shortage, electricity loss, unsanitary conditions, feeling isolated, and experiencing scams, were more common among people of color and individuals with lower education or income.

Conclusions. Many people in the United States, particularly from health disparity populations, are displaced because of natural disasters. Addressing SDOH and other vulnerability factors may help improve disaster preparedness and mitigate postdisaster impacts. (*Am J Public Health*. 2025;115(1):55–65. https://doi.org/10.2105/AJPH.2024.307854)

AJPH January 2025, Vol. 115, No. 1

Over the past 4 decades, the United States experienced 373 natural disasters that cost $1 billion or more.[1] The number of such billion-dollar disasters increased 4-fold from 3.3 events per year in the 1980s to 13.1 events per year in the 2010s. According to the Fifth National Climate Assessment, disasters such as hurricanes, extreme rainfall, drought, and wildfires are becoming more frequent and severe because of human-caused climate change.[2]

The increasing numbers of natural disasters are likely to intensify population displacement in the United States. Displacement can be temporary, as in the case of an evacuation where residents return after a hazard (e.g., a hurricane) has passed. Displacement can be long-term if damage to housing and other infrastructures is extensive and residents must wait to rebuild. Displacement becomes permanent if residents never return to their predisaster homes.

To our knowledge, there is no systematic monitoring of disaster displacements in the United States. The most comprehensive estimate available is from the Internal Displacement Monitor Center (IDMC), which estimates that 877 000 people were displaced in 2022 and 2023 primarily because of storms, wildfires, and flood.[3] According to the IDMC, the numbers are likely underestimated as they are obtained from the Federal Emergency Management Agency (FEMA) assistance database, evacuation orders, destroyed housing, shelter days, and media monitoring and have limitations.[3] For example, not all disasters or households may qualify for FEMA assistance, not everyone will stay in shelters, and not all disasters attract media attention. The estimates may also miss populations that never return to the disaster site.[4] In addition, IDMC data do not include individual-level socioeconomic characteristics of displaced individuals.

As a result, there is a limited understanding of the characteristics associated with populations who are displaced, duration of their displacement, and impacts that the displaced populations face, especially across various types of natural disasters. A 2020 systematic review of major hurricane disasters in the United States concluded that there is an absence of statistics on evacuation, displacement, and recovery of socially vulnerable populations compared with more advantaged individuals.[5] And much of what is known about characteristics of displaced populations is limited to age, race, and income. For example, studies of hurricanes, tornado, and wildfires have found changes in postdisaster population composition where neighborhoods become younger, wealthier, and more White as a result of higher population losses in minority and lower-income groups.[4,6–8] Reasons for long-term or permanent displacement of minorities and low-income households include predisaster social inequities, such as lack of insurance and resources to rebuild, delayed or limited access to assistance, housing affordability, and poor economic opportunities after the disaster.[9–11] Beyond a few commonly assessed demographic characteristics, there is limited knowledge on how other population groups, such as sexual minorities and those with disabilities, are impacted by natural disasters and displacement. In addition, only a handful of studies have looked at the intersection of individual-level social determinants of health (e.g., economic instability, food insecurity, energy insecurity) with natural disasters.[12–14]

Much of the current disaster research in the United States is based on an individual disaster or a type of disaster, such as hurricanes. While an in-depth study at a disaster location can provide valuable context-specific insights, an assessment across different types of natural disasters may provide a broader understanding of key commonalities to inform state and federal policies and resource allocations. Populations that experienced displacement may represent a vulnerable subgroup of disaster victims[15,16] regardless of disaster type. We acknowledge that each disaster is unique, and its impacts will depend on preexisting conditions and social inequities at the disaster location. However, patterns across disaster types could help shed light on deeper structural barriers, inform disaster management, and prepare the US population for future climate impacts.

We used data from the Household Pulse Survey (HPS) administered by the US Census Bureau to assess the extent of displacement because of natural disasters, its correlates, and adverse impacts. Our objective was to examine the extent to which natural disasters are impacting the US population and to contribute to a better understanding of a wider set of social vulnerabilities that may play a role across various disaster types.

METHODS

The HPS was first implemented in April 2020 to assess the social and economic impacts of the COVID-19 pandemic and other emergent issues affecting households. The survey sample is drawn from approximately 146 million housing units derived from the Census Master Address File with more than 85% matched phone or e-mail addresses. The File includes all living quarters in the United States, including housing units, group quarters (e.g., college housing and nursing facilities), and transitory locations (e.g., hotels, motels).[17] Adults in selected households are invited via text and e-mail to complete the survey online. When combined with survey weights provided by the HPS, the results provide estimates that are nationally representative of US households. The HPS uses an iterative raking ratio to match the interviewed respondents with census estimates (2021 American Community Survey, and 2022–2023 Population Estimates Program) of the population distributions on age, sex, race/ethnicity, and education within each state.[18]

Beginning in December 2022, the HPS added questions on displacement from natural disasters in the past 12 months. For those who reported displacement, the respondents were asked about duration of displacement, damage to property or possessions, and types of disaster. They were also asked if any of the following impacts were experienced within 1 month after the natural disaster: food shortage, drinkable water shortage, electricity loss, unsanitary conditions, feeling isolated, fear of crime, and offers that seemed like a scam.

Our study addressed 2 aims. In the first aim, we sought to assess the relationship between displacement because of natural disasters and sociodemographic characteristics. We obtained the dichotomous outcome variable (yes or no) for displacement from the question, "In the past year, were you displaced from your home because of a natural disaster?" This question was asked of all survey participants. We used predictors that have been reported in previous studies, including age, sex, race/ethnicity, education, household income, and household ownership or rental status. We also examined predictors that have been studied to a lesser extent, including sexual orientation, marital status, functional disabilities, and social determinants of health (SDOH). The SDOH captured by the HPS include unemployment in the past 7 days, being behind on rent or mortgage payment, food insecurity, and energy insecurity. See Appendix, Methods section (available as a supplement to the online version of this article at https://ajph.org) for additional details on how predictors such as food and energy insecurity were defined.

In the second aim, we investigated the relationship between disaster impacts and sociodemographic characteristics and natural disaster type among the subset of participants who reported displacement because of natural disaster. We examined a total of 9 impacts:

1. long-term displacement,
2. damage to property or possessions,
3. food shortage,
4. drinkable water shortage,
5. electricity loss,
6. unsanitary conditions,
7. feeling isolated,
8. fear of crime, and
9. offers that seem like scams.

Except for long-term displacement, all of these impacts refer to the first month after a disaster. We created a new variable for long-term displacement from the question, "How long were you displaced from your home?" Responses were "Less than a week," "More than a week but less than a month," "One to six months," "More than six months," and "Never returned to home." We defined long-term displacement as those who reported displacement for "More than six months" or "Never returned home." Property or possession damage responses were "No damage," "Some damage," "Moderate amount of damage," and "A lot of damage." In our analyses, we defined property damage as those who reported "Moderate amount of damage" or "A lot of damage." For all other remaining impacts, such as shortage of food and drinkable water, the responses were "Not at all," "A little," "Some," and "A lot." We defined the population as experiencing the impact for those who responded "Some" or "A lot." The survey responses for type of natural disaster were fire, hurricane, flood, tornado, and other (specify). As these questions are specific to natural disasters, we assumed "fire" to mean it originated from a natural source, such as forest fire, rather than something caused by a man-made structure, such as a stove or faulty electrical system. Written responses for the "other (specify)" category are only available on a restricted use basis. As respondents can check multiple disaster types, we created a new category, "Multiple disasters," for those who reported more than 1 disaster in the past 12 months.

We pooled data across 10 independent survey samples of the HPS from December 9, 2022, to September 4, 2023 (survey weeks 52–61). Independent samples were collected for each data-collection period, and each sampled housing unit was interviewed only once (i.e., no sample overlap).[18] The response rates for the 10 data collection periods ranged from 5.6% to 7.2%, and the average number of respondents was 67 473 per survey period. HPS uses person weights to create nationally representative estimates. For variance estimation, we used balanced repeated replication with 80 sets of replicate weights and Fay's[19] adjustment of 0.5. HPS creates replicate weights using a successive-differences replication method[20] within each state or metropolitan area to account for geographic clustering.

For our first aim, we used the Rao–Scott correction for the weighted χ^2 test to examine the bivariate relationship between displacement because of disaster and each of the predictor variables. We then ran 2 separate multivariable logistic regression models on displacement because experiencing a disaster may affect some variables. Model 1 was restricted to variables unlikely to be affected by displacement in the past 12 months, such as age, sex at birth, sexual orientation, and race and ethnicity. Model 2 includes all variables of interest, including variables that may be affected by displacement. For example, a respondent who is displaced may move into a friend or family's home with a different number of occupants, relocate to a different geographic region, become a renter, or experience food or energy insecurity.

For our second aim, we determined the prevalence of each impact for each natural disaster. We then ran separate logistic regressions where each of the 9 impacts represents a dependent variable. Predictor variables included demographic variables analyzed in model 1 as well as disaster type. We assessed collinearity among predictors in the multivariable regression models and concluded no serious multicollinearity as confirmed by variance inflation factor values below 2.

All data, including survey weights, are publicly available (https://www.census.gov/programs-surveys/household-pulse-survey/datasets.html). We used

Stata version 18 (StataCorp LLC, College Station, TX) for all analyses.

RESULTS

Table 1 provides sociodemographic characteristics of the weighted survey population of 213 234 003 adults. Their mean age was 49.2 years, a majority were non-Hispanic White, and nearly two thirds lived in a detached 1-family house. An estimated 3 166 500 (1.5%) adults reported being displaced from their home in the past 12 months because of a natural disaster (Table 2). Among those displaced, the numbers displaced by each type of disaster were fire: 385 541 (12.5%), hurricane: 1 121 818 (36.5%), flood: 318 216 (10.4%), tornado: 177 760 (5.8%), other disaster: 634 434 (20.6%), and multiple disasters: 435 417 (14.2%). The most common combinations of multiple disasters were hurricane and flood, reported by 278 866 (9.1%) adults, and flood and other disaster, reported by 97 307 (3.2%) adults.

On bivariate analysis (Table 2), several demographic characteristics were associated with displacement because of a natural disaster. For example, 2.3% of non-Hispanic Black participants reported being displaced compared with 1.3% of non-Hispanic White participants. On multivariable analysis, demographic variables independently associated with higher odds of displacement were being aged 75 years and older; being a member of a sexual and gender minority population; race and ethnicity Hispanic, non-Hispanic Black, or non-Hispanic other; and being widowed, divorced, or separated (model 1). Displacement was less common among those with higher levels of income.

TABLE 1— Characteristics of Census Bureau Household Pulse Survey Participants: United States, December 2022–September 2023

Characteristics	Weighted (n = 213 234 003), No. (%) or Mean ±SD
Age, y	49.2 ±16.9
Sex at birth	
Female	109 774 786 (51.3)
Male	104 313 223 (48.7)
Sexual orientation	
Heterosexual	185 142 712 (87.9)
Sexual and gender minority	25 512 286 (12.1)
Race/ethnicity	
Hispanic, any race	35 258 791 (16.5)
Non-Hispanic Asian	11 098 966 (5.2)
Non-Hispanic Black	22 563 307 (10.6)
Non-Hispanic other	8 818 308 (4.1)
Non-Hispanic White	135 494 630 (63.5)
Education	
≤ high-school graduate	76 657 668 (36.0)
Some college or associate degree	62 668 274 (29.4)
Bachelor's or graduate degree	73 908 061 (34.7)
Household income (past year), $	
< 35 000	44 263 320 (20.8)
35 000–74 999	56 306 344 (26.4)
75 000–149 999	56 817 488 (26.6)
≥ 150 000	33 849 891 (15.9)
Marital status	
Married	120 545 942 (56.8)
Widowed, divorced, or separated	39 710 499 (18.7)
Never married	52 146 883 (24.6)
Household size, no. persons	
1–2	91 031 246 (42.7)
3–4	81 208 341 (38.1)
≥ 5	40 994 417 (19.2)
No. of children in home	
None	135 172 896 (63.4)
1–2	61 530 692 (28.9)
≥ 3	16 530 415 (7.8)
House type	
Detached 1-family house	134 305 846 (63.0)
Attached 1-family house	14 650 767 (6.9)
A building with ≥ 2 apartments	37 298 528 (17.5)
Other (e.g., mobile home, boat, RV, van)	11 467 531 (5.4)
Home ownership	
Owner	140 598 969 (70.2)
Renter	59 564 711 (29.8)

Continued

AJPH January 2025, Vol. 115, No. 1

TABLE 1— Continued

Characteristics	Weighted (n = 213 234 003), No. (%) or Mean ±SD
Functional disabilities, no.	
None	171 194 117 (84.0)
1	24 183 890 (11.9)
≥ 2	8 382 641 (4.1)
Unemployed (past week)	
No	130 856 309 (61.7)
Yes	81 103 822 (38.3)
Behind on rent or mortgage payment	
No	183 824 937 (86.2)
Yes	15 331 548 (7.2)
Food insecure (past week)	
No	188 174 221 (88.7)
Yes	24 000 046 (11.3)
Energy insecure (past year)	
No	112 984 825 (53.0)
Yes	83 888 797 (39.3)
Census region	
Northeast	36 444 122 (17.1)
South	81 447 387 (38.2)
Midwest	44 121 028 (20.7)
West	51 221 466 (24.0)

In model 2, where demographic and SDOH variables that may be impacted by displacement are included, the significant demographic variables from model 1 remain statistically significant except for Hispanic ethnicity and household income. In addition, the highest education level, widowed, and never married categories have significantly higher odds of displacement compared with their reference categories. The odds of displacement also increase with the number of children in the household, specific housing characteristics, the number of functional disabilities, being behind on rent or mortgage payments, having food or energy insecurity, and being in the South or West.

Among different disaster types, multiple disasters were associated with the highest prevalence for 7 of the 9 impacts assessed. For example, the prevalence of property damage was 61.0% with multiple disasters (Figure 1; Appendix Table A2). Fire was associated with the highest prevalence of long-term displacement, and tornado was associated with the highest prevalence of electricity loss. Electricity loss is a common outcome with especially high prevalence across 4 disaster types: hurricane, tornado, other disaster, and multiple disasters.

On multivariable analysis (Table 3), disaster type and demographic factors were independently associated with disaster impacts. For example, individuals who reported multiple disasters in the past 12 months were nearly 3 times more likely to report food shortage compared with individuals who reported fire only. People of color and those with lower educational level or income were more likely to report food and water shortage, electricity loss, unsanitary conditions, and scams.

DISCUSSION

We estimate that more than 3 million American adults were displaced because of natural disasters in the past year. Both displacement and disaster impacts (such as food and water shortage) were more common among health disparity populations. Strengths of this study include a large and nationally representative sample, information on displacement and other disaster impacts, and the ability to examine a variety of individual, household, and geographic variables. We are not aware of previous surveys that captured the impacts of multiple natural disasters at a national scale.

We found that people of color, members of sexual and gender minority populations, and those with lower incomes, disabilities, or unfavorable SDOH were more likely to report displacement. Adverse impacts of disasters, such as food and water shortage, were also more common among people of color and those with lower income or education. Our findings align with previous studies that focused on an individual disaster or a type of disaster. Those studies also found that African Americans, Hispanics, low-income persons, elderly individuals, families with children, and those with disabilities are more likely to be impacted.[5,21,22] Other vulnerabilities associated with disproportionate impact included renting[23] and living in mobile homes.[24]

We found that sexual and gender minority populations were more likely to experience long-term displacement,

TABLE 2— Correlates of Displacement Because of Natural Disaster: United States, December 2022–September 2023

Characteristics	Bivariate Analysis,[a] Displaced No./Total No. (%)	Multivariable Analysis	
		Model 1, AOR (95% CI)	Model 2, AOR (95% CI)
Entire sample	3 166 500/213 234 003 (1.5)	...	...
Age, y			
18–34	765 408/52 960 079 (1.5)	1 (Ref)	1 (Ref)
35–49	874 358/55 352 596 (1.6)	1.20 (1.00, 1.44)	1.09 (0.90, 1.31)
50–64	778 225/55 283 423 (1.4)	1.02 (0.84, 1.23)	1.08 (0.90, 1.30)
65–74	498 422/36 214 150 (1.4)	0.99 (0.81, 1.21)	1.28 (1.04, 1.59)
≥75	250 087/13 423 756 (1.9)	1.35 (1.05, 1.74)	1.58 (1.19, 2.11)
Sex at birth			
Female	1 704 808/109 394 738 (1.6)	1.00 (0.91, 1.10)	0.96 (0.87, 1.06)
Male	1 461 691/103 839 266 (1.4)	1 (Ref)	1 (Ref)
Sexual orientation			
Heterosexual	2 532 913/185 142 712 (1.4)	1 (Ref)	1 (Ref)
Sexual/gender minority	583 349/25 512 286 (2.3)	1.70 (1.48, 1.94)	1.41 (1.22, 1.62)
Race/ethnicity			
Hispanic	615 034/35 258 791 (1.7)	1.24 (1.06, 1.45)	1.04 (0.89, 1.22)
Non-Hispanic Asian	144 072/11 098 966 (1.3)	1.07 (0.86, 1.35)	1.11 (0.85, 1.44)
Non-Hispanic Black	523 227/22 563 307 (2.3)	1.69 (1.44, 1.98)	1.19 (1.00, 1.43)
Non-Hispanic other	191 304/8 818 308 (2.2)	1.63 (1.29, 2.06)	1.37 (1.06, 1.76)
Non-Hispanic White	1 692 863/135 494 630 (1.3)	1 (Ref)	1 (Ref)
Education			
≤high-school graduate	1 368 157/76 657 668 (1.8)	1 (Ref)	1 (Ref)
Some college or associate degree	913 117/62 668 274 (1.5)	0.88 (0.78, 1.00)	1.00 (0.88, 1.14)
Bachelor's or graduate degree	885 225/73 908 061 (1.2)	0.87 (0.76, 0.99)	1.17 (1.03, 1.33)
Household income, $			
<35 000	989 698/44 263 320 (2.2)	1 (Ref)	1 (Ref)
35 000–74 999	796 505/56 306 344 (1.4)	0.71 (0.62, 0.81)	1.00 (0.86, 1.15)
75 000–149 999	572 031/56 817 488 (1.0)	0.56 (0.47, 0.66)	0.96 (0.80, 1.15)
≥150 000	350 018/33 849 891 (1.0)	0.60 (0.47, 0.77)	1.19 (0.92, 1.55)
Marital status			
Married	1 464 766/120 545 942 (1.2)	1 (Ref)	1 (Ref)
Widowed, divorced, or separated	850 934/39 710 499 (2.1)	1.42 (1.27, 1.59)	1.34 (1.20, 1.50)
Never married	831 918/52 146 883 (1.6)	0.99 (0.86, 1.15)	1.23 (1.04, 1.44)
Household size, no. persons			
1–2	1 214 438/91 031 246 (1.3)		1 (Ref)
3–4	1 170 321/81 208 341 (1.4)		0.98 (0.87, 1.11)
≥5	781 741/40 994 417 (1.9)		0.92 (0.77, 1.10)
No. of children in home			
None	1 787 893/135 172 896 (1.3)		1 (Ref)
1–2	960 117/61 530 692 (1.6)		1.19 (1.03, 1.37)
≥3	418 490/16 530 415 (2.5)		1.65 (1.31, 2.08)
House type			
Detached 1-family house	1 611 544/134 305 846 (1.2)		1 (Ref)
Attached 1-family house	233 571/14 650 767 (1.6)		1.21 (1.00, 1.47)

Continued

TABLE 2— Continued

Characteristics	Bivariate Analysis,[a] Displaced No./Total No. (%)	Multivariable Analysis	
		Model 1, AOR (95% CI)	Model 2, AOR (95% CI)
Building with ≥2 apartments	509 662/37 298 528 (1.4)		1.00 (0.84, 1.19)
Other	444 973/11 467 531 (3.9)		1.96 (1.68, 2.29)
Homeownership			
Owner	1 765 766/140 598 969 (1.3)		1 (Ref)
Renter	1 058 276/59 564 711 (1.8)		0.97 (0.85, 1.09)
Functional disabilities, no.			
None	2 018 893/171 194 117 (1.2)		1 (Ref)
1	485 332/24 183 890 (2.0)		1.25 (1.08, 1.44)
≥2	406 190/8 382 641 (4.9)		2.10 (1.78, 2.47)
Unemployed (past week)			
No	1 698 067/130 856 309 (1.3)		1 (Ref)
Yes	1 439 861/81 103 822 (1.8)		1.06 (0.97, 1.16)
Behind on rent or mortgage payment			
No	2 278 065/183 824 937 (1.2)		1 (Ref)
Yes	527 066/15 331 548 (3.4)		1.63 (1.44, 1.85)
Food insecure (past week)			
No	2 201 705/188 174 221 (1.2)		1 (Ref)
Yes	938 602/24 000 046 (3.9)		1.78 (1.58, 2.00)
Energy insecure (past year)			
No	988 271/112 984 825 (0.9)		1 (Ref)
Yes	1 794 027/83 888 797 (2.1)		1.67 (1.49, 1.88)
Census region			
Northeast	281 241/36 444 122 (0.8)		1 (Ref)
South	1 951 291/81 447 387 (2.4)		2.87 (2.37, 3.47)
Midwest	378 427/44 121 028 (0.9)		1.13 (0.89, 1.43)
West	555 540/51 221 466 (1.1)		1.35 (1.08, 1.70)

Note. AOR = adjusted odds ratio; CI = confidence interval.
[a]All bivariate *P* values were <.001 except for age (*P* = .18) and sex (*P* = .02).

unsanitary conditions, and fear of crime. These findings are important given limited documentation of the experiences of sexual and gender minority populations following disaster-induced displacement in the United States.[25] A review of natural disasters around the world found that heteronormative response and recovery policies can exacerbate adverse impacts and hinder recovery for sexual and gender minority communities with heightened vulnerabilities.[26] Examples of problems include experiences of discrimination, violence, and abuse at temporary shelters.[27] Our data are more recent and suggest that current disaster response and recovery policies may still be insufficient in addressing the needs of sexual and gender minority populations.

Our inclusion of SDOH identifies additional risk factors with a potential to inform interventions. We found that having housing, food, or energy insecurity was associated with displacement. It is possible that households with these adverse SDOH have fewer resources to prepare for and respond to disasters. We are only aware of 1 study with a small sample size of 185 low-income, primarily Hispanic adolescents in Texas that conducted a pre- and postdisaster assessment.[12] The study found that having food insecurity 2 days before a hurricane predicted more adverse outcomes, including lack of access to food, fresh water, and medicines; damaged homes; and displacement. More longitudinal studies, particularly pre- and postdisaster studies, with larger sample sizes and more

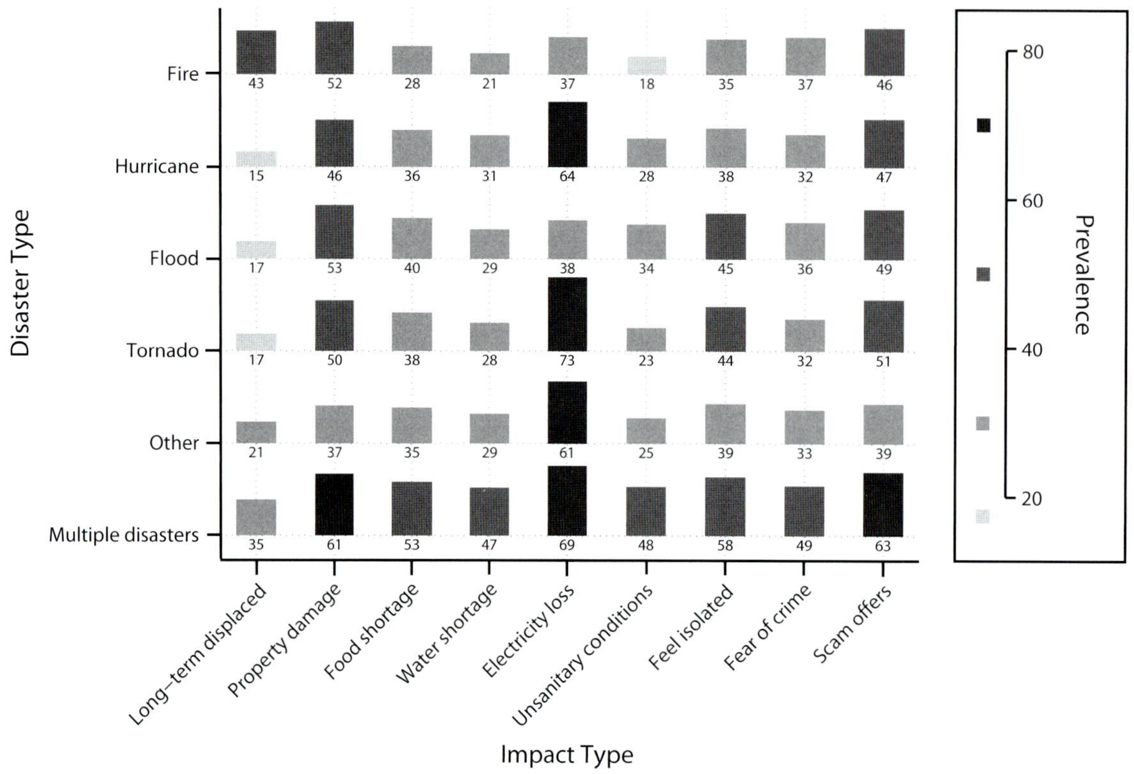

FIGURE 1— **Prevalence of Long-Term Displacement, Property Damage, Food or Water Shortage, Electricity Loss, Unsanitary Conditions, Feeling Isolated, Fear of Crime, and Scam Offers by Type of Natural Disaster: United States, December 2022 to September 2023**

Note. Numbers below each bar represent the percentage of each impact reported. Bar colors represent prevalence grouped into 4 colors ranging from light gray (≤ 20% prevalence), medium gray (21%–40%), dark gray (41%–60%), and black (≥ 61%).

diverse population groups are needed to better understand the mechanisms by which SDOH may modify the impacts of disasters.[6] We also recommend that researchers and policymakers evaluate SDOH that may play a role in enhancing community resilience and disaster preparedness, such as addressing transportation limitations and food insecurity.

We are not aware of any previous study that compared impacts across various disaster types. Our analyses provide insights for state and federal policymakers on preparedness needs depending on the hazard exposure relevant to the region of the country. For example, we found that electricity loss was especially common for hurricanes and tornadoes. Allocating resources to increase resilience of electrical infrastructure would be important for parts of the country where hurricanes and tornados are common or support for vulnerable populations most reliant on electricity, such as those who depend on durable medical equipment. Fires were associated with long-term or permanent displacement, indicating they may be more destructive to housing infrastructure and property. Disaster response to fires may need to consider policies and programs to address long-term or permanently displaced populations.

We found that populations who experienced multiple disasters in the past 12 months reported worse outcomes compared with those who experienced only 1 disaster. These findings support existing evidence that compound events (i.e., when multiple disasters or hazards occur close in time to each other) can have greater impacts than a single event.[2] This is because compound events can overwhelm local response and recovery efforts as well as lower the resilience of impacted populations who have not had time to recover from the first disaster. In addition, our analyses provide a unique opportunity to compare impacts from compound events with different types of single disaster events and across a variety of outcomes related to infrastructure failure (e.g., electricity loss), access to basic needs

TABLE 3— Multivariable Correlates of Impacts of Natural Disasters: United States, December 2022–September 2023

Characteristics	Impacts, AOR (95% CI)								
	Model 1: Long-Term Displaced	Model 2: Property Damage	Model 3: Food Shortage	Model 4: Water Shortage	Model 5: Electricity Loss	Model 6: Unsanitary Conditions	Model 7: Feel Isolated	Model 8: Fear of Crime	Model 9: Offers Like Scams
Disaster type (Ref = fire only)									
Hurricane only	0.26 (0.18, 0.37)	0.84 (0.63, 1.12)	1.75 (1.21, 2.53)	2.04 (1.25, 3.33)	3.25 (2.35, 4.49)	2.23 (1.44, 3.44)	1.18 (0.88, 1.59)	0.90 (0.65, 1.26)	1.22 (0.91, 1.64)
Flood only	0.24 (0.15, 0.38)	1.06 (0.68, 1.66)	1.34 (0.84, 2.15)	1.17 (0.68, 2.02)	0.92 (0.58, 1.45)	2.40 (1.35, 4.29)	1.26 (0.83, 1.91)	0.90 (0.54, 1.50)	1.13 (0.73, 1.77)
Tornado only	0.25 (0.14, 0.43)	0.99 (0.66, 1.48)	1.47 (0.92, 2.37)	1.48 (0.84, 2.61)	4.89 (2.87, 8.34)	1.57 (0.94, 2.64)	1.38 (0.84, 2.24)	0.88 (0.54, 1.45)	1.39 (0.93, 2.09)
Other only	0.33 (0.22, 0.50)	0.58 (0.40, 0.83)	1.47 (0.96, 2.24)	1.48 (0.90, 2.45)	2.65 (1.79, 3.94)	1.67 (1.02, 2.73)	1.11 (0.77, 1.59)	0.88 (0.60, 1.28)	0.77 (0.55, 1.09)
Multiple disasters	0.52 (0.34, 0.81)	1.55 (1.00, 2.39)	2.90 (1.71, 4.90)	3.02 (1.73, 5.28)	3.53 (2.26, 5.51)	4.18 (2.49, 7.01)	2.41 (1.56, 3.73)	1.42 (0.92, 2.20)	1.93 (1.23, 3.05)
Age, y (Ref = 18–34 y)									
35–49	1.45 (0.99, 2.12)	1.15 (0.84, 1.57)	1.14 (0.82, 1.59)	0.89 (0.66, 1.22)	0.93 (0.70, 1.23)	0.98 (0.69, 1.38)	1.21 (0.92, 1.58)	1.34 (0.99, 1.83)	0.98 (0.72, 1.33)
50–64	1.66 (1.13, 2.46)	1.46 (1.08, 1.98)	1.13 (0.83, 1.55)	1.03 (0.76, 1.40)	1.06 (0.80, 1.41)	0.98 (0.70, 1.36)	1.01 (0.74, 1.37)	1.58 (1.18, 2.12)	1.03 (0.71, 1.50)
65–74	1.61 (0.95, 2.70)	1.56 (1.08, 2.25)	0.89 (0.62, 1.26)	0.65 (0.43, 0.98)	0.90 (0.65, 1.23)	0.95 (0.66, 1.37)	0.78 (0.52, 1.17)	1.37 (0.99, 1.90)	1.19 (0.86, 1.64)
≥ 75	3.41 (2.16, 5.38)	1.73 (1.14, 2.63)	0.98 (0.63, 1.53)	1.07 (0.74, 1.54)	1.07 (0.72, 1.58)	1.34 (0.81, 2.22)	0.85 (0.55, 1.32)	1.06 (0.69, 1.63)	1.01 (0.67, 1.54)
Sex at birth (Ref = male)									
Female at birth	0.86 (0.68, 1.09)	0.93 (0.77, 1.12)	1.09 (0.89, 1.32)	1.07 (0.86, 1.33)	0.97 (0.79, 1.18)	1.03 (0.84, 1.26)	1.13 (0.95, 1.34)	0.82 (0.67, 0.99)	0.69 (0.55, 0.87)
Sexual orientation (Ref = heterosexual)									
Sexual/gender minority	1.83 (1.32, 2.53)	1.15 (0.84, 1.58)	1.27 (0.95, 1.69)	1.25 (0.93, 1.68)	1.11 (0.85, 1.45)	1.70 (1.33, 2.18)	1.26 (0.94, 1.69)	1.95 (1.48, 2.57)	1.23 (0.93, 1.64)
Race/ethnicity (Ref = non-Hispanic White)									
Hispanic	1.16 (0.84, 1.60)	0.88 (0.66, 1.19)	1.26 (0.96, 1.66)	1.76 (1.40, 2.19)	1.38 (1.03, 1.86)	1.89 (1.35, 2.64)	0.89 (0.67, 1.18)	1.39 (1.04, 1.85)	1.27 (0.93, 1.74)
Non-Hispanic Asian	1.95 (1.20, 3.19)	1.59 (1.00, 2.52)	0.82 (0.42, 1.60)	1.47 (0.86, 2.50)	0.89 (0.56, 1.40)	1.16 (0.66, 2.03)	0.86 (0.48, 1.55)	1.66 (1.04, 2.65)	1.65 (1.00, 2.73)
Non-Hispanic Black	1.08 (0.78, 1.50)	1.17 (0.91, 1.49)	2.10 (1.65, 2.68)	1.87 (1.44, 2.44)	1.40 (1.06, 1.83)	1.24 (0.96, 1.60)	1.10 (0.88, 1.38)	1.52 (1.14, 2.02)	1.65 (1.25, 2.18)
Non-Hispanic other	1.64 (0.99, 2.71)	1.08 (0.71, 1.62)	2.78 (1.78, 4.34)	1.96 (1.28, 3.00)	1.18 (0.77, 1.81)	1.70 (1.12, 2.56)	1.47 (0.98, 2.19)	1.49 (1.01, 2.19)	1.83 (1.20, 2.78)
Education (Ref ≤ high-school graduate)									
Some college or associate degree	0.66 (0.51, 0.86)	0.68 (0.55, 0.84)	0.60 (0.48, 0.76)	0.72 (0.56, 0.94)	0.85 (0.66, 1.08)	0.73 (0.57, 0.94)	1.07 (0.85, 1.33)	0.89 (0.75, 1.06)	0.92 (0.74, 1.14)
Bachelor's or graduate degree	0.65 (0.48, 0.88)	0.78 (0.61, 0.99)	0.48 (0.36, 0.64)	0.63 (0.49, 0.81)	0.75 (0.58, 0.97)	0.73 (0.56, 0.95)	1.10 (0.85, 1.42)	0.82 (0.66, 1.01)	0.75 (0.60, 0.94)
Marital status (Ref = married)									
Widowed, divorced, or separated	1.56 (1.17, 2.07)	1.09 (0.83, 1.43)	1.64 (1.26, 2.15)	1.12 (0.87, 1.44)	1.15 (0.91, 1.45)	1.27 (0.98, 1.64)	1.48 (1.19, 1.83)	1.34 (1.08, 1.65)	1.76 (1.33, 2.34)
Never married	1.55 (1.06, 2.26)	0.75 (0.55, 1.02)	1.26 (0.90, 1.76)	1.26 (0.93, 1.71)	1.34 (1.03, 1.74)	1.28 (0.95, 1.73)	1.44 (1.12, 1.84)	1.11 (0.87, 1.40)	1.04 (0.76, 1.43)
Household income, $ (Ref < 35 000)									
35 000–74 999	0.54 (0.39, 0.74)	0.88 (0.65, 1.18)	0.53 (0.39, 0.72)	0.55 (0.41, 0.73)	0.71 (0.54, 0.93)	0.58 (0.45, 0.77)	0.52 (0.38, 0.71)	0.55 (0.43, 0.69)	0.58 (0.44, 0.77)
75 000–149 999	0.48 (0.33, 0.70)	0.73 (0.53, 1.01)	0.39 (0.27, 0.57)	0.43 (0.29, 0.65)	0.92 (0.68, 1.24)	0.49 (0.35, 0.70)	0.36 (0.25, 0.52)	0.44 (0.33, 0.58)	0.49 (0.36, 0.65)
≥ 150 000	0.71 (0.48, 1.06)	0.54 (0.39, 0.75)	0.28 (0.17, 0.46)	0.58 (0.36, 0.95)	0.71 (0.50, 1.00)	0.48 (0.33, 0.69)	0.39 (0.25, 0.60)	0.54 (0.37, 0.77)	0.54 (0.39, 0.75)

Note. AOR = adjusted odds ratio; CI = confidence interval.

(e.g., food shortage), and social impacts (e.g., feeling isolated). As compound events are likely to increase with climate change,[28] there is an urgent need to strengthen disaster preparedness and recovery efforts, particularly for socially vulnerable populations.

Many scholars have called attention to the structural inequities and racism[29] that may contribute to the disproportionate impacts of natural disasters. Studies have found that people of color and with lower income are likely to live in places that increase their exposure to hazards, such as areas more prone to flooding.[30,31] Our findings support the existence of these structural barriers as we found that people of color and low-income households were more likely to experience adverse impacts.

Limitations and Strengths

Several limitations must be considered in interpreting our results. We relied on self-reported data for displacement, impacts from natural disasters, and potential correlates. Previous studies have also relied on self-reported data on exposure to natural disaster events, displacement, and impacts.[32,33] The HPS excludes people who do not have e-mail or mobile phones or cannot be identified. This may potentially exclude some of the most socially vulnerable populations, including those who lack digital access and technologies and people experiencing homelessness.

The survey response rate was low, and it is possible that nonparticipants experienced higher or lower rates of displacement than participants. The Census Bureau attempts to minimize nonresponse bias by applying nonresponse weighting adjustments and controlling to independent population controls using census estimates by occupied housing units and various demographic factors.[34] Despite iterative raking used in the HPS weighting procedure, coverage ratios are not perfect for some demographic groups, such as those with no high-school diploma and individuals aged 18 to 24 years.[18] As such, respondents may not be fully representative of the general US population. It is important to note that response rates for many surveys have decreased in recent years, and larger decreases among low socioeconomic subgroups suggest that our results may underestimate impacts in this subgroup.[35]

It is possible that problems related to COVID-19 (such as prolonged illness, loss of a job, or financial strain) led to displacement that survey participants incorrectly attributed to natural disasters. It is also possible that problems related to COVID-19 increased the likelihood of subsequent displacement because of a natural disaster. Our cross-sectional design also limits our ability to determine if certain factors (e.g., food insecurity) preceded and increased the risk of displacement from disasters or followed and were the consequences of disasters. This limitation applies to the model 2 analyses in Table 2 but not to the model 1 analyses in Table 2 or the analyses presented in Figure 1 or Table 3. Our sample size was too small to conduct multivariable analyses restricted to individuals affected by the same natural disaster.

Despite these limitations, we believe that the strengths of the HPS outweigh its weaknesses relative to other data sources such as the IDMC. We recommend systematic monitoring of natural disaster–induced population displacements. Given that the populations most likely to experience long-term or permanent displacement often consist of socially vulnerable populations, there is a need to understand and address their unique needs.

Public Health Implications

Our study quantifies for the first time, to our knowledge, the magnitude of displacement and impacts associated with natural disasters in the United States. We also identified important associations between multiple SDOH domains and disasters and encourage further work to explore this intersection to improve disaster preparedness and mitigate postdisaster impacts. AJPH

ABOUT THE AUTHORS

Ther W. Aung and Ashwini R. Sehgal are with Population Health and Equity Research Institute, The MetroHealth System, Cleveland, OH, and School of Medicine, Case Western Reserve University, Cleveland. A. R. Sehgal is also with the Institute for Health Opportunity, Partnership, and Empowerment, The MetroHealth System, Cleveland.

CORRESPONDENCE

Correspondence should be sent to Ther W. Aung, 2500 MetroHealth Dr, Cleveland, OH 44109 (e-mail: twa21@case.edu). Reprints can be ordered at https://www.ajph.org by clicking the "Reprints" link.

PUBLICATION INFORMATION

Full Citation: Aung TW, Sehgal AR. Prevalence, correlates, and impacts of displacement because of natural disasters in the United States from 2022 to 2023. *Am J Public Health*. 2025;115(1):55–65.

Acceptance Date: August 13, 2024.

DOI: https://doi.org/10.2105/AJPH.2024.307854

ORCID iD:
Ther W. Aung https://orcid.org/0000-0001-9984-9810

CONTRIBUTORS

T. W. Aung and A. R. Sehgal contributed equally to conceptual development, writing, data interpretation, and final revision of the article. T. W. Aung led the statistical analyses.

CONFLICTS OF INTEREST

The authors declare no conflicts of interest.

HUMAN PARTICIPANT PROTECTION

The study is a secondary analysis of de-identified and publicly available data and, therefore, is exempted from institutional review board review.

REFERENCES

1. National Centers for Environmental Information. US billion-dollar weather and climate disasters. National Oceanic and Atmospheric Administration. Available at: https://www.ncei.noaa.gov/access/billions. Accessed August 15, 2024.
2. Crimmins AR, Avery CW, Easterling DR, Kunkel KE, Stewart BC, Maycock TK, eds. *Fifth National Climate Assessment*. Washington, DC: US Global Change Research Program; 2023. https://doi.org/10.7930/NCA5.2023
3. Internal Displacement Monitor Center. Global Internal Displacement Database. Available at: https://www.internal-displacement.org/countries/united-states. Accessed August 15, 2024.
4. Palinkas LA. The California wildfires. In: *Global Climate Change, Population Displacement, and Public Health: The Next Wave of Migration*. Cham, Switzerland: Springer International Publishing; 2020:53–67. https://doi.org/10.1007/978-3-030-41890-8_4
5. Benevolenza MA, DeRigne L. The impact of climate change and natural disasters on vulnerable populations: a systematic review of literature. *J Hum Behav Soc Environ*. 2019;29(2):266–281. https://doi.org/10.1080/10911359.2018.1527739
6. MacNabb E, Fletcher BJ. Hurricanes, disasters, and food insecurity: the intersection of two social events. In: Rivera FI, ed. *Emerging Voices in Natural Hazards Research*. Oxford, England: Butterworth-Heinemann; 2019:121–144. https://doi.org/10.1016/B978-0-12-815821-0.00012-6
7. Raker EJ. Natural hazards, disasters, and demographic change: the case of severe tornadoes in the United States, 1980–2010. *Demography*. 2020;57(2):653–674. https://doi.org/10.1007/s13524-020-00862-y
8. Groen JA, Polivka AE. Going home after Hurricane Katrina: determinants of return migration and changes in affected areas. *Demography*. 2010;47(4):821–844. https://doi.org/10.1007/BF03214587
9. Wilson B, Tate E, Emrich CT. Flood recovery outcomes and disaster assistance barriers for vulnerable populations. *Frontiers in Water*. 2021;3:752307. https://doi.org/10.3389/frwa.2021.752307
10. Fussell E, Harris E. Homeownership and housing displacement after Hurricane Katrina among low-income African-American mothers in New Orleans. *Soc Sci Q*. 2014;95(4):1086–1100. https://doi.org/10.1111/ssqu.12114
11. Hamideh S, Sen P. Experiences of vulnerable households in low-attention disasters: Marshalltown, Iowa (United States) after the EF3 Tornado. *Glob Environ Change*. 2022;77:102595. https://doi.org/10.1016/j.gloenvcha.2022.102595
12. Arlinghaus KR, Hernandez DC, Johnston C. Food insecurity as a predictor of hurricane exposure among underserved adolescents. *Health Behav Res*. 2019;2(4). https://doi.org/10.4148/2572-1836.1047
13. Clay LA, Ross AD. Factors associated with food insecurity following Hurricane Harvey in Texas. *Int J Environ Res Public Health*. 2020;17(3):762. https://doi.org/10.3390/ijerph17030762
14. Lim H, Shin SH, Ji H. The effect of natural disasters on household economic hardship during a pandemic. *J Consum Aff*. 2022;56(4):1525–1560. https://doi.org/10.1111/joca.12480
15. Mitchell CM, Esnard AM, Sapat A. Hurricane events, population displacement, and sheltering provision in the United States. *Nat Hazards Rev*. 2012;13(2):150–161. https://doi.org/10.1061/(ASCE)NH.1527-6996.0000064
16. Uscher-Pines L. Health effects of relocation following disaster: a systematic review of the literature. *Disasters*. 2009;33(1):1–22. https://doi.org/10.1111/j.1467-7717.2008.01059.x
17. Sullivan TA, Cork DL, eds.; National Academies of Sciences, Engineering, and Medicine. *Assessing the 2020 Census: Final Report*. Washington, DC: The National Academies Press; 2023. https://doi.org/10.17226/27150
18. US Census Bureau. Source of the data and accuracy of the estimates for the Household Pulse Survey. Household Pulse Survey technical documentation. 2023. Available at: https://www.census.gov/programs-surveys/household-pulse-survey/technical-documentation/source-accuracy.2023.html#list-tab-1670696597. Accessed November 16, 2023.
19. Judkins DR. Fay's method for variance estimation. *J Off Stat*. 1990;6(3):223–239.
20. Fay RE, Train GF. Aspects of survey and model-based postcensal estimation of income and poverty characteristics for states and counties. In: *Proceedings of the Governments Statistics Section*. Boston, MA: American Statistical Association; 1995:154–159.
21. Chakraborty J, Grineski SE, Collins TW. Hurricane Harvey and people with disabilities: disproportionate exposure to flooding in Houston, Texas. *Soc Sci Med*. 2019;226:176–181. https://doi.org/10.1016/j.socscimed.2019.02.039
22. Coleman N, Esmalian A, Mostafavi A. Equitable resilience in infrastructure systems: empirical assessment of disparities in hardship experiences of vulnerable populations during service disruptions. *Nat Hazards Rev*. 2020;21(4):4020034. https://doi.org/10.1061/(ASCE)NH.1527-6996.0000401
23. Lee JY, Van Zandt S. Housing tenure and social vulnerability to disasters: a review of the evidence. *J Plann Lit*. 2018;34(2):156–170. https://doi.org/10.1177/0885412218812080
24. Rumbach A, Sullivan E, Makarewicz C. Mobile home parks and disasters: understanding risk to the third housing type in the United States. *Nat Hazards Rev*. 2020;21(2):05020001. https://doi.org/10.1061/(ASCE)NH.1527-6996.0000357
25. Dominey-Howes D, Gorman-Murray A, McKinnon S. Queering disasters: on the need to account for LGBTI experiences in natural disaster contexts. *Gend Place Cult*. 2014;21(7):905–918. https://doi.org/10.1080/0966369X.2013.802673
26. Gorman-Murray A, McKinnon S, Dominey-Howes D. Queer domicide: LGBT displacement and home loss in natural disaster impact, response, and recovery. *Home Cult*. 2014;11(2):237–261. https://doi.org/10.2752/175174214X13891916944751
27. D'Ooge C. Queer Katrina: gender and sexual orientation matters in the aftermath of the disaster. In: Willinger B, ed. *Katrina and the Women of New Orleans*. New Orleans, LA: Tulane University; 2008:22–24.
28. AghaKouchak A, Chiang F, Huning LS, et al. Climate extremes and compound hazards in a warming world. *Annu Rev Earth Planet Sci*. 2020;48:519–548. https://doi.org/10.1146/annurev-earth-071719-055228
29. Raker EJ, Arcaya MC, Lowe SR, Zacher M, Rhodes J, Waters MC. Mitigating health disparities after natural disasters: lessons from The RISK Project. *Health Aff (Millwood)*. 2020;39(12):2128–2135. https://doi.org/10.1377/hlthaff.2020.01161
30. Tate E, Rahman MA, Emrich CT, Sampson CC. Flood exposure and social vulnerability in the United States. *Nat Hazards*. 2021;106(1):435–457. https://doi.org/10.1007/s11069-020-04470-2
31. Handwerger LR, Sugg MM, Runkle JD. Present and future sea level rise at the intersection of race and poverty in the Carolinas: a geospatial analysis. *J Climate Change Health*. 2021;3:100028. https://doi.org/10.1016/j.joclim.2021.100028
32. López-Cepero A, O'Neill HJ, Marrero A, et al. Association between adverse experiences during Hurricane María and mental and emotional distress among adults in Puerto Rico. *Soc Psychiatry Psychiatr Epidemiol*. 2022;57(12):2423–2432. https://doi.org/10.1007/s00127-022-02355-2
33. Belleville G, Ouellet MC, Lebel J, et al. Psychological symptoms among evacuees from the 2016 Fort McMurray wildfires: a population-based survey one year later. *Front Public Health*. 2021;9:655357. https://doi.org/10.3389/fpubh.2021.655357
34. Peterson S, Toribio N, Farber J, Hornick D. Nonresponse bias report for the 2020 Household Pulse Survey. US Census Bureau. 2021. Available at: https://www2.census.gov/programs-surveys/demo/technical-documentation/hhp/2020_HPS_NR_Bias_Report-final.pdf. Accessed November 16, 2023.
35. Krieger N, LeBlanc M, Waterman PD, Reisner SL, Testa C, Chen JT. Decreasing survey response rates in the time of COVID-19: implications for analyses of population health and health inequities. *Am J Public Health*. 2023;113(6):667–670. https://doi.org/10.2105/AJPH.2023.307267

Manhattan's Street Trees: An Unfinished Public Health Story

John M. Harris Jr, MD, MBA

Stephen Smith launched a 40-year effort to bring trees to New York City streets in 1872, the year he founded the American Public Health Association (APHA). Smith argued that street trees would mitigate the adverse health effects of Manhattan's summer heat and help purify the air. The young APHA endorsed Smith's position and gave trees a prominent role in urban sanitation, but public health turned away from trees and urban reform movements as it adopted a biomedical public health model in the late 19th century. Nevertheless, Smith wrote and campaigned for a successful 1902 law requiring the New York City Parks Department to assume management of street trees in the name of public health. He then led a 1914 campaign to force the department to uphold his law. New York's street tree program has had an erratic trajectory, but it now generally follows Smith's vision. Public health could play a bigger role in creating greener cities and mitigating climate change with more field research and the health in all policies approach that Smith used to bring trees to Manhattan's streets in 1914. (*Am J Public Health*. 2025;115(1):66–74. https://doi.org/10.2105/AJPH.2024.307856)

AJPH January 2025, Vol. 115, No. 1

American public health professionals may be familiar with Stephen Smith (1823–1922), the New York City surgeon who organized and served as the first president of the American Public Health Association (APHA).[1–3] However, they would likely not attribute the handsome trees bordering the 10-story New York City Health Building, where Smith's name is carved into the façade, or Manhattan's 64 000 other street trees, to him and to public health. What follows is a case study of Smith's 40-year effort to bring public health into New York City's tree maintenance policies and a brief commentary on public health's unrealized opportunities in today's urban reforestation efforts.[4]

Sonja Dümpelmann explored the complex history of New York City's street trees in 2019 and recognized Smith as a guiding force in New York's turn-of-the-20th century street tree–planting movement.[5] However, Dümpelmann did not describe how Smith's community-based public health perspective, which differed from that of many of his laboratory-oriented peers, shaped his efforts, nor did she explore the practical details of his work to make street trees a city responsibility. Her sweeping account presented the botanic, economic, aesthetic, and cultural complexities of street trees in New York City from the mid-19th century through the next hundred years, leaving public health as a contributing but unexplored sidebar.

STREET TREES AND 19TH CENTURY AMERICAN PUBLIC HEALTH

Smith had been a member of the New York City Board of Health and its predecessor, the Metropolitan Board of Health, since 1868. The Board asked him to investigate Manhattan's well-documented increase in summer death rates in 1871, and he delivered a detailed 30-page report in 1872, the year he launched the APHA. Smith's analysis focused on temporal correlations between mortality and ambient temperature, which he supported with animal data showing the negative effects of heat stress. He concluded: "Heat is the principal, if not the sole exciting cause of the excessive summer mortality in New York."[6(p381)] Smith noted that heat affected the most vulnerable individuals first, and diarrheal diseases and heat stroke followed. All of this was worsened by life in foul and unventilated tenements.[6]

Smith recognized that urbanization made Manhattan hotter than the surrounding countryside and proposed three solutions: shade trees along city streets, periodically flooding the streets with river water for cleaning and cooling, and more public baths—as the Romans had done. The solution to which he devoted the most attention was street trees. He offered information on the temperature-mitigating and moisture-providing properties of trees. He noted that they removed poisonous gasses from the atmosphere, including carbon dioxide and the (presumably miasmatic) infectious agent of malaria. He added that trees would also beautify the city.[6]

Smith argued that urban tree planting, like other aspects of public health, should be placed under government authority: "If it is left to individual citizens to select their own trees, and cultivate them as they may think proper, there will be no improvement upon the present system."[6(p398)] He could have suggested that New York's Department of Public Works, which managed city streets, assume tree-planting responsibilities, but New York's notoriously corrupt Democratic political machine, Tammany Hall, ran this graft-ridden unit,[7] so Smith recommended that the Department of Public Parks oversee Manhattan's street trees.[6] He introduced a bill to the 1873 legislature, but it went nowhere.[8]

Smith reprinted his report as a public health monograph in 1873, and the press picked it up.[9] The *New York Times* summarized the message in April, citing Smith's data connecting summer heat and mortality while paying particular attention to street trees. The editor wrote, "Trees in a crowded city are a self-acting sanitarium."[10] Wire services passed the *Times* piece along, and Smith's pronouncement about the health virtues of street trees was soon published across the country.[11,12] The *Times* continued the call, editorializing in August 1873 that, "No city in the United States has so few shade trees in its streets as New York [which then meant Manhattan]"[13] (Figure 1).

Smith was hardly the first to connect trees with human health. The Roman architect Vitruvius praised the purifying properties of urban greenery in the first century BCE, and city planners had made similar statements to justify their beautification efforts ever since.[14,15] Where Smith's report differed was the specificity of his health issue—increased heat-related mortality, the supporting scientific detail, and his argument for government intervention. This was more consistent with the messages of the country's nascent public health movement than with longstanding civic beautification projects favoring parks and tree-lined boulevards.[16,17]

Smith tried to bring street trees into the newly formed APHA. His organizing group met in September 1872 and assigned Frederick Law Olmsted, Central Park's well-known landscape architect, to a committee "on the sanitary value and uses of shade trees, parks, and forests."[18(p.xv)] But Olmsted never attended an APHA meeting nor seriously pushed Smith's public health agenda. Olmsted later incorporated the sanitation concepts of public health, but his primary emphasis remained the spiritual and social benefits of nature.[19]

And Smith had more pressing issues to address. His city health board led a frontal assault on New York's fly-infested public markets in July 1873, tearing down illegal stalls. At the same time, the board moved to clean up tenements and cellars.[20] He had to manage a member rebellion that almost destroyed the young APHA in November 1873.[21] Then Smith returned to his surgery practice in 1875, his

FIGURE 1— Stephen Smith in 1873

Source. National Library of Medicine, public domain.

primary source of income. He resigned his seat on the New York City Board of Health and the APHA presidency, handing his presidential gavel to Joseph Toner of Washington, DC.[22,23]

Toner seconded Smith's street tree advocacy in his 1875 APHA presidential address. He named tree-planting one of the leading public health matters facing the country, along with pure water and sanitation: "Too much importance cannot be attached to the planting and preservation of trees, not only in the country but along all streets, and in every practicable locality in cities."[23(p12)] Toner's support was understandable because he lived in the most aggressively reforested city in the country. President Grant had charged his drinking buddy, Boss (Alexander) Shepherd, with a national capital makeover beginning in 1872 that, among other accomplishments, put 63 000 trees on 120 miles of Washington's streets between 1872 and 1887.[24]

But no one within public health picked up Smith and Toner's baton. Two APHA members spoke about trees at the 1877 APHA meeting in Chicago, Illinois, where the city motto was *Urbs in Horto*, "City in a Garden." However, they mostly repeated platitudes about the virtues of forests. When Yale botanist William Brewer rose to advise the APHA on tree-planting in 1877, he was unaware of Smith's 1873 monograph, lamenting: "Thus far the subject of shade-trees in our cities and about our dwellings has been discussed almost entirely from the aesthetic and sentimental sides, and I have failed thus far in getting definite, recorded observations, or even carefully formed opinions, on the sanitary questions involved."[25(p43)]

Science discovered the sources of many historic killers in the 1880s, and the laboratory-based biomedical model became public health's future, leaving trees behind.[26] When APHA members discussed urban shade trees at the 1889 meeting, no one maintained that they were a public health priority, and members argued that trees often did more harm than good. John Rauch, of Chicago, a founding member and past president of the APHA, summed up a common sentiment: "I have noticed that at times there is too much tree-planting. In the course of my official duties, I have destroyed trees, and I have noticed that it has been beneficial."[27(p230)] Once Smith left its ranks, the New York City Board of Health never discussed street trees again.

STREET-TREE LAWMAKING IN NEW YORK

Yet, Smith still lived in hot, treeless Manhattan, and he returned to public health several times during the rest of the century. He lobbied for a national board of health in 1878 and served on the ill-fated National Board from 1879 to 1883. He authored New York's State Board of Health Act in 1880. He represented the United States at the Ninth International Sanitary Conference in Paris in 1894. He brought public health principles to mental illness care as State Commissioner on Lunacy from 1882 to 1888 and as a member of the State Board of Charities from 1888 to 1918. Because Smith's civic work had its roots in mid-19th century urban reform rather than laboratory medicine, he remained committed to the cross-disciplinary alliances that "scientific" public health no longer needed.[28,29]

Smith quietly advocated for street trees between his other duties. He presented his 1872 arguments to the New York County Medical Society in 1886.[30] When the State Forestry Association invited him to speak in preparation for New York's newly launched Arbor Day in 1890, he encouraged the audience to plant trees on city streets to help mitigate temperature extremes.[31] He signed on when a group of New York City luminaries formed the Tree Planting Association in 1896.[32,33]

The Tree Planting Association's purpose was to raise funds and encourage community involvement in the spirit of Arbor Day. But trees were a public health matter for Smith, and voluntarism was not the way he saw public health. He used the Association's visibility to propose a bill in Albany that would give the City Parks Department control of street trees in 1899, much as he had in 1873.[34] He launched a public relations campaign to support this bill that left a lasting mark.

One part of his publicity effort was speaking to civic groups,[35] but his most far-reaching promotional contribution was an 18-page article in the February 1899 issue of *Popular Science Monthly*, titled "Vegetation a Remedy for the Summer Heat of Cities."[36] This was a readable version of his 1872 report, emphasizing the botanical science of heat abatement and atmospheric cleansing and the need to make street trees a civic responsibility. Smith's paper presented the science-based health arguments that a new generation of tree advocates needed. The Tree Planting Association passed it around, and tree experts cited from it from 1903 to 1977.[37–40]

Smith's tree-planting bill sailed through the 1899 legislature, only to be vetoed by Mayor Van Wyck, the first mayor of Greater New York City and a Tammany Hall politician. The same thing happened in 1900. The Tree

Planting Association's landscape architect, John Culyer, blasted the mayor and called attention to Smith, "an experienced and recognized sanitary authority," as the bill's author.[41] Smith resubmitted his bill in 1902, following the election of reform Mayor Seth Low, and the legislature, governor, and mayor approved it, creating the aptly named Act to Extend the Jurisdiction of the Park Board of the City of New York to the Preservation, Planting and Cultivation of Trees and Vegetation in the Streets Thereof for the Purpose of Improving the Public Health.[42,43] The Parks Department responded by adopting eight new ordinances regulating street tree care and planting.[44]

But adopting ordinances was all the Parks Department did. The city controller told Smith and Culyer shortly after the bill passed that the Parks Department had no funds to plant street trees and no authority to plant them in Brooklyn or Queens even if it had funds, beginning a 12-year stalemate.[45] Smith angrily watched from the sidelines as Culyer and the Tree Planting Association pressured the Parks Department and offered organizational support to voluntary tree-planting.[8,46,47]

Smith represented the Tree Planting Association before an ad hoc group of reform-minded Fifth Avenue merchants, the Fifth Avenue Association, in 1910. The Fifth Avenue group opposed trees because of the large number of subterranean vaults and passages along its famous thoroughfare, but Smith's health arguments convinced the members to reconsider.[48] The Fifth Avenue Association accepted tree planting as part of its master plan a month later—acknowledging street trees as a component of the newly trendy City Beautiful Movement.[49] A few months after the Fifth Avenue meeting, the Tree Planting Association asked 88-year-old Smith to be its president, assuring the public that the Fifth Avenue plans were moving ahead and Smith would follow in the former president's footsteps.[50]

But Smith had no intention of following in the former president's footsteps because, for him, street trees were part of a managed City Healthy, not a voluntary City Beautiful. Smith wanted the Parks Department to comply with his 1902 law, and now he had a respected organization behind him.

The problem was that the Parks Department prioritized its tree-care budget for parks, not street trees. The Department reported in 1910 that Manhattan's street tree stock was constantly diminishing because no one seemed to care: "the desire to maintain trees on the street in the business or residential sections is scarcely ever found."[51(p49)] Property owners wanted street trees gone because they obstructed signage and views. Except for a few parkways, the Department had never planted street trees.[51] Smith could do nothing to change the Department's frustrating policies.

Smith pushed his message while he waited for a change in Parks Department leadership. He joined Department President Charles Stover on a sunny October 30, 1912, to honor the oldest tree in Manhattan, the 225-year-old Inwood Tulip. Smith told Stover and the audience that New York City would have the most wonderful climate in the world if it cultivated trees.[52] He authored a piece on trees and health for the Tree Planting Association's 1913 bulletin, which *The Outlook* picked up for its December issue.[53] When the *New York Times* interviewed him on January 4, 1914, for a full-page article on his distinguished career in medicine and public service, writing, "his place in world of affairs is probably without precedent," the reporter got Smith's presentation on trees.[54]

Smith's moment had finally arrived when he met with the *Times* in January. Parks Department President Stover resigned in late 1913,[55] and Smith gave the reporter a scoop that his Tree Planting Association had recently asked the State College of Forestry at Syracuse to do a survey of Manhattan's street trees. He commented on his unfulfilled 1902 law: "It is humiliating to state that this law, with all its possible benefits to the city, has been a dead letter on the statute book more than a decade." He cited Olmsted's struggles with Central Park, saying that his Association planned to stir the voice of reform with "shame, disgust, and indignation."[54]

When Smith had approached Syracuse about a tree survey in 1913, he could only hope that Stover's replacement would be more sympathetic to street trees. He got his wish when the newly elected mayor appointed Cabot Ward, a 38-year-old Manhattan lawyer, to take Stover's place in January 1914.[56] Unlike Stover, Ward favored street trees, and, also unlike Stover, Ward was a meticulous planner.

Anticipating Ward's needs, Smith wrote the *Times* in March 1914 that the Tree Planting Association had sent a detailed plan for a Bureau of Tree Culture to the Park Board, including a budget of $72 000, which the College of Forestry had approved.[57] To smooth the path forward, he hosted a soirée at the Colony Club a few days later, where Tree Planting Association members and spouses rubbed elbows with the mayor, Park Board President Ward, and other VIPs.[58,59]

Smith sent another letter to the *Times* in May claiming that even former

Tammany boss Richard Croker favored trees in New York streets and that: "there is no more pathetic sight in this city than the thousands of those dying objects [trees], without which human life would be impossible."[60] He wrote a third letter a month later, reminding everyone that the Tree Planting Association had been working for years to get the Parks Department behind street trees, reporting that the Forestry College had completed a tree survey of the boroughs, and noting that New York could soon rival Washington and Paris in its trees.[61]

Smith was not above bending facts to support his cause. The Parks Board did get a proposal for a Bureau of Tree Culture, but there is no evidence that it arrived in 1913 or early 1914. Nor is there evidence that the notoriously corrupt Boss Croker was a fan of trees, but Croker was living in Ireland in 1914 and not likely to contradict Smith.[62] Smith's most elastic assertion was that the Forestry College had already completed a tree survey in June when Syracuse did not start its first tree survey of New York City until July 1914[63] (Figure 2).

FIGURE 2— **Stephen Smith in 1914**

Source. Library of Congress, public domain.

Dümpelmann later recounted how Smith's 1914 tree survey changed the trajectory of street-tree planting in New York City. The 1914 report was more an overview than a tree census, but it visually documented the poor state of Manhattan's trees and allowed Ward to order a detailed Rockefeller-financed survey the following year. The second survey gave Ward all he needed and led to a Bureau of Tree Culture within the Parks Department in 1917, which established the City's street tree mission. This survey's author, Laurie Cox, became one of the founders of the new discipline of urban forestry. Dümpelmann described how subsequent New York street tree efforts centered on standardization and how ongoing debates about the economic (not public health) advantages and disadvantages of street trees shaped later policies. Her concluding observation was that there was renewed interest in urban trees in 21st century New York City, citing its public–private Million Trees Campaign as an example[5] (Figure 3, Figure 4).

Smith's tree advocacy work ended with the Tree Planting Association's 1914 *Report on the Street Trees of the City of New York.*[64] His labors reflected an understanding of how public policy advocacy works and a commitment to public health activism that are considered essential lawmaking activities today. Burris et al. presented five steps required to develop and enforce laws to improve public health, all of which Smith's tree-planting efforts demonstrated:

1. Define the problem with evidence and expertise.
2. Translate policy solutions into a technically sound and politically acceptable legal form.
3. Build political momentum by forming community coalitions, engaging in communications, and spending face time with legislators.
4. Plan for effective enforcement.
5. Make sure the law works.[65]

But Smith's tree-planting work has more implications for today's public health professionals than exemplifying the long game of collaborative legislative advocacy.[66]

FIGURE 3— **Pitt and Rivington Streets in Manhattan's Lower East Side in 1909**

Source. Library of Congress, public domain.

FIGURE 4— **Pitt and Rivington Streets in 2023**

Source. Author's collection.

PUBLIC HEALTH'S STREET TREE OPPORTUNITIES

Smith's community-based view of public health was shaped before the biomedical model transformed his discipline, and it persisted after the transformation was well under way. He is a historical exemplar of what is now framed as a "health in all policies approach."[4] Smith brought public health concepts and priorities into housing reform, mental health, and, as recounted here, urban beautification.

One of the practical implications of Smith's public health perspective was that street trees required professional administrative management. New York State forester William Fox picked up this message, stating in 1903, "The planting and care of street trees belongs to the city government as much as street paving."[38(29)] Smith and Fox's Progressive Era message was eventually adopted by New York City, and the New York City Department of Parks and Recreation now plants and maintains street trees and puts heat-reducing shade trees in underserved neighborhoods, much as Smith envisioned.[67,68] A recent survey of two New York City neighborhoods found that most residents agreed that urban trees were a government duty.[69]

But government duty is not the norm. Many cities rely on private assistance to plant and maintain street trees.[70] Portland, Oregon, requires property owners to care for adjacent street trees, meaning maintenance can be spotty, and neighborhood income levels influence tree distribution and condition.[71] Los Angeles, California, has a public–private "million tree" campaign, which depends on uneven financing and faces myriad local constraints and priorities.[72] A public health approach to urban reforestation might help cities better control and professionalize their street tree programs.

However, a health in all policies approach to street trees also requires better data and more cross-disciplinary collaboration to maximize outcomes. Most analyses of urban trees have focused on macro-level effects, and most of these analyses have emphasized the positive bio-physical properties of trees, not their health properties.[73,74] A recent scoping review of urban trees and human health found only three papers (of 201) dealing with street trees and a dearth of rigorous study designs.[75] The foresters and planners who work with street trees consistently plead for greater public health engagement.[73,76,77]

There is some progress but room for much more. A recent review of 28 urban planning decision-support tools, which included the US Department of Agriculture's widely used I-Tree, found that none of the existing tools comprehensively integrated health, environmental, and economic effects of trees[78]—perhaps understandably, because estimating the health effects of trees is a complicated business. Another recent study suggested that increasing urban tree cover to 30% in 93 European cities would reduce summer deaths in adults by about 4.3%. This is the type of effect Smith proposed, and such an estimate is a helpful start. However, this model was based on just three months of mortality data and large-scale estimates of the cooling effects of trees.[79] There is evidence that many health effects of trees are localized, and, moreover, trees come with health liabilities that such models often ignore: allergenic pollens, emission of volatile organics, production of organic detritus, and falling limbs, to name a few.[80,81] We need more data on all of these variables.

Stephen Smith's street tree story need not be a public health sidebar. We tend to take for granted the isolating role of laboratory science in public health and public health's apolitical advocacy for individual reform.[29] Yet public health has a bigger role to play in shaping policies, cultures, practices, norms, and histories that affect health.[82] This role requires field research and the kind of alliances and persistent political work that Smith used to bring trees to Manhattan's streets in 1914. Smith's tree story is a reminder that what we take as progress may not be inevitable and that public health can shape its destiny.[83] AJPH

ABOUT THE AUTHOR

John M. Harris Jr is a retired physician executive living in Tucson, Arizona.

CORRESPONDENCE

Correspondence should be sent to John M. Harris Jr, MD, MBA, 5944 E Miramar Dr, Tucson, AZ 85715 (e-mail: jharrisjrmd@outlook.com). Reprints can be ordered at https://www.ajph.org by clicking the "Reprints" link.

PUBLICATION INFORMATION

Full Citation: Harris JM Jr. Manhattan's street trees: an unfinished public health story. *Am J Public Health*. 2025;115(1):66–74.

Acceptance Date: August 18, 2024.

DOI: https://doi.org/10.2105/AJPH.2024.307856

ORCID iD:

John M. Harris Jr https://orcid.org/0000-0001-6877-4983

ACKNOWLEDGMENTS

J. M. Harris is the author of *Pestilence, Insanity, and Trees: How Stephen Smith Changed New York* (New York, NY: Routledge; 2023).

CONFLICTS OF INTEREST

The author has no conflicts of interest.

REFERENCES

1. Glasser JH, Fee E, Brown TM. Stephen Smith (1823–1922): founder of the American Public Health Association. *Am J Public Health*.

2011;101(11):2058. https://doi.org/10.2105/AJPH.2009.188920
2. Dumont AE. Thoughts prompted by the centennial of the American Public Health Association. *Ann Surg*. 1973;178(1):113–114. https://doi.org/10.1097/00000658-197307000-00022
3. Roses DF. Stephen Smith—pioneer of American surgery and public health. *Bull Am Coll Surg*. 1991;76(12):10–17.
4. Rudolph L, Caplan J, Ben-Moshe K, Dillon L. *Health in All Policies: A Guide for State and Local Governments*. Washington, DC, and Oakland, CA: American Public Health Association and Public Health Institute; 2013.
5. Dümpelmann S. *Seeing Trees: A History of Street Trees in New York City and Berlin*. New Haven, CT: Yale University Press; 2019.
6. Smith S. Report of the Sanitary Committee: on the effects of high temperature upon the public health of New York, and on measures of prevention. In: *Second Annual Report of the Board of Health of the Health Department, City of New York*. New York, NY: David H. Gildersleeve, Printer; 1872:374–403.
7. New city government. *New York Herald*. April 11, 1870: 10.
8. Smith S. Trees in the city [letter]. *New York Times*. July 6, 1903: 6.
9. Smith S. *On the Effects of High Temperature Upon the Public Health and on Measures of Prevention*. New York, NY: Thomas L. Clacher; 1873.
10. Shade-trees as disinfectants. *New York Times*. April 7, 1873: 4.
11. Trees as disinfectants. *Chetopa Advance*. April 30, 1873: 1.
12. Trees as disinfectants. *The San Francisco Examiner*. April 3, 1874: 2.
13. Our shade-trees. *New York Times*. August 19, 1873: 2.
14. Morgan MH, ed. *Vitruvius: The Ten Books on Architecture*. Cambridge, MA: Harvard University Press; 1914; No. 5.
15. Konijnendijk CC, Nilsson K, Randrup TB, Schipperijn J, eds. *Urban Forests and Trees*. New York, NY: Springer; 2005. https://doi.org/10.1007/3-540-27684-X
16. Lawrence HW. From private allée to public shade tree; the historic roots of the urban forest. *Arnoldia*. 1997;57(2):2–10. https://doi.org/10.5962/p.251179
17. Laurian L. Planning for street trees and human–nature relations: lessons from 600 years of street tree planting in Paris. *J Plann Hist*. 2019; 18(4):282–310. https://doi.org/10.1177/1538513218820525
18. Smith S. Historical sketch of the American Public Health Association. *Public Health Reports and Papers*. 1880;5:vii–liv.
19. Nicholson CJ. Elegance and grass roots: the neglected philosophy of Frederick Law Olmsted. *Transactions of the Charles S Peirce Society*. 2004;40(2):335–348.
20. *Fourth Annual Report of the Board of Health of the Health Department of the City of New York*. New York, NY: D. Appleton and Company; 1874.
21. Sanitary reform—American Health Association. *New York Times*. November 14, 1873: 2.
22. *Fifth and Sixth Annual Reports of the Board of Health of the Health Department of the City of New York*. New York, NY: Martin B. Brown, Printer; 1876.
23. *Public Health Reports and Papers*. Vol 2. New York, NY: Hurd and Houghton; 1876.
24. Henderson P. Street trees of Washington. *Harper's New Monthly Magazine*. 1888;77:285–287.
25. *Public Health Reports and Papers*. Vol 4. Boston, MA: Houghton, Mifflin and Company; 1880.
26. Ravenel M. The American Public Health Association: past, present, and future. In: Ravenel M, ed. *A Half Century of Public Health*. New York, NY: American Public Health Association; 1921:13–55. https://doi.org/10.2105/AJPH.11.12.1031-a
27. *Public Health Papers and Reports*. Vol 15. Concord, NH: Republican Press Association; 1890.
28. Harris JM Jr. *Pestilence, Insanity, and Trees: How Stephen Smith Changed New York*. New York, NY: Routledge; 2023. https://doi.org/10.4324/9781003458913
29. Fairchild AL, Rosner D, Colgrove J, Bayer R, Fried L. The exodus of public health: what history can tell us about the future. *Am J Public Health*. 2010; 100(1):54–63. https://doi.org/10.2105/AJPH.2009.163956
30. Deaths in the hot season. *New York Times*. March 23, 1886: 2.
31. State Forestry Association. *Buffalo Courier*. April 27, 1890: 1.
32. Trees for city streets—a society to plant them has been started in the Wool Club. *WORLD*. 1896:9.
33. Shade trees in city streets. *New York Tribune*. July 12, 1896: 14.
34. Care of trees in city streets. *New-York Tribune*. April 24, 1899: 4.
35. Want trees in the streets. *New York Times*. January 26, 1899: 4.
36. Smith S. Vegetation a remedy for the summer heat of cities. In: *Appletons' Popular Science Monthly*. Vol 54. New York, NY: D. Appelton and Company; 1899:433–450.
37. Tree culture in cities. *New York Times*. May 13, 1900: 21.
38. Fox WF. *Tree Planting on Streets and Highways*. Albany, NY: J.B. Lyon Company; 1903.
39. Solotaroff W. *Shade-Trees in Towns and Cities*. New York, NY: John Wiley & Sons; 1911.
40. Smith WH. Removal of atmospheric particulates by urban vegetation: implications for human and vegetative health. *Yale J Biol Med*. 1977;50(2):185–197.
41. Culyer JY. The boulevard trees [letter]. *New York Times*. October 7, 1900: 18.
42. City care of trees. *New-York Tribune*. April 28, 1902: 7.
43. An Act to Extend the Jurisdiction of the Park Board of the City of New York to the Preservation, Planting and Cultivation of Trees and Vegetation in the Streets Thereof for the Purpose of Improving the Public Health. Laws of New York - Chapter 453. 1902.
44. *Report for the Year 1902*. New York, NY: The City of New York Department of Parks; 1903.
45. Budget hearings close; Board of Estimate to act. *The Brooklyn Daily Eagle*. October 20, 1902: 20.
46. Culyer JY. How to get trees in street [letter]. *New York Times*. April 19, 1908: 47.
47. Culyer JY. Tree planting in Berlin and New York [letter]. *New York Times*. March 5, 1908: 6.
48. No trees for Fifth Avenue. *New-York Tribune*. November 2, 1910: 2.
49. Beautify Fifth Avenue and handle its traffic. *New York Times*. December 4, 1910: 43.
50. Fighting to beautify Fifth Avenue with trees. *New York Times*. April 30, 1911: 41.
51. *Annual Report*. New York, NY: The City of New York Department of Parks; 1911:49–50.
52. City's oldest tree honored at Inwood. *New York Times*. October 31, 1912: 22.
53. Trees and life. In: *The Outlook*. Vol 105. New York, NY: The Outlook Company; 1913:937–938.
54. New York is being surveyed for planting of trees. *New York Times*. January 4, 1914;5:6.
55. Will-o-the-wisp Charles B. Stover is in New Orleans. *The Evening World*. December 1, 1913: 3.
56. Mitchel names his city helpers. *New York Times*. January 1, 1914: 1.
57. Smith S. Want city bureau for tree culture [letter]. *New York Times*. March 15, 1914: 19.
58. Tree planters meet. *New York Times*. March 25, 1914: 11.
59. Plans for Colony Club. *New York Times*. September 18, 1914: 11.
60. Smith S. City street trees: if official neglect continues they will soon disappear [letter]. *New York Times*. May 26, 1914: 10.
61. Smith S. A tree culture bureau [letter]. *New York Times*. June 25, 1914: 8.
62. Croker letter raps Murphy. *New York Times*. February 10, 1914: 2.
63. Urges city tree planting. *New York Times*. August 18, 1914: 16.
64. Francis HR. *Report on the Street Trees of the City of New York*. Syracuse, NY: The New York State College of Forestry at Syracuse University; 1914.
65. Burris S, Ashe M, Blanke D, et al. Better health law faster: the five essential public health law services. *Public Health Rep*. 2016;131(6):747–753. https://doi.org/10.1177/0033354916667496
66. McGowan AK, Greeley S, Griffis R, Polan SL. Thirty-six years after the 1988 IOM *Future of Public Health:* stop ruminating and start taking action. *Am J Public Health*. 2024;114(5):486–488. https://doi.org/10.2105/AJPH.2024.307634
67. New York City Department of Parks and Recreation. Street tree planting. Available at: https://www.nycgovparks.org/trees/street-tree-planting. Accessed April 16, 2024.
68. New York City Mayor's Office of Climate and Environmental Justice. Extreme heat adaptation. Available at: https://climate.cityofnewyork.us/initiatives/extreme-heat-adaptation. Accessed April 16, 2024.
69. Moskell C, Allred SB. Residents' beliefs about responsibility for the stewardship of park trees and street trees in New York City. *Landsc Urban Plan*. 2013;120:85–95. https://doi.org/10.1016/j.landurbplan.2013.08.002
70. Young RF, McPherson EG. Governing metropolitan green infrastructure in the United States. *Landsc Urban Plan*. 2012;109(1):67–75. https://doi.org/10.1016/j.landurbplan.2012.09.004
71. DiSalvo A, Fukuda J, Ransey J. *Street Tree Inventory Report: City of Portland*. Portland, OR: Portland Parks and Recreation Urban Forestry; 2017.
72. Pincetl S, Gillespie T, Pataki DE, Saatchi S, Saphores J-D. Urban tree planting programs,

function or fashion? Los Angeles and urban tree planting campaigns. *GeoJournal.* 2013;78(3): 475–493. https://doi.org/10.1007/s10708-012-9446-x

73. Donovan GH. Including public health benefits of trees in urban-forestry decision making. *Urban for Urban Green.* 2017;22:120–123. https://doi.org/10.1016/j.ufug.2017.02.010
74. Salmond JA, Tadaki M, Vardoulakis S, et al. Health and climate related ecosystem services provided by street trees in the urban environment. *Environ Health.* 2016;15(suppl 1):36. https://doi.org/10.1186/s12940-016-0103-6
75. Wolf KL, Lam ST, McKeen JK, Richardson GRA, van den Bosch M, Bardekjian AC. Urban trees and human health: a scoping review. *Int J Environ Res Public Health.* 2020;17(12):4371. https://doi.org/10.3390/ijerph17124371
76. Kumar P, Drukman A, Gallagher J, et al. The nexus between air pollution, green infrastructure, and human health. *Environ Int.* 2019;133(Pt A): 105181. https://doi.org/10.1016/j.envint.2019.105181
77. McDonald R, Kroeger T, Boucher T, Longzhu W, Salem R. *Planting Healthy Air: A Global Analysis of the Role of Urban Trees in Addressing Particulate Matter Pollution and Extreme Heat.* Arlington, VA: The Nature Conservancy; 2016.
78. Tefera Y, Soebarto V, Bishop C, Kandulu J, Williams C. A scoping review of urban planning decision support tools and processes that account for the health, environment, and economic benefits of trees and greenspace. *Int J Environ Res Public Health.* 2023;21(1):48. https://doi.org/10.3390/ijerph21010048
79. Iungman T, Cirach M, Marando F, et al. Cooling cities through urban green infrastructure: a health impact assessment of European cities. *Lancet.* 2023;401(10376):577–589. https://doi.org/10.1016/S0140-6736(22)02585-5
80. Roman LA, Conway TM, Eisenman TS, et al. Beyond 'trees are good': disservices, management costs, and tradeoffs in urban forestry. *Ambio.* 2021;50(3):615–630. https://doi.org/10.1007/s13280-020-01396-8
81. Vailshery LS, Madhumitha J, Nagendra H. Effect of street trees on microclimate and air pollution in a tropical city. *Urban For Urban Green.* 2013; 12(3):408–415. https://doi.org/10.1016/j.ufug.2013.03.002
82. Galea S, Vaughn R. Expanding the scope of health in all policies approach. *Am J Public Health.* 2021;111(10):1733–1735. https://doi.org/10.2105/AJPH.2021.306479
83. Morabia A. This is how important history is. *Am J Public Health.* 2018;108(2):152–153. https://doi.org/10.2105/AJPH.2017.304228

Adding Nativity, Citizenship, and Immigration Status to Health Monitoring and Survey Data

Fatma E. Marouf, JD, MPH, Krista M. Perreira, PhD, and Huyen Pham, JD

Immigration status and related policies have a significant impact on health outcomes. Yet major national health surveys currently provide little or no information about immigration status, rendering subgroups of noncitizens largely invisible. Even measures of citizenship, nativity, country of birth, and years in the United States, which provide critical information about immigration history, are not consistently included in national data sets.

The main objections to asking directly about immigration status are that (1) such questions are too stigmatizing, risking lower response rates and inaccurate responses; and (2) answering the questions may expose respondents to possible immigration or criminal consequences. Our analysis shows that these objections are unfounded or can be mitigated.

National health surveys have evolved over the past decades to include questions about mental health, substance use, sexual orientation, and gender identity—topics once assumed to be too stigmatizing to ask about, with possible negative legal consequences. We argue that the time has come to obtain more detailed information about immigration status as well as to consistently include the measures of immigration history mentioned so that we can better evaluate the health consequences of immigrant-related policy choices. (*Am J Public Health*. 2025;115(1):75–82. https://doi.org/10.2105/AJPH.2024.307867)

AJPH January 2025, Vol. 115, No. 1

According to the US Census Bureau, approximately 14% of persons in the United States are foreign born, approximately half of whom are naturalized citizens. The health of foreign-born persons can be affected by their place of birth, years in the United States, citizenship status, and immigration status. However, few national health data sets collect data on these various aspects of nativity, despite their profound influence on health.[1] Moreover, the small sample size of foreign-born persons in national surveys limits research and prevents analysis by ethnoracial categories, more specific Asian or Hispanic backgrounds, gender, and immigration status.[2,3] Not knowing whether certain subgroups of immigrants, such as asylum seekers, are included among the foreign-born population can also make it difficult to determine whether results are biased by the makeup of the foreign-born population.[2] In most analyses, all US-born persons are simply compared with all foreign-born persons, leading to potentially erroneous conclusions about associations between nativity and health.

To remedy this, large national data sets should oversample foreign-born populations and collect data on nativity as well as on foreign-born persons' place of birth, years in the United States, citizenship status, and immigration status. Among these aspects of nativity, the effects of immigration status on health and health care access are the least understood. Immigration status has been recognized as a social determinant of health. Immigration status affects health through experiences of discrimination and stigma; stressful federal immigration enforcement policies; and exclusionary federal, state, and local government policies that restrict immigrants' access to health insurance and other health care resources.[4,5]

Not all categories of immigrants are equally affected by government policies.

For example, at the federal level, individuals who have been granted refugee status or asylum are eligible for full-scope Medicaid, the Children's Health Insurance Program, and the Supplemental Nutrition Assistance Program (i.e., food stamps); however, those with pending asylum applications and others with liminal status—such as those granted deferred action status or temporary protected status (TPS)—are excluded. The categories of immigrants allowed to purchase health insurance through Patient Protection and Affordable Care Act marketplaces are broader, including individuals with pending asylum applications who have received work permits and those with deferred action status and TPS.

However, before a policy change in May 2024, Deferred Action for Childhood Arrivals (DACA) recipients were ineligible to buy insurance through Patient Protection and Affordable Care Act marketplaces, despite having a type of deferred action status. If researchers wanted to examine this policy change's impact, they would have to impute who has DACA status based on other variables, because of the lack of direct information about immigration status. Researchers may also want to distinguish undocumented individuals from those with some type of liminal legal status such as DACA or TPS. Individuals with liminal status can typically get a work permit and a driver's license, whereas undocumented individuals cannot obtain these essential documents that affect access to health resources.

The lack of data on immigration status and other aspects of nativity limits not only the extent to which research can inform policy debates and programmatic interventions but also the ability of studies to detect health-related disparities among different categories of immigrants. Moreover, the absence of these data impedes our ability to understand intergenerational patterns of health and well-being. Approximately 1 in 4 children living in the United States had an immigrant parent in 2022, making it extremely important to study mixed-status families.

The federal government recently recognized "the importance of having data available for detailed groups to measure differences in healthcare outcomes."[6(p22186)] This recognition comes as part of the revision of the Office of Management and Budget Statistical Policy Directive 15, which adds a race and ethnicity category for individuals who identify as Middle Eastern and North African on the US Census and other federal forms.[6] Similarly, collecting more immigration data would foster research and programs to address health inequities for specific populations of immigrants that are currently invisible in data sets.

LIMITATIONS OF PROXY MEASURES AND IMPUTATION

Because few national surveys directly ask people about their immigration status, most analyses of immigration status rely on proxy measures or imputations. For example, researchers have assigned undocumented status based on country of birth, years in the United States, state of residence, occupation, educational attainment, age, and sex.[7,8] Studies have also relied on the absence of a social security number or on emergency Medicaid usage as proxies for undocumented status.[9,10] But these proxies are problematic; for example, as the Department of Homeland Security has acknowledged, millions of US citizens and permanent residents do not have social security numbers.[11] Even when undocumented status is convincingly assigned to survey participants, it is not randomly assigned, making it difficult to draw causal conclusions related to undocumented status without the use of more sophisticated analytical methods like propensity score matching.[5]

Similarly, researchers interested in examining the health effects of DACA have had to impute DACA eligibility in various ways. One DACA study using the National Health Interview Survey (NHIS) relied on an estimate of the percentage of noncitizens who are undocumented because of a lack of information about immigration status, noting that other DACA eligibility criteria (e.g., age at time of migration and criminal history) were also unavailable.[12] Another study was available to control for DACA status by drawing survey respondents from a pool of individuals who attended 1 or more DACA workshops between 2012 and 2014 but acknowledged that this method "does not allow the development of population estimates."[13] The authors noted that "no current data set allows representative sampling of individual-level characteristics of DACA applicants."[13(p40)]

One of the only national surveys that asks about immigration status is the US Census Bureau's Survey on Income and Program Participation (SIPP), which includes a question about immigration status at the time of entry into the United States. However, because immigration status can change over time, researchers still must use proxy measures or imputation techniques to estimate current immigration status. Another limitation of SIPP is that the Census Bureau uses a statistical technique called "hot-deck imputation" to handle missing responses on legal status questions, assigning responses based on responses from "similar" individuals. Bachmeier et al. question the validity of this approach and employ different methods for assigning legal status to foreign-born respondents in the SIPP.[14] The 2008 SIPP was the only version that contained specific questions on migration history. Several subsequent studies have used SIPP data to impute immigration status in other data sets.[8,15,16] But as the 2008 SIPP data get older, these imputations become less accurate.

Previous articles have mentioned several challenges in using proxy measures for undocumented status. Some have raised concerns that failing to ask about legal status leads to omitted variable bias.[14,17] Proxy measures can also reinforce stereotypes about the undocumented population and make it harder to examine minority (e.g., non-Hispanic) groups in the undocumented population.[18] The "residual method" that is generally used to determine the size of the undocumented population in the United States also has weaknesses related to uncertainties in underlying assumptions about emigration rates and, to a lesser extent, about coverage error and mortality rates.[19] The Census Bureau itself has also acknowledged that "as-reported ACS [American Community Survey] citizenship responses are reasonably good, but the edits and imputes are less reliable."[20(p35)]

By contrast, directly asking about immigration status would avoid many of the pitfalls associated with trying to impute legal status. Several surveys have successfully collected immigration data by asking participants about their status. The National Agricultural Worker Survey, which the US Department of Labor conducts annually, surveys farmworkers and includes a categorical variable for current legal status, with possible responses of "citizen," "green card," "other work authorization," and "unauthorized."

The Kaiser Family Foundation/Los Angeles Times Survey of Immigrants, a nationally representative survey of 3358 immigrant adults, asked foreign-born respondents if they had naturalized, were lawful permanent residents, or had a work permit.[21] Those who did not fall into any of these categories were identified as "likely undocumented." The Hispanic Community Health Study/Study of Latinos (HCHS/SOL), which includes more than 16 000 Latinos in 4 US metropolitan areas, added questions about immigration status in 2016 asking about naturalization, lawful permanent resident status, pending applications for permanent resident status, other visa statuses, and pending visa applications.[22]

Additionally, the Los Angeles Family and Neighborhood Survey (L.A.FANS), which collected data from approximately 3000 families in Los Angeles County, recorded even more detailed categories of immigration status, including TPS and "does not have papers." The success of these large surveys in collecting immigration status data demonstrates that such data can be successfully collected in national health surveys.

COMMON OBJECTIONS TO ASKING ABOUT IMMIGRATION STATUS

Although asking directly about immigration status has important research benefits, researchers may be reluctant to collect these data because they fear decreased response rates or invalid responses. Researchers may also worry that collecting immigration data will increase the risk of criminal or immigration enforcement for respondents. However, these concerns are either insignificant or can be mitigated.

Response Rates

Researchers often avoid asking about immigration status because they fear stigmatizing participants by such sensitive questions, which can lower response rates. Although immigration status can be a stigmatizing issue in certain contexts, the surveys we have discussed provide evidence that people are willing to answer questions about legal status for health surveys. On the 2 national surveys that include questions about immigration status—the National Agricultural Worker Survey and SIPP—researchers have found no impact on response rate and no "chilling effect" on subsequent questions; nor have questions about immigration status had a negative impact on state and local surveys, such as L.A.FANS.[14] Bachmeier et al.[14] reported that of all the foreign-born respondents in L.A.FANS, only 4.3% had an ambiguous immigration status, owing to nonresponse to the series of questions about status. Similarly, HCHS/SOL added questions on immigration status in 2014 and found minimal nonresponse (< 3%).[22] These findings indicate that asking about immigration status on health surveys is not as stigmatizing as some researchers may think.

Additionally, we can look to surveys that ask about citizenship status. Since its inception in 1998, the ACS has included a question on each household member's citizenship. In the past decade, nonresponse rates for the citizenship question have varied from 6% among non-Hispanic Whites to 15.5%

among Hispanics.[23] Thus, the overwhelming majority of respondents answered the citizenship question, even under the Trump administration, when anti-immigrant rhetoric was pervasive. As might be expected, nonresponse to the citizenship question on the ACS is higher among households that include noncitizens than among households with all citizen members.[23,24]

The evolution of survey questions related to sexual orientation and gender identities (SOGI) provides helpful historical context in understanding how questions once considered too "sensitive" can become destigmatized over time, especially once we become aware of the harmful effects of omitting them. Until 2013, national health surveys such as the NHIS did not include any questions on SOGI. A question was added that year after a 2011 report by the Institute of Medicine observed that little health research had been done on LGBT (lesbian, gay, bisexual, transgender) individuals.[25] The committee identified several challenges associated with conducting health research on LGBT populations, including potential reluctance to answer questions and problems recruiting a large enough sample for meaningful analysis. These challenges are similar to those researchers face regarding immigration status. Despite these challenges, the Institute of Medicine called for collection of SOGI data in federally funded surveys.

After extensive testing, the NHIS added a question on sexual orientation in 2013. Having found during the testing phase that there was no benefit in asking the question in a private, self-administered mode, the question was incorporated into the face-to-face mode. Although researchers expected SOGI questions to be particularly sensitive, it turned out that respondents did not view them that way and were willing to answer.[26] Similarly, following National Academies of Sciences, Engineering, and Medicine recommendations, the HCHS/SOL incorporated questions on SOGI in 2020.[27] Missing data on these questions were minimal (< 1%), and their inclusion did not reduce response rates.[28] Efforts to collect comprehensive data on SOGI gradually expanded to "parallel the evolution of measures to assess other aspects of identity . . . such as race, ethnicity, primary language, and disability."[29(p73)]

The time has come for the measurement of immigration status in federally supported surveys to evolve as well. The Coming Out as Undocumented campaign that emerged in the immigrant rights' movement since 2010 focused on increasing visibility. Instead of hiding their status, undocumented youths "came out" as a way of asserting their dignity and countering dehumanizing discourses. The National Immigrant Youth Alliance even started the National Coming Out of the Shadows Week of Action. National surveys that fail to ask about legal status may unintentionally reinforce an old message that being undocumented is something shameful and stigmatizing—the antithesis of the message embraced by the immigrant rights' movement.

The political climate may, of course, affect the sensitivity of questions on citizenship and immigration status. When President Trump politicized the issue and proposed adding citizenship questions to the 2020 census while also engaging in anti-immigrant rhetoric, researchers found greater sensitivity and nonresponse to the questions. Respondents, especially those who were foreign born, feared that their answers to Census Bureau questions would be shared with other government agencies and used against them.[30] Although immigration status may remain politicized, collecting anonymized data and ensuring confidentiality should help mitigate these fears.

Because the US census is used to define political districts, it is also much more politicized than any national health survey; undercounting communities of color in the census reduces their political representation. Given the less politicized nature of a national health survey, adding immigration questions would likely have a smaller chilling effect.

Response Validity

A separate but related concern is that asking about immigration status would produce invalid responses. In other words, people may not tell the truth about their immigration status, especially if they are undocumented. The Census Bureau has analyzed the accuracy of self-reported citizenship on the ACS by comparing responses to administrative records from numerous sources, including Department of Homeland Security databases with immigration information, Department of State passport information, Social Security records, and Internal Revenue Service records. Among those with records corroborating US citizenship, the Census Bureau found that self-reported ACS citizenship responses were highly accurate, with only 0.71% misreporting as noncitizens. But among those identified as noncitizens based on the administrative records, 12.21% self-reported as citizens on the ACS.[20]

This invalidity percentage is not particularly high, especially if one considers that the administrative records may be incomplete or not fully up-to-date.

In fact, an earlier Census Bureau analysis, using a more limited set of administrative records, suggested that individuals self-reported as citizens in 23.8% to 34.7% of cases in which the administrative records indicated that the person was not a citizen.[23] The reduction to 12.21% with the inclusion of more detailed immigration records underscores the importance of using accurate records. Ultimately, even if a small percentage of respondents do misreport themselves as US citizens, there are important benefits to be gained from research that includes citizenship and immigration status.

Additionally, missing values and misreporting are common challenges for many variables in survey-based research. One of the most widely used variables in surveys, income, tends to have the highest levels of missing data as well as misreported data of any variable on a survey. For example, one study found correlations of 0.75 to 0.89 between self-reported income on SIPP and Social Security Administration detailed earnings records for annual earnings between 1990 and 1999.[31] Other studies show that missing income data rates in the NHIS and other surveys range from 6% to 33%, depending on the question format.[32,33] Nevertheless, income is still included in most health surveys because of its importance in understanding a variety of health outcomes and health disparities. To address issues of missing and misreported data, researchers have worked to develop strategies to improve recall and completeness, such as using computer-assisted self-interviews, providing an explanation for questions, and providing memory cues.[34–36]

Concerns about the validity of surveys on substance use have also existed for decades, yet these questions are appropriately included in national and federally funded surveys.[37] Substance use underreporting tends to increase with the perceived stigma of the substance being discussed; for alcohol, which is arguably the least stigmatized substance, state-level estimates of alcohol use from self-reports correlate fairly strongly with the estimates from sales and tax data.[37] By analogy, we may find that respondents accurately report forms of legal status such as DACA and TPS, which are less stigmatized than being undocumented. As the stigma associated with being undocumented is reduced, people may be more likely to report that status as well.

Immigration Threats or Criminal Consequences

A third objection is that collecting information about immigration status could put survey participants at risk for deportation and criminal prosecution if data are turned over to law enforcement and immigration authorities. Every undocumented person faces some risk of deportation, and although being undocumented is not a crime, illegal entry or reentry into the United States are among the most commonly prosecuted federal crimes. These concerns are very important, especially in today's polarized environment, but they can be addressed by making the collection of immigration information completely anonymized wherever possible and by providing strong privacy and confidentiality protections against disclosure.

For cross-sectional surveys, information about immigration status can be collected in anonymized ways so that the status cannot be linked back to specific individuals, even with an algorithm, code, or pseudonym. To be able to identify and detain an individual for deportation or criminal prosecution, law enforcement agencies need to know the individual's name, location (home, work, or school), and the approximate times that the individual will be at the location. Without personally identifiable information, the immigration status information collected in surveys will not be a useful basis for law enforcement action. For example, instead of asking for a respondent's name and home and work addresses, a survey could ask for their zip code; doing so would provide the geographical information that researchers need without providing the personally identifiable information that could be used by law enforcement.

For longitudinal surveys in which completely anonymized data collection is not possible, immigration status information can be safeguarded by privacy and confidentiality laws. Current laws offer substantial protection to protect against disclosure to law enforcement and immigration authorities. Existing laws are necessary, in part because numerous surveys already ask about illegal activities. For example, the National Survey on Drug Use and Health includes detailed questions on drug use, theft, and assault; the Behavioral Risk Factor Surveillance System asks about illicit behavior (e.g., drug use) by family members; and the National Survey of Family Growth asks about abortion, which is now criminalized in many states.

The Confidential Information Protection and Statistical Efficiency Act, which applies whenever the federal government collects data for statistical purposes, prohibits the use of those data for any nonstatistical purpose and prohibits disclosing confidential data in identifiable form without consent.[38] The penalties for disclosing confidential information under this act are imprisonment for up to 5 years and a fine of up to $250 000.

Federal agencies such as the National Center for Health Statistics (NCHS) have also adopted stringent legal protections that minimize the risk of information disclosure to third parties. The NCHS requires all staff to pass rigorous annual training on protecting data and to sign an affidavit to protect privacy. Additionally, under the Public Health Service Act, access to identifiable information is granted only to NCHS staff, its designated agents, and the collaborators mentioned in the initial consent statement. This act also limits the use of information to the purposes for which it was collected. The NCHS confidentiality brochure specifically promises never to give any information to state or federal agencies, including the police or immigration services.[39]

Similarly, responses to US census questions cannot be used for any purpose in a legal or administrative proceeding without consent, nor can they be used to the detriment of a respondent under 13 USC sections 9(a) and 8(c). Presidential proclamations under both Democratic and Republican administrations have affirmed that census information cannot be used in the regulation of immigration.[39] The Supreme Court also held in *Baldridge v Shapiro* (455 US 345, 1982), that the Census Act protects all raw data from disclosure, even if the data do not reveal the respondent's identity, including disclosure through Freedom of Information Act requests.

For surveys funded by federal agencies, we can look to the protections offered by certificates of confidentiality. Under 42 USC section § 241, Congress authorizes agencies that are part of the Public Health Service, including the National Institutes of Health, to issue certificates of confidentiality that allow researchers to refuse to disclose identifying information about participants in civil, criminal, administrative, or other proceedings at the federal, state, or local levels. Because the researchers, in most cases, have sole possession of the data, third parties seeking the data would need to resort to judicial or similar proceedings to try to obtain access. The National Institutes of Health automatically issues these certificates for the research it funds and has the discretionary authority to issue the certificates for other types of research as well. Researchers can therefore request these certificates to provide additional protection to survey respondents in the event that a third party, such as a governmental entity, seeks to access the data.

These federal laws and the capacity to collect anonymized data make it extremely unlikely that any harm would come to respondents who shared their immigration status as part of a federal survey.

CONCLUSIONS

Collecting data on key aspects of nativity, including place of birth, years in the United States, US citizenship status, and immigration status, is necessary to understand health challenges affecting specific immigrant subgroups and to inform policy decisions. Oversampling the foreign-born population, in the same way that we oversample certain racial and ethnic minorities, will provide the power needed to detect significant differences. We can no longer rely on conventional assumptions that undocumented status is too stigmatizing to ask about or that such questions will yield lower response rates or invalid answers. Such concerns must be rigorously tested and weighed against the knowledge lost—and poor health policy decisions that may be made—as a result of not asking. It is time for national health surveys to evolve to account more precisely for immigrant identities, just as they have evolved to record more detailed information about other sensitive topics. AJPH

ABOUT THE AUTHORS

Fatma E. Marouf and Huyen Pham are with the Texas A&M University School of Law, Fort Worth. Krista M. Perreira is with the Department of Social Medicine, University of North Carolina School of Medicine, Chapel Hill.

CORRESPONDENCE

Correspondence should be sent to Fatma E. Marouf, Texas A&M School of Law, 1515 Commerce St, Fort Worth, TX 76102 (e-mail: fatma.marouf@law.tamu.edu). Reprints can be ordered at https://www.ajph.org by clicking the "Reprints" link.

PUBLICATION INFORMATION

Full Citation: Marouf FE, Perreira KM, Pham H. Adding nativity, citizenship, and immigration status to health monitoring and survey data. *Am J Public Health*. 2025;115(1):75–82.

Acceptance Date: August 31, 2024.

DOI: https://doi.org/10.2105/AJPH.2024.307867

ORCID iDs:
Fatma E. Marouf https://orcid.org/0009-0000-7875-3369

Krista M. Perreira https://orcid.org/0000-0003-2906-0261

CONTRIBUTORS

F. E. Marouf drafted the article. F. E. Marouf and K. M. Perreira led the idea formulation and overall direction and planning of the article. K. M. Perreira and H. Pham participated in the research and in writing and editing the article. All authors provided critical feedback and approved the final version to be published.

ACKNOWLEDGMENTS

K. M. Perreira was supported by the Eunice Kennedy Shriver National Institute of Child Health and Human Development, National Institutes of Health (NIH; grant P2C HD050924).

Note. The content of this article is solely the responsibility of the authors and does not necessarily represent the official views of the NIH.

CONFLICTS OF INTEREST

No competing financial interests exist for the authors.

HUMAN PARTICIPANT PROTECTION

This study did not involve human participant research, so no protocol approval was necessary.

REFERENCES

1. Allen CD. A systematic review of datasets to research the effect of policy and place on immigrants' health. *MedRxiv.* January 31, 2022. Available at: https://www.medrxiv.org/content/10.1101/2022.01.30.22270115v1. Accessed April 1, 2024.
2. Dedania R, Gonzales G. Disparities in access to health care among US-born and foreign-born US adults by mental health status, 2013–2016. *Am J Public Health.* 2019;109(suppl 3):S221–S227. https://doi.org/10.2105/AJPH.2019.305149
3. Takeuchi DT, Alegría M, Jackson JS, Williams DR. Immigration and mental health: diverse findings in Asian, Black, and Latino populations. *Am J Public Health.* 2007;97(1):11–12. https://doi.org/10.2105/AJPH.2006.103911
4. Morey BN. Mechanisms by which anti-immigrant stigma exacerbates racial/ethnic health disparities. *Am J Public Health.* 2018;108(4):460–463. https://doi.org/10.2105/AJPH.2017.304266
5. Perreira KM, Pedroza JM. Policies of exclusion: implications for the health of immigrants and their children. *Annu Rev Public Health.* 2019;40:147–166. https://doi.org/10.1146/annurev-publhealth-040218-044115
6. Office of Management and Budget. Revisions to OMB's Statistical Policy Directive No. 15: standards for maintaining, collecting, and presenting federal data on race and ethnicity. *Fed Regist.* 2024;89(62):22182–22196.
7. Passel JS. Measuring illegal immigration: how Pew Research Center counts unauthorized immigrants in the US. July 12, 2019. Available at: https://www.pewresearch.org/short-reads/2019/07/12/how-pew-research-center-counts-unauthorized-immigrants-in-us. Accessed April 1, 2024.
8. Van Hook J, Bachmeier JD, Coffman DL, Harel O. Can we spin straw into gold? An evaluation of immigrant legal status imputation approaches. *Demography.* 2015;52(1):329–354. https://doi.org/10.1007/s13524-014-0358-x
9. Richardson DM, Andrea SB, Ziring A, Robinson C, Messer LC. Pregnancy outcomes and documentation status among Latina women: a systematic review. *Health Equity.* 2020;4(1):158–182. https://doi.org/10.1089/heq.2019.0126
10. Hainmueller J, Lawrence D, Martén L, et al. Protecting unauthorized immigrant mothers improves their children's mental health. *Science.* 2017;357(6355):1041–1044. https://doi.org/10.1126/science.aan5893
11. US Department of Homeland Security. Privacy impact assessment for the DHS immigration-related information sharing with US Census Bureau. November 23, 2020. Available at: https://www.dhs.gov/sites/default/files/publications/privacy-pia-dhs079-sharingwithcensus-november2020.pdf. Accessed April 1, 2024.
12. Venkataramani AS, Shah SJ, O'Brien R, Kawachi I, Tsai AC. Health consequences of the US Deferred Action for Childhood Arrivals (DACA) immigration programme: a quasi-experimental study. *Lancet Public Health.* 2017;2(4):e175–e181. https://doi.org/10.1016/j.socscimed.2017.03.009
13. Patler C, Laster Pirtle W. From undocumented to lawfully present: do changes to legal status impact psychological wellbeing among Latino immigrant young adults? *Soc Sci Med.* 2018;199:39–48. https://doi.org/10.1016/j.socscimed.2017.03.009
14. Bachmeier JD, Van Hook J, Bean FD. Can we measure immigrants' legal status? Lessons from two US surveys. *Int Migr Rev.* 2014;48(2):538–566. https://doi.org/10.1111/imre.12059
15. Kaiser Family Foundation. ACA eligibility analysis, technical appendix b: immigration status imputation. October 2015. Available at: https://files.kff.org/attachment/technical-appendix-b-new-estimates-of-eligibility-for-aca-coverage-among-the-uninsured. Accessed July 16, 2024.
16. Capps R, Bachmeier JD, Van Hook J. Estimating the characteristics of unauthorized immigrants using US Census data: combined sample multiple imputation. *Annals Am. Acad. Pol.* 2018;677(1):165–179. https://doi.org/10.1177/0002716218767383
17. Massey DS, Bartley K. The changing legal status distribution of immigrants: a caution. *Int Migr Rev.* 2005;39(2):469–484. https://doi.org/10.1111/j.1747-7379.2005.tb00274.x
18. Young MT, Madrigal DS. Documenting legal status: a systematic review of measurement of undocumented status in health research. *Public Health Rev.* 2017;38:26. https://doi.org/10.1186/s40985-017-0073-4
19. Van Hook J, Morse A, Capps R, Gelatt J. Uncertainty about the size of the unauthorized foreign-born population in the United States. *Demography.* 2021;58(6):2315–2336. https://doi.org/10.1215/00703370-9491801
20. Abowd JM, Bell WR, Brown JD, et al. *Determination of the 2020 US Citizen Voting Age Population (CVAP) Using Administrative Records and Statistical Methodology.* Center for Economic Studies working paper 20-33. October 30, 2020. Available at: https://www2.census.gov/ces/wp/2020/CES-WP-20-33.pdf. Accessed October 14, 2024.
21. Schumacher S, Hammel L, Artiga S, et al. Understanding the US immigrant experience: the 2023 KFF/LA Times Survey of immigrants. September 18, 2023. Available at: https://www.kff.org/racial-equity-and-health-policy/poll-finding/kff-la-times-survey-of-immigrants. Accessed April 1, 2024.
22. Ross J, Hua S, Perreira KM, et al. Association between immigration status and anxiety, depression, and use of anxiolytic and antidepressant medications in the Hispanic Community Health Study/Study of Latinos. *Ann Epidemiol.* 2019;37:17–23.e3. https://doi.org/10.1016/j.annepidem.2019.07.007
23. Abowd JM. Memorandum from John M. Abowd to Wilbur L. Ross Jr. Technical review of the Department of Justice request to add citizenship question to the 2020 Census. January 19, 2018. Available at: https://epic.org/wp-content/uploads/foia/censusbureau/EPIC-18-03-22-Census-Bureau-FOIA-20180611-Production-Technical-Review-Memo.pdf. Accessed October 16, 2024.
24. Brown JL, Swartzendruber A, DiClemente RJ. Application of audio computer-assisted self-interviews to collect self-reported health data: an overview. *Caries Res.* 2013;47(suppl 1):40–45. https://doi.org/10.1159/000351827
25. US Institute of Medicine. Collecting sexual orientation and gender identity data in electronic health records: workshop summary. 2013. Available at: https://nap.nationalacademies.org/catalog/18260/collecting-sexual-orientation-and-gender-identity-data-in-electronic-health-records. Accessed October 14, 2024.
26. Baker KE, Streed CG Jr, Durso LE. Ensuring that LGBTQI+ people count—collecting data on sexual orientation, gender identity, and intersex status. *N Engl J Med.* 2021;384(13):1184–1186. https://doi.org/10.1056/NEJMp2032447
27. Poteat T, Gallo LC, Harkness A, et al. Influence of stress, gender, and minority status on cardiovascular disease risk in the Hispanic/Latino community: protocol for a longitudinal observational cohort study. *JMIR Res Protoc.* 2021;10(5):e28997. https://doi.org/10.2196/28997
28. University of North Carolina Collaborative Studies Center. Stress Gender and Minority Status in the Study of Latinos (SGM SOL). Ancillary Studies Management Report. March 2024. Available at: https://sites.cscc.unc.edu/hchs/SGM-SOL. Accessed April 1, 2024.
29. Patterson CJ, ed. *Understanding the Well-Being of LGBTQI+ Populations.* Washington, DC: National Academies Press; 2020.
30. McGeeney K, Kriz B, Mullenax S, et al. *2020 Census Barriers, Attitudes, and Motivators Study Survey Report: A New Design for the 21st Century.* January 24, 2019. Available at: https://www2.census.gov/programs-surveys/decennial/2020/program-management/final-analysis-reports/2020-report-cbams-study-survey.pdf. Accessed July 16, 2024.
31. Abowd JM, Stinson MH. Estimating measurement error in annual job earnings: a comparison of survey and administrative data. *Rev Econ Stat.* 2013;95(5):1451–1467. https://doi.org/10.1162/REST_a_00352
32. Schenker N, Raghunathan TE, Chiu PL, Makuc DM, Zhang G, Cohen AJ. Multiple imputation of missing income data in the National Health Interview Survey. *J Am Stat Assoc.* 2006;101(475):924–933. https://doi.org/10.1198/016214505000001375

33. Pleis JR, Dahlhamer JM, Meyer PS. Unfolding the answers? Income nonresponse and income brackets in the National Health Interview Survey. Proceedings of the ASA Section on Survey Research Methods. 2006. Available at: http://www.asasrms.org/Proceedings/y2006/Files/JSM2006-000277.pdf. Accessed October 17, 2024.
34. De Leeuw ED, Hox J, Huisman M. Prevention and treatment of item nonresponse. *J Off Stat.* 2003;19(2):153.
35. Randolph JJ, Virnes M, Jormanainen I, Eronen PJ. The effects of a computer-assisted interview tool on data quality. *J Educ Technol Soc.* 2006;9(3):195–205.
36. Lor M, Bowers BJ, Krupp A, Jacobson N. Tailored explanation: a strategy to minimize nonresponse in demographic items among low-income racial and ethnic minorities. *Surv Pract.* 2017;10(3): https://doi.org/10.29115/SP-2017-0015
37. Johnson TP. Sources of error in substance use prevalence surveys. *Int Sch Res Notices.* 2014; 2014:923290. https://doi.org/10.1155/2014/923290
38. Percival K. Federal laws that protect census confidentiality. 2019. Available at: https://www.brennancenter.org/sites/default/files/2019-08/Report_Federal_Laws_Census_Confidentiality.pdf. Accessed July 10, 2024.
39. National Center for Health Statistics. Protecting the public's privacy. 2021. Available at: https://www.cdc.gov/nchs/data/nhanes/participant/Confidentiality-Brochure-2021.pdf. Accessed April 1, 2024.

Effect of the Communities That HEAL Intervention on Overdose Education and Naloxone Distribution: A Cluster-Randomized, Wait-List Controlled Trial

Patricia R. Freeman, PhD, Alexander Y. Walley, MD, MSc, T. John Winhusen, PhD, Emmanuel A. Oga, MD, MPH, Jennifer Villani, PhD, MPH, Timothy Hunt, PhD, Redonna K. Chandler, PhD, Douglas R. Oyler, PharmD, Brittni Reilly, MSW, Kitty Gelberg, PhD, Christian Douglas, DrPH, Michael S. Lyons, MD, JaNae Holloway, MSPH, Nathan A. Vandergrift, PhD, Joella W. Adams, PhD, Katherine Asman, MSPH, Trevor J. Baker, MS, Candace J. Brancato, MS, Debbie M. Cheng, ScD, Janet E. Childerhose, PhD, James L. David, MS, Daniel J. Feaster, PhD, Louisa Gilbert, PhD, LaShawn M. Glasgow, DrPH, Dawn A. Goddard-Eckrich, EdD, Charles Knott, MPA, Hannah K. Knudsen, PhD, Michelle R. Lofwall, MD, Katherine R. Marks, PhD, Jason T. McMullan, MD, Carrie B. Oser, PhD, Monica F. Roberts, PharmD, Abigail B. Shoben, PhD, Michael D. Stein, MD, Scott T. Walters, PhD, Josie Watson, CPhT, Gary A. Zarkin, PhD, Rebecca D. Jackson, MD, Jeffrey H. Samet, MD, Sharon L. Walsh, PhD, and Nabila El Bassel, PhD

See also Doe-Simkins and Wheeler, p. 6, and Marshall, p. 9.

Objectives. To determine whether the Communities That HEAL (CTH) intervention is effective in increasing naloxone distribution compared with usual care.

Methods. The HEALing (Helping to End Addiction Long-Term) Communities Study (HCS) is a cluster-randomized, parallel-arm, wait-list controlled implementation science trial testing the impact of the CTH intervention on increasing the use of evidence-based practices to lower opioid-related overdose deaths. Communities (n = 67) highly impacted by opioid overdose in Kentucky, Massachusetts, New York, and Ohio were allocated to CTH intervention (n = 34) or wait-list comparison (usual care; n = 33) arms. The primary outcome for this study was the number of naloxone units distributed in HCS communities during the comparison period (July 1, 2021–June 30, 2022), examined using an intent-to-treat negative binomial regression model.

Results. Naloxone distribution was 79% higher in the CTH intervention versus usual care arm (adjusted relative rate = 1.79; 95% confidence interval = 1.28, 2.51; *P* = .001; adjusted rates of naloxone distribution 3378 vs 1884 naloxone units per 100 000 residents), when controlling for urban–rural status, state, baseline opioid-related overdose death rate, and baseline naloxone distribution rate.

Conclusions. The CTH intervention increased naloxone distribution compared with usual care in communities highly impacted by the opioid crisis.

Trial Registration. ClinicalTrials.gov identifier: NCT04111939. (*Am J Public Health*. 2025;115(1):83–94. https://doi.org/10.2105/AJPH.2024.307845)

The public health crisis of drug overdose continues unabated in the United States. Nearly 107 000 drug overdose deaths occurred in 2021, an almost 5-fold increase since 2001.[1,2] Deaths are driven by synthetic opioids, primarily fentanyl, now ubiquitous in the illicit drug supply. Accelerating disparities in opioid-related overdoses are evident, with American Indian/Alaska Native and Black populations most impacted.[3] The continued escalation

AJPH January 2025, Vol. 115, No. 1

and widening disparities in opioid overdose demand innovative approaches in public health response to reduce drug overdose mortality.

The HEALing (Helping to End Addiction Long-Term) Communities Study (HCS) is a cluster-randomized, parallel-arm, wait-list controlled implementation science trial testing the impact of the Communities That HEAL (CTH) intervention on increasing the use of evidence-based practices (EBPs) to lower opioid-related overdose deaths.[4,5] The CTH intervention has 3 components: (1) a coalition-driven community-engagement process to select and support the implementation of strategies to facilitate the uptake of EBPs[6]; (2) the Opioid-overdose Reduction Continuum of Care Approach (ORCCA), a menu of strategies and technical assistance guide for implementing EBPs of overdose education and naloxone distribution (OEND), medication for opioid use disorder (MOUD), and prescription opioid safety[7]; and (3) communication campaigns designed to reduce stigma and increase awareness of and demand for OEND and MOUD.[8]

Overdose education and naloxone distribution, an EBP that decreases opioid-related overdose deaths, is a harm-reduction strategy that was focused initially on people who use drugs and bystanders who were most likely to witness and respond to opioid overdoses.[9] As the opioid crisis escalated, expanding access to OEND became a focus of US health policy interventions. Naloxone access laws were implemented by states to allow naloxone dispensing from pharmacies via standing order or direct prescribing,[10] and federal leaders encouraged OEND for a wider array of community members.[11] Despite this expansion of OEND, modeling data show in most states there is insufficient access to naloxone,[12] particularly for rural populations[13] and among Black and Hispanic persons.[14,15]

As efforts to reduce opioid-related overdose mortality through expanded OEND continue, it is imperative to identify effective strategies for increasing OEND. In this study, we examined the effect of the CTH intervention on OEND in 67 communities highly impacted by opioid overdose. We conducted analyses to evaluate 3 hypotheses:

Hypothesis 1: CTH intervention communities will distribute, overall, significantly higher rates of naloxone units compared to usual care.

Hypothesis 2: CTH intervention communities will distribute, via community-based organizations and events, significantly higher rates of naloxone units compared to usual care.

Hypothesis 3: CTH intervention communities will distribute, via pharmacy dispensing, significantly higher rates of naloxone units compared to usual care.

METHODS

The HCS is a cluster-randomized, parallel-arm, wait-list controlled implementation science trial testing the impact of the CTH intervention on increasing the use of EBPs to lower opioid-related overdose deaths.

Participants

The study consisted of 67 communities (48 counties and 19 cities or towns) in Kentucky, Massachusetts, New York, and Ohio. To participate in the study, communities had to be both highly impacted by opioid-related overdose deaths and willing to partner with behavioral health, criminal justice, and health care settings to implement MOUD and OEND. Within each state, at least 30% of the communities had to be classified as rural, and across each state, a threshold of at least 150 opioid-related overdose deaths (with rural communities accounting for 15% of deaths) and an overdose death rate of at least 25 per 100 000 people was required, based on 2016 data.

Randomization

Study arm allocation was assigned using a covariate-constrained randomization procedure balancing urban–rural classification, opioid-related overdose death rate, and community population size within each state using a macro described by Greene.[4,16] The HCS Data Coordinating Center Study System Developer ran the randomization code, assigned communities to the study arms, and notified the states of the assignment. Thirty-four communities were allocated to wave 1 (CTH intervention arm), and 33 communities were allocated to wave 2 (waitlist control [usual care] arm). The study follows the Consolidated Standards of Reporting Trials (CONSORT) reporting guideline for randomized clinical trials.[17]

Intervention

HCS communities allocated to wave 1 received the CTH intervention, an adaptation of the Communities That Care model,[18] from January 2020 through June 2022. An iterative 7-step process guided community coalitions in the creation of data-driven action plans to reduce opioid-related overdose deaths.[6] As part of the action plan, community coalitions selected strategies from the ORCCA to increase community OEND. Specifically, the CTH required community coalitions to choose at least 1 active OEND strategy, which involved proactive delivery to at-risk individuals and their social networks and delivery in high-risk venues including behavioral health, criminal justice, and health care sectors.[7] Passive OEND strategies were optional and included making OEND more accessible by referral (e.g., a health care provider refers someone to a pharmacy for OEND) or self-request (e.g., a person requests OEND at a pharmacy or community event) and increasing naloxone availability for immediate use in overdose hotspots (e.g., installation of opioid emergency boxes containing naloxone). Community coalitions could also choose an optional strategy of increasing capacity for first-responder naloxone administration. The unique strategy–sector–venue triad combinations used to assess strategy implementation and the strategies initially selected for implementation by wave 1 communities in their action plans have been reported in detail.[19] The actual strategies to promote the uptake of OEND that were actively implemented (i.e., strategies that reached the service delivery stage of implementation) by communities during the intervention period are reported herein.

Outcomes

The primary outcome (hypothesis 1) evaluated in this study was the total number of naloxone units distributed in communities. Secondary outcomes included the number of naloxone units distributed through community programs (hypothesis 2) and the number of naloxone units dispensed by retail pharmacies (hypothesis 3). The overall primary outcome for the HCS trial is opioid-related overdose deaths and was evaluated separately.[5] We assessed outcomes during a 12-month comparison period from July 1, 2021, through June 30, 2022, to allow time for community selection and implementation of strategies to promote OEND.

Total naloxone distribution was measured by the sum of the number of naloxone units distributed through community programs with support by state and federal funding (including HCS funding) and the number of naloxone units dispensed by retail pharmacies located within the communities, as previously described.[20] Data were captured from the IQVIA Xponent database for retail pharmacy dispensing and from administrative data from state agencies and HCS study records for community program distribution (see Supplementary Methods, pp. 1–2, available as a supplement to the online version of this article at https://ajph.org). One unit of naloxone equals 1 carton or kit containing 2 doses. Per the ORCCA, all naloxone distributed was accompanied by overdose education; education could be accomplished through a variety of approaches including, for example, in-person training or the use of training videos or educational pamphlets.

Statistical Analysis

The HCS was designed to have high power (> 99%) to detect a 40% reduction for the overall primary outcome, opioid-related overdose deaths, with a total sample size of 67 communities randomized into wave 1 (n = 34) and wave 2 (n = 33).[5]

For each community-level outcome of distribution counts and total community population size during 2020, we estimated the comparison of rates between wave 1 and wave 2 communities during the comparison period by fitting a negative binomial regression model adjusting for urban–rural status; state (KY, MA, NY, OH); community-level opioid-related overdose death rate (defined across the study as the number of overdose deaths per 100 000 adults) for January 1, 2019, through December 31, 2019 (baseline); and the community-level rate (per 100 000 residents) of the outcome variable at baseline.[21] We used the natural log of the community population as the offset. We used small, sample-adjusted, empirical standard errors for all inference testing.[22,23]

For each outcome, we calculated the marginal adjusted rates of wave 1 and wave 2 communities, adjusted relative rate (RR; wave 1 rate over wave 2 rate), and associated 95% confidence intervals (CIs) and *P* values. We conducted these analyses in both the intent-to-treat and per-protocol (which excludes 1 community that withdrew from the study before the intervention) populations. The results were consistent for the 2 approaches; thus, only the intent-to-treat analyses are presented.

For 2 potential effect modifiers of the CTH intervention, state and urban–rural status, we fitted separate models. Each model included fixed effects for the stratification variable as well as an interaction between wave and the stratification variable. For state, urban–rural status, and overall, we computed means and standard deviations for community-level naloxone units, population size, and rates per 100 000 residents by randomized group and outcome. In addition, we evaluated the comparisons of the raw rates between wave 1 and wave 2 communities. To account for multiple comparisons arising from these subgroup analyses, we controlled the false discovery rate for all effect modification interaction tests between wave and the stratification variable as well as pairwise tests between levels of stratification variables using the Benjamini–Hochberg correction.[24] We considered results statistically significant for *P* values < .05.

The statistical analysis plan was prespecified. We conducted all analyses using SAS version 9.4 (SAS Institute, Cary, NC).

RESULTS

All randomized communities (n = 67) were included in the intent-to-treat analysis (16 each from KY, MA, and NY, and 19 from OH). The CONSORT diagram is shown in Appendix Figure A (available as a supplement to the online version of this article at https://ajph.org). Baseline (January 2019–December 2019) characteristics of wave 1 (n = 5 595 837 residents) and wave 2 (n = 4 833 976 residents) communities are summarized in Table 1. The 2 study arms were balanced on urban–rural status and opioid-related overdose death rate at baseline. Overall, baseline mean rates of total naloxone distribution were similar between wave 1 (mean = 1229.9; SD = 1109.9) and wave 2 (mean = 1320.8; SD = 1196.3) communities. When stratified by state, baseline mean rates of total naloxone distribution were similar between wave 1 and wave 2 for Kentucky and New York but differed by nearly 50% in Massachusetts (mean = 1342.9; SD = 1075.3 vs mean = 2187.4; SD = 1846.0) and Ohio (mean = 1219.2; SD = 1363.6 vs mean = 655.1; SD = 423.9).

Wave 1 CTH intervention communities implemented 254 strategies to increase OEND (Table 2). Variation existed among the number of strategies implemented by state (KY = 104; OH = 58; MA = 54; NY = 38) and urban–rural status (urban = 145; rural = 109). Communities implemented far more active (68.9%) than passive (28.0%) OEND strategies, with more strategies implemented within high-risk venues (59.4%) than for at-risk individuals (40.6%), although the latter varied considerably by state. Overall, communities implemented more strategies in behavioral health (52.4%) than in criminal justice (24.0%) or health care (23.6%) sectors. Specific examples of the strategies to increase OEND that were implemented by wave 1 communities can be found in Appendix Table A.

Table 3 presents results of the efficacy outcomes analyses for the 3 hypotheses. The adjusted rate of total naloxone distribution was 79% higher for the wave 1 CTH intervention versus wave 2 usual care arm (adjusted RR = 1.79; 95% CI = 1.28, 2.51; *P* = .001; adjusted rates of naloxone distribution were 3378 vs 1884 naloxone units per 100 000 residents for CTH vs usual care), when controlling for urban–rural status, state, baseline opioid-related overdose death rate, and baseline naloxone distribution rate. The rate of naloxone distributed by community programs was 104% higher in CTH versus usual care communities (adjusted RR = 2.04; 95% CI = 1.32, 3.17; *P* = .002). There were no significant differences in the rates of naloxone dispensed from retail pharmacies (adjusted RR = 0.99; 95% CI = 0.75, 1.30; *P* = .917).

State and urban–rural status were evaluated as prespecified potential effect modifiers by fitting separate models testing the interaction between each of these factors and intervention group. Observed mean rates (per 100 000 residents) of total naloxone distribution varied considerably by state, ranging from 9971.6 (SD = 6126.2) in Kentucky to 2255.5 (SD = 2338.7) in Ohio wave 1 communities and 3279.0 (SD = 2171.1) to 1398.3 (SD = 1098.3) in Kentucky and Ohio wave 2 communities, respectively (Table 4). Raw RRs of total naloxone distribution in wave 1 over wave 2 communities varied by state, ranging from 3.04 in Kentucky to 1.18 in New York, although the test of effect modification for state was not statistically significant. Observed mean rates of total naloxone distribution were higher in urban communities (wave 1: 4682.9; SD = 5368.0; wave 2: 2599.0; SD = 1729.4) compared with rural communities (wave 1: 4025.0; SD = 3528.4; wave 2: 1811.5; SD = 1729.8). The raw RRs of total naloxone distribution in wave 1 over wave 2 urban (1.80) and rural (2.22) communities were similar, however, and the test of effect modification for urban–rural status was not statistically significant. While variability by state and urban–rural status was also noted for community program distribution and retail pharmacy dispensing, because all interactions were nonsignificant, we conducted no post hoc analyses.

DISCUSSION

As hypothesized, the CTH intervention significantly increased OEND compared with usual care. Increased naloxone distribution was driven by OEND provided by community programs, with no significant effect observed on the rate of naloxone dispensed by retail pharmacies. The CTH intervention offers a flexible way for communities to select strategies to significantly increase OEND, which is critical given access to this life-saving medication is suboptimal in most communities highly impacted by opioid-related overdose deaths.[12] The finding that the CTH intervention

TABLE 1— Baseline Demographic Characteristics of Communities Participating in the HEALing Communities Study, by Intervention Wave: 4 US States, January 2019–December 2019

	Intervention Wave		
	Wave 1	Wave 2	Overall
Randomized communities, no. (%)			
Overall	34	33	67
Kentucky	8 (23.5)	8 (24.2)	16 (23.9)
Massachusetts	8 (23.5)	8 (24.2)	16 (23.9)
New York	8 (23.5)	8 (24.2)	16 (23.9)
Ohio	10 (29.4)	9 (27.3)	19 (28.4)
Urban–rural classification, no. (%)			
Urban	19 (55.9)	19 (57.6)	38 (56.7)
Rural	15 (44.1)	14 (42.4)	29 (43.3)
Total population,[a] no.			
Overall	5 595 837	4 833 976	10 429 813
Kentucky	782 758	1 044 354	1 827 112
Massachusetts	439 910	447 385	887 295
New York	1 357 580	1 247 888	2 605 468
Ohio	3 015 589	2 094 349	5 109 938
Rate of opioid-related overdose deaths, mean (SD)[b]			
Overall	38.4 (22.8)	37.4 (21.0)	37.9 (21.8)
Kentucky	43.2 (16.6)	37.5 (21.8)	40.4 (19.0)
Massachusetts	46.0 (14.2)	54.1 (23.0)	50.1 (18.9)
New York	19.3 (5.6)	29.3 (12.8)	24.3 (10.8)
Ohio	43.8 (33.0)	29.6 (17.9)	37.1 (27.2)
Rate of total naloxone units distributed, mean (SD)[c]			
Overall	1 229.9 (1 109.9)	1 320.8 (1 196.3)	1 274.7 (1 145.4)
Kentucky	1 039.6 (663.1)	894.3 (422.1)	966.9 (542.2)
Massachusetts	1 342.9 (1 075.3)	2 187.4 (1 846.0)	1 765.2 (1 523.2)
New York	1 320.4 (1 324.8)	1 629.7 (1 003.2)	1 475.1 (1 146.4)
Ohio	1 219.2 (1 363.6)	655.1 (423.9)	952.0 (1 045.6)
Rate of naloxone units distributed through community-based programs, mean (SD)[c]			
Overall	796.3 (907.0)	888.7 (869.2)	841.8 (883.1)
Kentucky	458.3 (252.4)	596.7 (346.7)	527.5 (301.5)
Massachusetts	902.3 (982.7)	1 346.9 (1 106.2)	1 124.6 (1 036.5)
New York	1 178.4 (1 302.2)	1 384.5 (990.6)	1 281.4 (1 122.7)
Ohio	676.2 (799.8)	300.1 (238.4)	498.1 (618.3)
Rate of naloxone units dispensed by retail community pharmacies, mean (SD)[c]			
Overall	433.6 (472.2)	432.1 (722.4)	432.9 (603.7)
Kentucky	581.3 (576.5)	297.6 (119.7)	439.4 (428.1)
Massachusetts	440.6 (357.4)	840.4 (1 413.8)	640.5 (1 017.4)
New York	142.0 (60.3)	245.2 (93.2)	193.6 (92.7)
Ohio	543.0 (590.3)	354.9 (303.0)	453.9 (473.7)

Note. HEAL = Helping to End Addiction Long-Term. The sample size was n = 67 communities. Percentages may not add up to 100 because of rounding. There are no missing data.

[a]For communities that represent counties (n = 48 of 67), population estimates are from 2019 Bridged-Race Population Estimates retrieved via https://www.cdc.gov/nchs/nvss/bridged_race.htm on March 17, 2023. For communities that represent units smaller than counties (n = 19 of 67), population estimates are from 2015 to 2019 American Community Survey 5-Year Estimates retrieved via https://data.census.gov/cedsci on March 17, 2023.

[b]Rate per 100 000 community residents aged ≥ 18 years.

[c]Rate per 100 000 community residents.

TABLE 2— Actively Implemented Overdose Education and Naloxone Distribution (OEND) Strategies for Wave 1 Communities Participating in the HEALing Communities Study: 4 US States, April 8, 2020–June 30, 2022

	State				Urban-Rural Classification		
	KY	MA	NY	OH	Urban	Rural	Total
No. of communities	8	8	8	9	18	15	33
No. of OEND strategies implemented	104	54	38	58	145	109	254
Strategy, no. (%)							
Active OEND	58 (55.8)	38 (70.4)	28 (73.7)	51 (87.9)	101 (69.7)	74 (67.9)	175 (68.9)
At-risk individuals[a]	9 (15.5)	19 (50.0)	22 (78.6)	21 (41.2)	40 (39.6)	31 (41.9)	71 (40.6)
High-risk venues[a]	49 (84.5)	19 (50.0)	6 (21.4)	30 (58.8)	61 (60.4)	43 (58.1)	104 (59.4)
Passive OEND	44 (42.3)	12 (22.2)	9 (23.7)	6 (10.3)	42 (29.0)	29 (26.6)	71 (28.0)
Referral[b]	0 (0)	2 (16.7)	0 (0)	1 (16.7)	1 (2.4)	2 (6.9)	3 (4.2)
Self-request[b]	37 (84.1)	7 (58.3)	2 (22.2)	2 (33.3)	30 (71.4)	18 (62.1)	48 (67.6)
Naloxone availability for immediate use in overdose hotspots[b]	7 (15.9)	3 (25.0)	7 (77.8)	3 (50.0)	11 (26.2)	9 (31.0)	20 (28.2)
Capacity for first-responder administration	2 (1.9)	3 (5.6)	1 (2.6)	1 (1.7)	1 (0.7)	6 (5.5)	7 (2.8)
Other[c]	0 (0)	1 (1.9)	0 (0)	0 (0)	1 (0.7)	0 (0)	1 (0.4)
Sector, no. (%)							
Health care	18 (17.3)	15 (27.8)	9 (23.7)	18 (31.0)	34 (23.4)	26 (23.9)	60 (23.6)
Behavioral health	55 (52.9)	35 (64.8)	23 (60.5)	20 (34.5)	76 (52.4)	57 (52.3)	133 (52.4)
Criminal justice	31 (29.8)	4 (7.4)	6 (15.8)	20 (34.5)	35 (24.1)	26 (23.9)	61 (24.0)

Note. HEAL = Helping to End Addiction Long-Term. The sample size was n = 33 communities; n = 1 community randomized to wave 1 withdrew before strategy selection. Summary of unique strategy–sector–venue triad combinations that were actively implemented (defined as strategies that reached the service delivery stage of implementation) during wave 1. The most recent entry for each triad is chosen. Duplicate triad entries are rolled to the triad level. Results are based on data pulled from the Opioid-overdose Reduction Continuum of Care Approach (ORCCA) Tracker on March 24, 2023.
[a]Percentage out of active OEND strategies.
[b]Percentage out of passive OEND strategies.
[c]Other strategy: Never Use Alone helpline.

resulted in a 104% increase in naloxone distribution by community programs compared with control communities receiving usual care is particularly noteworthy given that the intervention was implemented during a time in which opioid overdose mortality was increasing and calls for increased naloxone access as a public health response grew louder.[11] A 2022 report to Congress on State Opioid Response (SOR) grants indicates that from April 1, 2021, to March 30, 2022, grantees reported distributing 2 177 367 naloxone kits.[25] Naloxone distribution increased from baseline in the wave 2 usual care communities during the comparison period, in part attributable to SOR-funded naloxone distribution and other ongoing public health efforts that were occurring across all communities regardless of their participation status in the HCS. The policy landscape supporting naloxone distribution in the HCS states has been described in detail.[26]

The HCS is the largest implementation study in the field of addiction science and the first randomized controlled trial to examine the impact of a community-engaged intervention designed to promote the uptake of EBPs to reduce opioid-related overdose mortality. HCS communities participating in the CTH intervention selected and implemented strategies to increase uptake of OEND as part of a broader data-driven community action plan to reduce opioid-related overdose deaths. The HCS Consortium recently reported that opioid-related overdose deaths were 9% lower in communities implementing the CTH intervention compared with usual care.[5] While the results did not reach statistical significance, the estimated 483 deaths averted in the intervention communities represents a meaningful public health impact. The HCS was designed to have

TABLE 3— Analyses Testing the Effect of the Communities That HEAL Intervention on the Rate of Each Efficacy Outcome Between Wave 1 and Wave 2 Communities During the Comparison Period: 4 US States, July 1, 2021–June 30, 2022

Outcome	Adjusted Rate (95% CI)[a]		Adjusted RR (95% CI)[b]
	Wave 1	Wave 2	
Hypothesis 1: Total no. of naloxone units distributed in communities	3378.1 (2663.1, 4285.0)	1884.4 (1466.9, 2420.7)	1.79 (1.28, 2.51)
Hypothesis 2: No. of naloxone units distributed through community-based programs	2754.1 (2081.9, 3643.3)	1348.4 (962.4, 1889.3)	2.04 (1.32, 3.17)
Hypothesis 3: No. of naloxone units dispensed by retail community pharmacies	524.0 (447.8, 613.1)	531.6 (421.7, 670.2)	0.99 (0.75, 1.30)

Note. CI = confidence interval; HEAL = Helping to End Addiction Long-Term; RR = relative rate. A separate negative binomial model was fit for each hypothesis adjusting for urban–rural classification (urban, rural), state (KY, MA, NY, OH), baseline opioid-related overdose death rate, and baseline outcome rate using the intention-to-treat population (n = 67 communities). The natural log of the community population was used as the offset. Dispersion parameters for each of the hypotheses' models are: k = 0.36 (95% CI = 0.26, 0.49) for hypothesis 1; k = 0.93 (95% CI = 0.67, 1.29) for hypothesis 2; and k = 0.25 (95% CI = 0.18, 0.35) for hypothesis 3.
[a]Model estimated marginal event rate expressed as per 100 000 community residents.
[b]Adjusted RR of wave 1 communities over wave 2 communities.

high power (> 99%) to detect a 40% reduction in opioid-related mortality. The HCS consortium acknowledges that a 40% reduction was an ambitious goal and that the study was likely underpowered to detect smaller reductions in mortality. Ongoing research is evaluating the impact of the CTH on other overdose-related outcomes, including nonfatal overdoses and opioid-related overdoses in combination with stimulants.

In total, wave 1 communities implemented 254 unique OEND strategies, which represented a 40% increase in the number of strategies initially selected and included in action plans.[19] Although the number and type of strategies implemented varied by state, all communities implemented OEND strategies across behavioral health, health care, and criminal justice sectors. More than two thirds of the strategies implemented were active OEND strategies designed to reach people at high risk for opioid overdose and their social networks and be deployed at high-risk venues. This distribution of strategies was expected given that proactively providing OEND to those at high risk for overdose is most effective[27] and that active OEND strategies were a required component of the ORCCA.[7] Common high-risk venues where active OEND strategies were implemented included addiction treatment centers (behavioral health sector), syringe service programs (behavioral health sector), emergency departments (health care sector), and jails and other criminal justice settings (criminal justice sector). The implementation of active OEND strategies in criminal justice settings was especially important during the period of the study that coincided with the COVID-19 public health emergency and expedited release of individuals from carceral settings, a known risk factor for fatal overdose.[28] As such, wave 1 communities fast-tracked the implementation of OEND strategies in jails, syringe service programs, and other high-risk venues.

The absence of a significant difference in the rate of naloxone dispensed from retail pharmacies is not completely unexpected. Implementation of passive OEND strategies, which were more commonly pharmacy-based, was optional in the ORCCA and implemented far less often compared with the required active strategies (71 vs 175 actively implemented strategies, respectively). To increase naloxone dispensing from pharmacies during the intervention period, communities would have needed to implement strategies to encourage practitioners to write more prescriptions for naloxone or encourage pharmacists to increase their direct prescribing or initiation of naloxone prescriptions via standing order, collaborative care agreements, or protocols as allowed by state law.[10] The CTH intervention was conducted during the COVID-19 pandemic, when retail pharmacies had adopted an expansive role in testing, vaccinating, and providing COVID-19 treatment. Additional factors, such as insurance formularies, prior authorization requirements, and individual cost-sharing expectations, may have influenced naloxone accessibility in retail pharmacies.[26] Finally, research has suggested that pharmacists may not be adequately trained or comfortable dispensing naloxone, and people seeking naloxone may face stigma or discrimination from pharmacy staff.[29]

TABLE 4— Descriptive Statistics for Efficacy Outcomes, Overall and by State and Rurality, During the Comparison Period Using the Intention-to-Treat Population in the HEALing Communities Study: 4 US States, July 1, 2021–June 30, 2022

	Wave 1 (n = 34)		Wave 2 (n = 33)		Raw Rate Ratio[c]
	Naloxone Units[a]	Raw Rate[b]	Naloxone Units[a]	Raw Rate[b]	
Total no. of naloxone units distributed in communities					
Overall					
Mean (SD)	4 946.8 (5 474.0)	4 392.6 (4 594.4)	3 841.8 (8 530.1)	2 264.9 (1 747.6)	1.94
Median (Q1, Q3)	2 968.0 (823.0, 8 065.0)	2 716.7 (1 557.5, 5 528.2)	1 065.0 (631.0, 2 078.0)	1 937.3 (956.2, 3 388.8)	1.40
State, mean (SD)					
Kentucky	6 382.8 (2 854.8)	9 971.6 (6 126.2)	2 977.9 (4 919.0)	3 279.0 (2 171.1)	3.04
Massachusetts	1 606.9 (1 235.0)	3 198.5 (2 227.4)	1 336.4 (1 529.0)	2 219.2 (1 744.9)	1.44
New York	6 153.4 (8 064.6)	2 679.1 (1 705.1)	4 629.1 (6 320.0)	2 271.4 (1 637.5)	1.18
Ohio	5 504.8 (6 194.4)	2 255.5 (2 338.7)	6 137.0 (14 809.2)	1 398.3 (1 098.3)	1.61
Urban–rural classification, mean (SD)					
Urban	7 136.4 (6 251.2)	4 682.9 (5 368.0)	6 039.3 (10 813.7)	2 599.0 (1 729.4)	1.80
Rural	2 173.4 (2 375.0)	4 025.0 (3 528.4)	859.6 (750.1)	1 811.5 (1 729.8)	2.22
No. of naloxone units distributed through community-based programs					
Overall					
Mean (SD)	4 085.9 (4 732.8)	3 631.3 (3 890.8)	3 029.8 (7 065.2)	1 664.0 (1 577.1)	2.18
Median (Q1, Q3)	2 575.0 (761.0, 6 405.0)	2 346.4 (945.1, 5 054.7)	821.0 (281.0, 1 789.0)	1 263.6 (535.0, 2 176.0)	1.86
State, mean (SD)					
Kentucky	5 408.3 (2 318.8)	8 448.1 (4 981.4)	2 048.3 (3 261.1)	2 353.5 (2 155.6)	3.59
Massachusetts	1 388.0 (1 180.5)	2 789.7 (2 194.8)	981.6 (1 137.6)	1 650.2 (1 468.6)	1.69
New York	5 687.6 (7 576.6)	2 427.2 (1 703.0)	3 948.3 (5 569.4)	1 879.8 (1 478.8)	1.29
Ohio	3 904.8 (4 677.1)	1 414.2 (1 483.7)	4 906.4 (12 333.9)	871.5 (924.4)	1.62
Urban–rural classification, mean (SD)					
Urban	5 939.2 (5 444.0)	3 924.3 (4 475.5)	4 810.2 (8 977.4)	1 931.9 (1 600.4)	2.03
Rural	1 738.3 (2 031.4)	3 260.0 (3 108.9)	613.5 (600.8)	1 300.4 (1 526.1)	2.51
No. of naloxone units dispensed by retail community pharmacies					
Overall					
Mean (SD)	861.0 (1 167.1)	761.4 (1 131.0)	812.0 (1 578.2)	600.9 (430.0)	1.27
Median (Q1, Q3)	335.5 (159.0, 873.0)	386.0 (287.0, 612.4)	289.0 (163.0, 630.0)	551.8 (305.3, 759.5)	0.70
State, mean (SD)					
Kentucky	974.5 (917.1)	1 523.5 (1 934.6)	929.6 (1 717.4)	925.6 (514.0)	1.65
Massachusetts	218.9 (119.7)	408.7 (103.3)	354.8 (429.1)	569.0 (421.7)	0.72
New York	465.8 (512.1)	251.9 (61.1)	680.9 (847.4)	391.6 (219.2)	0.64
Ohio	1 600.0 (1 732.4)	841.3 (950.4)	1 230.6 (2 481.0)	526.8 (393.0)	1.60
Urban–rural classification, mean (SD)					
Urban	1 197.2 (1 386.0)	758.5 (1 311.7)	1 229.1 (1 990.2)	667.1 (474.6)	1.14
Rural	435.1 (627.0)	765.0 (896.1)	246.1 (218.4)	511.2 (358.1)	1.50

Note. HEAL = Helping to End Addiction Long-Term.
[a]Raw mean (SD) of the community-level number of naloxone units in that group in that wave.
[b]Raw mean (SD) of the community-level rates per 100 000 individuals in that group in that wave. Population means used for rate calculations are presented in Table B (available as a supplement to the online version of this article at https://ajph.org).
[c]Raw rate ratio calculated as the raw rate in wave 1 over the raw rate in wave 2.

Comprehensive efforts are needed to bridge the training gap among pharmacists, combat stigma within the health care community, and raise awareness about naloxone's vital role in preventing opioid-related overdose deaths.

In March 2023, the US Food and Drug Administration approved the first over-the-counter (OTC) naloxone product, a 4-milligram naloxone nasal spray, which became available at pharmacies and other retail outlets in September 2023.[30] While the goal of making naloxone available OTC is increased accessibility, the impact of OTC status on naloxone availability may be limited because of cost. At the time of writing, the manufacturer's suggested retail price for a 2-dose carton of OTC Narcan Nasal Spray was $44.99,[31] which may limit accessibility for many unless insurance companies provide coverage for OTC naloxone products. As such, continued free distribution through community organizations will likely be needed to ensure access for individuals at highest risk (e.g., those who are actively using drugs) for whom cost, stigma, and discrimination encountered at the pharmacy may be deterrents.

Although we did not detect any statistically significant differences when assessing effect modification of the CTH intervention by state or urban–rural status, we noted differences in observed mean rates of naloxone distribution both at baseline and follow-up. These differences may be important to consider given that previous modeling studies have indicated that increasing naloxone distribution rates as part of a multicomponent intervention with engagement and retention in MOUD treatment is necessary to achieve opioid overdose prevention goals.[32] Further investigation into the specific factors that may be associated with increases in naloxone distribution, including the number of strategies, specific strategies deployed, how they were implemented, and other factors such as communication campaign messaging, is warranted and will be the focus of future publications in this implementation science trial. HCS researchers adapted the Reach, Effectiveness, Adoption, Implementation, and Maintenance (RE-AIM)/Practical, Robust, Implementation, and Sustainability (PRISM) implementation science framework to guide our assessment of contextual factors that affect CTH implementation and outcomes.[33,34] Future analyses of qualitative data from the study may help elucidate the relationships among community context, coalition characteristics, and EBP adoption among partner organizations.

Because this study primarily used administrative data from state agencies to capture OEND, demographic information about individuals who received OEND was not consistently collected. Analysis of available data in one state suggests that the demographic makeup of individuals who received OEND was similar to that of the county where OEND was delivered, although this varied by facility type (e.g., criminal justice vs behavioral health).[35] Additional data-capture methodologies were implemented in wave 2 to collect demographic information about OEND recipients consistently across the consortium, and future studies will specifically examine the impact of the CTH on vulnerable populations.

Strengths and Limitations

This study had numerous strengths. Our community-engaged intervention guided community coalitions through a phased, data-driven approach to create community action plans to promote the uptake of EBPs, including OEND. This process allowed communities to build on strengths, address gaps, and develop action plans uniquely tailored to deliver the maximum impact on scaling up naloxone distribution. Our study included a large sample of communities in both urban and rural areas highly impacted by opioid overdose.

Despite these strengths, the study is subject to limitations. We used administrative data from state agencies to capture naloxone distribution by community programs. These data may not capture all naloxone distributed in the community as naloxone purchased with support from private donations, foundations, or locally awarded federal funding may not be captured in state administrative data. For example, Ohio captured community naloxone distributed through Project DAWN (Deaths Avoided With Naloxone); however, during the intervention period, efforts to blanket the state with naloxone were conducted. These surges provided naloxone to some community agencies not affiliated with Project DAWN, resulting in likely undercounting of naloxone distribution in Ohio study communities.

In this study, we were unable to verify if the individuals who received the naloxone were HCS community residents or if individuals received more than 1 unit of naloxone. Retail pharmacy naloxone dispensing data were provided by IQVIA in aggregate with no information on the number of pharmacies in the community that dispensed the naloxone. IQVIA suppression rules preclude the reporting of data for geographic areas with fewer than 4 retail pharmacies, resulting in reporting a weighted mean number of naloxone units dispensed based on population size for 3 Massachusetts communities. Dispensed naloxone prescriptions in IQVIA are attributed to communities based on the dispensing pharmacy address rather than the customer's residence, which may result in an overcount of naloxone in a community with pharmacies that serve residents of non-HCS communities, or an undercount if there is a pharmacy located outside an HCS community that serves HCS residents.

Public Health Implications

This community-level, cluster-randomized controlled implementation science trial showed that compared with usual care, the CTH intervention significantly increased OEND, an EBP that reduces opioid-related overdose mortality, in US communities highly affected by opioid overdose. The CTH intervention, including the ability to tailor selection and implementation of strategies to promote the uptake of OEND to individual communities, can serve as a model for other communities to adopt as part of ongoing public health response efforts to reduce opioid-related overdose mortality. *AJPH*

ABOUT THE AUTHORS

Patricia R. Freeman and Douglas R. Oyler are with the University of Kentucky College of Pharmacy, Department of Pharmacy Practice and Science, Lexington. Alexander Y. Walley, Trevor J. Baker, and Jeffrey H. Samet are with the Boston Medical Center, Boston, MA. T. John Winhusen is with the University of Cincinnati Department of Psychiatry and Behavioral Neuroscience, Cincinnati, OH. Emmanuel A. Oga, Christian Douglas, JaNae Holloway, Nathan A. Vandergrift, Joella W. Adams, Katherine Asman, LaShawn M. Glasgow, Charles Knott, and Gary A. Zarkin are with RTI International, Research Triangle Park, NC. Jennifer Villani and Redonna K. Chandler are with the National Institute on Drug Abuse, National Institutes of Health, Bethesda, MD. Timothy Hunt, Kitty Gelberg, James L. David, Louisa Gilbert, Dawn A. Goddard-Eckrich, and Nabila El Bassel are with the Columbia University School of Social Work, Social Intervention Group, New York, NY. Brittni Reilly is with the Massachusetts Department of Public Health, Boston. Michael S. Lyons is with Ohio State University Department of Emergency Medicine, Columbus. Candace J. Brancato is with the University of Kentucky College of Public Health, Department of Biostatistics, Lexington. Debbie M. Cheng is with the Boston University School of Public Health, Department of Biostatistics, Boston, MA. Janet E. Childerhose is and Rebecca D. Jackson was with the Ohio State University College of Medicine, Department of Internal Medicine, Columbus. Daniel J. Feaster is with the University of Miami Miller School of Medicine, Department of Public Health Sciences, Miami, FL. Hannah K. Knudsen, Michelle R. Lofwall, Katherine R. Marks, and Sharon L. Walsh are with the University of Kentucky College of Medicine, Department of Behavioral Science, Lexington. Jason T. McMullan is with the University of Cincinnati Department of Emergency Medicine, Cincinnati, OH. Carrie B. Oser is with the University of Kentucky, Department of Sociology, Lexington. Monica Roberts and Josie Watson are with the University of Kentucky Substance Use Priority Research Area, Lexington. Abigail B. Shoben is with the Ohio State University College of Public Health, Division of Biostatistics, Columbus. Michael D. Stein is with the Boston University School of Public Health, Department of Health Law, Policy, and Management, Boston, MA. Scott T. Walters is with the University of North Texas Health Science Center, School of Public Health, Fort Worth.

CORRESPONDENCE

Correspondence should be sent to Patricia R. Freeman, PhD, Department of Pharmacy Practice and Science, 267 Healthy Kentucky Research Building, 760 Press Ave, Lexington, KY 40536 (e-mail: trish.freeman@uky.edu). Reprints can be ordered at https://www.ajph.org by clicking the "Reprints" link.

PUBLICATION INFORMATION

Full Citation: Freeman PR, Walley AY, Winhusen TJ, et al. Effect of the communities that HEAL intervention on overdose education and naloxone distribution: a cluster-randomized, wait-list controlled trial. *Am J Public Health*. 2025;115(1):83–94.

Acceptance Date: August 14, 2024.

DOI: https://doi.org/10.2105/AJPH.2024.307845

ORCID iDs:

Patricia R. Freeman https://orcid.org/0000-0002-4749-6563

Emmanuel A. Oga https://orcid.org/0000-0002-0744-5681

Jennifer Villani https://orcid.org/0000-0003-2337-2504

Douglas R. Oyler https://orcid.org/0000-0002-6153-831X

Brittni Reilly https://orcid.org/0000-0002-4980-8938

Kitty Gelberg https://orcid.org/0000-0002-3734-3280

Michael S. Lyons https://orcid.org/0000-0002-4774-1899

JaNae Holloway https://orcid.org/0009-0009-1609-8237

Nathan A. Vandergrift https://orcid.org/0000-0001-9994-5466

Janet E. Childerhose https://orcid.org/0000-0003-0985-1306

James L. David https://orcid.org/0009-0009-6738-8031

LaShawn M. Glasgow https://orcid.org/0000-0003-3336-7039

Dawn A. Goddard-Eckrich https://orcid.org/0000-0002-3456-2322

Charles Knott https://orcid.org/0000-0002-3340-1850

Hannah K. Knudsen https://orcid.org/0000-0002-0137-9337

Katherine R. Marks https://orcid.org/0000-0001-5936-7497

Carrie B. Oser https://orcid.org/0000-0001-8658-9335

Abigail B. Shoben https://orcid.org/0000-0001-9347-4755

Michael D. Stein https://orcid.org/0000-0002-2466-5192

Josie Watson https://orcid.org/0009-0004-3910-0612

Sharon L. Walsh https://orcid.org/0000-0002-9722-5681

CONTRIBUTORS

As principal investigators of this multisite study, R. D. Jackson, J. H. Samet, S. L. Walsh, and N. El Bassel contributed equally as co-senior authors. T. J. Baker, C. J. Brancato, R. K. Chandler, D. M. Cheng, N. El Bassel, P. R. Freeman, L. Gilbert, L. M. Glasgow, T. Hunt, R. D. Jackson, H. K. Knudsen, M. R. Lofwall, M. S. Lyons, K. R. Marks, E. A. Oga, C. B. Oser, D. R. Oyler, B. Reilly, M. Roberts, J. H. Samet, A. B. Shoben, M. D. Stein, N. A. Vandergrift, J. Villani, A. Y. Walley, S. L. Walsh, S. T. Walters, J. Watson, T. J. Winhusen, and G. A. Zarkin contributed to the concept and design. J. E. Childerhose, J. L. David, C. Douglas, D. J. Feaster, P. R. Freeman, K. Gelberg, J. Holloway, T. Hunt, C. Knott, M. R. Lofwall, J. T. McMullan, D. R. Oyler, A. Y. Walley, and S. L. Walsh contributed to acquisition, analysis, or interpretation of data. R. K. Chandler, C. Douglas, N. El Bassel, P. R. Freeman, K. Gelberg, J. Holloway, T. Hunt, E. A. Oga, D. R. Oyler, J. Villani, A. Y. Walley, S. L. Walsh, and T. J. Winhusen drafted the article. T. J. Baker, C. J. Brancato, D. M. Cheng, J. E. Childerhose, J. L. David, D. J. Feaster, L. Gilbert, L. M. Glasgow, D. A. Goddard-Eckrich, C. Knott, H. K. Knudsen, M. R. Lofwall, M. S. Lyons, K. R. Marks, J. T. McMullan, C. B. Oser, B. Reilly, M. Roberts, J. H. Samet, A. B. Shoben, M. D. Stein, N. A. Vandergrift, S. T. Walters, J. Watson, and G. A. Zarkin critically revised the article for important intellectual content. D. M. Cheng, C. Douglas,

J. Holloway, A. B. Shoben, and N. A. Vandergrift performed the statistical analysis. N. El Bassel, D. J. Feaster, R. D. Jackson, C. Knott, K. R. Marks, J. H. Samet, S. L. Walsh, and T. J. Winhusen obtained funding.

ACKNOWLEDGMENTS

This research was supported by the National Institutes of Health (NIH) and the Substance Abuse and Mental Health Services Administration through the NIH HEAL (Helping to End Addiction Long-Term) initiative under award numbers UM1DA049394, UM1DA049406, UM1DA049412, UM1DA049415, and UM1DA049417. R. K. Chandler and J. Villani were substantially involved in UM1DA049394, UM1DA049406, UM1DA049412, UM1DA049415, and UM1DA049417, consistent with their roles as scientific officers.

Co-author Rebecca D. Jackson died October 11, 2022.

We wish to acknowledge the participation of the HEALing Communities Study communities, community coalitions, community partner organizations and agencies, and community advisory boards and state government officials who partnered with us on this study. We acknowledge the Kentucky Pharmacists Association; the Massachusetts Department of Public Health, Bureau of Substance Addiction Services, and State Office for Pharmacy Services; the New York State Department of Health, Office of Drug User Health; and the Ohio Department of Health, Project DAWN for providing state administrative data on naloxone distribution. Finally, we acknowledge our faculty and colleagues in the HEALing Communities Study who contributed to the study's overall design and conduct.

Note. The content is solely the responsibility of the authors and does not necessarily represent the official views of the NIH, the Substance Abuse and Mental Health Services Administration, or the NIH HEAL Initiative. The statements, findings, conclusions, views, and opinions contained and expressed herein are based in part on data obtained from IQVIA and are not necessarily those of IQVIA or any of its affiliated or subsidiary entities.

CONFLICTS OF INTEREST

M. R. Lofwall reported serving as scientific advisor/consultant to Berkshire Biomedical, Braeburn Pharmaceuticals, and Journey Colab for medications in development. S. L. Walsh reported serving as a consultant/advisor to Pocket Naloxone and Opiant, who are developing overdose reversal products, neither of which was used in this study.

HUMAN PARTICIPANT PROTECTION

The study protocol (Pro00038088) was approved by Advarra Inc, the HEALing Communities Study single institutional review board. A data and safety monitoring board, chartered by the National Institute on Drug Abuse, monitored the study. The study is registered at ClinicalTrials.gov under the identifier NCT04111939.

REFERENCES

1. Spencer MR. Drug overdose deaths in the United States, 2001–2021. *NCHS Data Brief*; no. 457. Hyattsville, MD: National Center for Health Statistics; 2022. https://doi.org/10.15620/cdc:122556
2. Ahmad FB, Cisewski JA, Rossen LM, Sutton P. Provisional drug overdose death counts. National Center for Health Statistics. January 5, 2023. Available at: https://www.cdc.gov/nchs/nvss/vsrr/drug-overdose-data.htm. Accessed February 3, 2023.
3. Han B, Einstein EB, Jones CM, Cotto J, Compton WM, Volkow ND. Racial and ethnic disparities in drug overdose deaths in the US during the COVID-19 pandemic. *JAMA Netw Open*. 2022;5(9):e2232314. https://doi.org/10.1001/jamanetworkopen.2022.32314
4. HEALing Communities Study Consortium. The HEALing (Helping to End Addiction Long-Term) Communities Study: protocol for a cluster randomized trial at the community level to reduce opioid overdose deaths through implementation of an integrated set of evidence-based practices. *Drug Alcohol Depend*. 2020;217:108335. https://doi.org/10.1016/j.drugalcdep.2020.108335
5. Samet JH, El-Bassel N, Winhusen TJ, et al.; The HEALing Communities Study Consortium. Community-based cluster-randomized trial to reduce opioid overdose deaths. *N Engl J Med*. 2024; 391(11):989–1001. https://doi.org/10.1056/NEJMoa2401177
6. Sprague Martinez L, Rapkin BD, Young A, et al. Community engagement to implement evidence-based practices in the HEALing communities study. *Drug Alcohol Depend*. 2020;217:108326. https://doi.org/10.1016/j.drugalcdep.2020.108326
7. Winhusen T, Walley A, Fanucchi LC, et al. The Opioid-overdose Reduction Continuum of Care Approach (ORCCA): evidence-based practices in the HEALing Communities Study. *Drug Alcohol Depend*. 2020;217:108325. https://doi.org/10.1016/j.drugalcdep.2020.108325
8. Lefebvre RC, Chandler RK, Helme DW, et al. Health communication campaigns to drive demand for evidence-based practices and reduce stigma in the HEALing Communities Study. *Drug Alcohol Depend*. 2020;217:108338. https://doi.org/10.1016/j.drugalcdep.2020.108338
9. Doe-Simkins M, Walley AY, Epstein A, Moyer P. Saved by the nose: bystander-administered intranasal naloxone hydrochloride for opioid overdose. *Am J Public Health*. 2009;99(5):788–791. https://doi.org/10.2105/AJPH.2008.146647
10. Davis C, Carr D. State legal innovations to encourage naloxone dispensing. *J Am Pharm Assoc (2003)*. 2017;57(2S):S180–S184. https://doi.org/10.1016/j.japh.2016.11.007
11. US Department of Health and Human Services. US Surgeon General's Advisory on Naloxone and Opioid Overdose. April 3, 2018. Available at: https://www.hhs.gov/surgeongeneral/reports-and-publications/addiction-and-substance-misuse/advisory-on-naloxone/index.html. Accessed June 22, 2023.
12. Irvine MA, Oller D, Boggis J, et al. Estimating naloxone need in the USA across fentanyl, heroin, and prescription opioid epidemics: a modelling study. *Lancet Public Health*. 2022;7(3):e210–e218. https://doi.org/10.1016/S2468-2667(21)00304-2
13. Faul M, Dailey MW, Sugerman DE, Sasser SM, Levy B, Paulozzi LJ. Disparity in naloxone administration by emergency medical service providers and the burden of drug overdose in US rural communities. *Am J Public Health*. 2015;105(suppl 3):e26–e32. https://doi.org/10.2105/AJPH.2014.302520
14. Khan MR, Hoff L, Elliott L, et al. Racial/ethnic disparities in opioid overdose prevention: comparison of the naloxone care cascade in White, Latinx, and Black people who use opioids in New York City. *Harm Reduct J*. 2023;20(1):24. https://doi.org/10.1186/s12954-023-00736-7
15. Nolen S, Zang X, Chatterjee A, et al. Evaluating equity in community-based naloxone access among racial/ethnic groups in Massachusetts. *Drug Alcohol Depend*. 2022;241:109668. https://doi.org/10.1016/j.drugalcdep.2022.109668
16. Greene EJ. A SAS macro for covariate-constrained randomization of general cluster-randomized and unstratified designs. *J Stat Softw*. 2017;77(Code Snippet 1, CS1). https://doi.org/10.18637/jss.v077.c01
17. EQUATOR Network. CONSORT 2010 Statement: updated guidelines for reporting parallel group randomised trials. Available at: https://www.equator-network.org/reporting-guidelines/consort. Accessed February 24, 2023.
18. Oesterle S, Kuklinski MR, Hawkins JD, Skinner ML, Guttmannova K, Rhew IC. Long-term effects of the communities that care trial on substance use, antisocial behavior, and violence through age 21 years. *Am J Public Health*. 2018;108(5):659–665. https://doi.org/10.2105/AJPH.2018.304320
19. Chandler R, Nunes EV, Tan S, et al. Community selected strategies to reduce opioid-related overdose deaths in the HEALing (Helping to End Addiction Long-term) Communities Study. *Drug Alcohol Depend*. 2023;245:109804. https://doi.org/10.1016/j.drugalcdep.2023.109804
20. Slavova S, LaRochelle MR, Root ED, et al. Operationalizing and selecting outcome measures for the HEALing Communities Study. *Drug Alcohol Depend*. 2020;217:108328. https://doi.org/10.1016/j.drugalcdep.2020.108328
21. Westgate PM, Cheng DM, Feaster DJ, Fernández S, Shoben AB, Vandergrift N. Marginal modeling in community randomized trials with rare events: utilization of the negative binomial regression model. *Clin Trials*. 2022;19(2):162–171. https://doi.org/10.1177/17407745211063479
22. Mancl LA, DeRouen TA. A covariance estimator for GEE with improved small-sample properties. *Biometrics*. 2001;57(1):126–134. https://doi.org/10.1111/j.0006-341X.2001.00126.x
23. Kauermann G, Carroll RJ. A note on the efficiency of sandwich covariance matrix estimation. *J Am Stat Assoc*. 2001;96(456):1387–1396. https://doi.org/10.1198/016214501753382309
24. Benjamini Y, Hochberg Y. Controlling the false discovery rate: a practical and powerful approach to multiple testing. *J R Stat Soc B*. 1995;57(1):289–300. https://doi.org/10.1111/j.2517-6161.1995.tb02031.x
25. Substance Abuse and Mental Health Services Administration. *2022 Report to Congress on the State Opioid Response Grants (SOR)*. 2022. Available at: https://www.samhsa.gov/sites/default/files/2022-state-opioid-response-grants-report.pdf. Accessed July 15, 2024.
26. Bohler RM, Freeman PR, Villani J, et al. The policy landscape for naloxone distribution in four states highly impacted by fatal opioid overdoses. *Drug Alcohol Depend Rep*. 2023;6:100126. https://doi.org/10.1016/j.dadr.2022.100126

27. Walley AY, Xuan Z, Hackman HH, et al. Opioid overdose rates and implementation of overdose education and nasal naloxone distribution in Massachusetts: interrupted time series analysis. *BMJ*. 2013;346:f174. https://doi.org/10.1136/bmj.f174
28. Mital S, Wolff J, Carroll JJ. The relationship between incarceration history and overdose in North America: a scoping review of the evidence. *Drug Alcohol Depend*. 2020;213:108088. https://doi.org/10.1016/j.drugalcdep.2020.108088
29. Abbas B, Marotta PL, Goddard-Eckrich D, et al. Socio-ecological and pharmacy-level factors associated with naloxone stocking at standing-order naloxone pharmacies in New York City. *Drug Alcohol Depend*. 2021;218:108388. https://doi.org/10.1016/j.drugalcdep.2020.108388
30. Commissioner of the FDA. FDA approves first over-the-counter naloxone nasal spray. US Food and Drug Administration. March 29, 2023. Available at: https://www.fda.gov/news-events/press-announcements/fda-approves-first-over-counter-naloxone-nasal-spray. Accessed April 23, 2023.
31. Emergent BioSolutions Inc. Emergent BioSolutions' NARCAN nasal spray launches over the counter making it possible for everyone to help save a life from an opioid overdose emergency. Available at: https://investors.emergentbiosolutions.com/news-releases/news-release-details/emergent-biosolutions-narcanr-nasal-spray-launches-over-counter. Accessed November 9, 2023.
32. Linas BP, Savinkina A, Madushani RWMA, et al. Projected estimates of opioid mortality after community-level interventions. *JAMA Netw Open*. 2021;4(2):e2037259. https://doi.org/10.1001/jamanetworkopen.2020.37259
33. Glasgow RE, Harden SM, Gaglio B, et al. RE-AIM Planning and Evaluation Framework: adapting to new science and practice with a 20-year review. *Front Public Health*. 2019;7:64. https://doi.org/10.3389/fpubh.2019.00064
34. Knudsen HK, Drainoni ML, Gilbert L, et al. Model and approach for assessing implementation context and fidelity in the HEALing Communities Study [erratum in *Drug Alcohol Depend*. 2021;224:108742]. *Drug Alcohol Depend*. 2020;217:108330. https://doi.org/10.1016/j.drugalcdep.2020.108330
35. Oyler DR, Knudsen HK, Oser CB, et al. Equity of overdose education and naloxone distribution provided in the Kentucky HEALing Communities Study. *Drug Alcohol Depend Rep*. 2024;10:100207. https://doi.org/10.1016/j.dadr.2023.100207

Long-Acting Reversible Contraception (LARC) and Early Childbearing Revisited: Births and Birth Intendedness After LARC Removal in a State Medicaid Population (2012–2020)

Michael S. Rendall, PhD, Mieke C. W. Eeckhaut, PhD, Katie Gifford, PhD, and Constanza Hurtado-Acuna, PhD

Objectives. To analyze births and birth intendedness after long-acting reversible contraception (LARC) removal among Medicaid-insured women.

Methods. We linked all Delaware women with a Medicaid-covered LARC removal in 2012 to 2020 (n = 8047) to birth records and to Pregnancy Risk Assessment Monitoring System (PRAMS) pregnancy intendedness survey responses (n = 241).

Results. Births within 3 years of a Medicaid-covered LARC removal were much more likely to be to women in their 20s compared with all Medicaid births (63.5% vs 53.4%; $P < .001$). The intended proportion for births within 3 years of Medicaid-covered LARC removal (65.2%) was higher than for all Medicaid-covered births (58.8%; $P = .08$) and was consistently above 60% across all age groups younger than 30 years.

Conclusions. A state Medicaid-insured population's use of highly effective reversible contraception was associated with births being concentrated among women in their 20s and with consistently high fractions of intended births across younger ages at birth.

Public Health Implications. Programs and policies may consider LARC access for its potential to increase low-income women's reproductive autonomy by enhancing their ability to achieve births at the age of their choosing. (*Am J Public Health*. 2025;115(1):95–102. https://doi.org/10.2105/AJPH.2024.307844)

AJPH January 2025, Vol. 115, No. 1

The use of long-acting reversible contraception (LARC) in the United States has grown substantially in the past 2 decades. Among women using any contraceptive method, LARC accounted for only 2% in 2002 and 6% in 2006 to 2008,[1] whereas it accounted for 16% of contraceptive users in 2017 to 2019, a fraction surpassed only by sterilization (28%) and the pill (21%).[2] The contraceptive failure rate of LARC is much lower than that of other reversible methods and is comparable to that of sterilization.[3] This low failure rate has led to LARC's promotion as a first-line contraceptive choice by health organizations such as the American College of Obstetricians and Gynecologists,[4] the Centers for Disease Control and Prevention,[5] and the American Academy of Pediatrics.[6]

Criticisms of "LARC-first" efforts have highlighted their focus on LARC rather than on women's preferences, potentially endangering women's reproductive autonomy.[7] Health organizations such as the American College of Obstetricians and Gynecologists have therefore recently shifted direction to emphasize patient-centered contraceptive counseling.[8,9] Paralleling this change in policy, recent research has shifted its focus to women's contraceptive autonomy and preferences.[10] This has included a shift from investigations of LARC use to reduce unintended pregnancies and births to investigations exploring the likelihood that women will have an intended birth after LARC removal.[11]

Encouragingly, a national study found that births were 20 percentage points more likely to be intended when the last contraceptive method used was a LARC device than when the last method used was either a moderately effective method such as the pill or a less effective method such as condoms.[12] More consideration of births and birth intendedness subsequent to LARC use is therefore merited.

Contraceptive access initiatives[13–15] and changes to state policies,[16] including in Delaware between 2015 and 2020,[17–20] have focused on increasing LARC access to younger and lower-income women. Following this emphasis, and noting that previous investigations have not examined intended births specifically among disadvantaged groups, we investigated women's births and birth intendedness in Delaware following Medicaid-covered LARC removals. We paid particular attention to the women's ages at LARC removal and to the relationship of this both to distributions of ages at birth and to intended birth fractions by age of the woman whose birth followed a Medicaid-covered LARC removal.

METHODS

Our main sources of data were the Delaware Medicaid administrative database and the Delaware Pregnancy Risk Assessment Monitoring System (PRAMS), both for 2012 to 2020. The major strengths of the Delaware Medicaid administrative database are its large sample sizes and complete state coverage, including all Medicaid-insured women in Delaware, and the links from this database to all Delaware births and to sampled Delaware PRAMS survey records, also in the years 2012 through 2020. Our Medicaid administrative database analytical samples consisted of all women who had a LARC device removal that was covered by Medicaid between 2012 and 2020 (n = 8047).

We used record links to all births of these women that occurred in Delaware between 2012 and 2020 (n = 2738), irrespective of whether the births were covered by Medicaid, and compared these to all Medicaid-covered births, as observed in the 2012 to 2020 PRAMS data (n = 3537). Additionally, for the approximately 9% of post–LARC removal births that were included in the Delaware PRAMS sample (n = 241), we used the PRAMS birth intendedness question responses. We focused on the intended fractions of births occurring within 3 years of LARC removal (n = 187). More information on the coding and record links for these data are provided in Appendix A (available as a supplement to the online version of this article at http://www.ajph.org).

One limitation of our study is that we were not able to link Medicaid Database records to records of births occurring outside Delaware. A limitation of the Delaware Medicaid administrative database is its relative lack of detail about the women. We nevertheless had information in this database on their age at, and year of, LARC removal, their race/ethnicity, and whether the LARC device they had removed was an intrauterine device (IUD) or an implant.

For more sociodemographic detail on women who recently discontinued LARC use and for comparisons of Delaware to the United States and between Medicaid-insured and privately insured women, we used the National Survey of Family Growth (NSFG) 2011 to 2013 through 2017 to 2019 cycles.[21] In the NSFG, we identified women who recently discontinued LARC use by means of its contraceptive calendar (n = 824), and we identified their health insurance type in the year before the survey interview, including those who were Medicaid insured (n = 245). More information on the coding and analyses of the NSFG data are provided in Appendix B (available as a supplement to the online version of this article at http://www.ajph.org).

We investigated what fraction of women go on to have a birth following LARC removal, considering the possibility that some may restart LARC or choose sterilization instead. We analyzed these birth outcomes and restarting LARC or opting for sterilization for up to 8 years following LARC removal. We derived the fraction having a birth at each duration using a multidecrement life table,[22] which allowed us to use all 8047 Medicaid-covered LARC removals in the estimation up until the point when the observation period ended in 2020 (Appendix A, Table B).

Among those who were estimated to have a birth within 3 years of LARC removal (years 0, 1, and 2), we investigated the fraction of births that were intended. To be congruent with previous research, we coded an intended pregnancy as one in which the respondent indicated the pregnancy resulting in birth was one that occurred for them at the right time or later than desired or that they were unsure about.[11,23] Our limiting of intendedness to births within 3 years of LARC removal connected those births more closely to LARC as the last-used method.[12] We show that approximately two thirds of all births estimated to occur within 8 years of LARC removal occurred in the first 3 years. More information on our estimation and simulation to derive these quantities is provided in Appendix A.

We used the 2012 to 2020 PRAMS data[24] to estimate the age distribution and intendedness of all births to Delaware Medicaid-insured women, using age groups equivalent to those in our Medicaid LARC-removal sample. We defined "Medicaid insured" in our PRAMS sample as women covered by Medicaid during their pregnancy. Using this definition, an average of 47% of Delaware births between 2012 and 2020 were covered by Medicaid (results not shown). We achieved an approximate equivalence in age groups at the time of the birth between the PRAMS data and the Medicaid Database–linked birth records following LARC removal by adding 2 years to the PRAMS age groups. We made this adjustment to match a median duration to birth of 2 years following LARC removal that we estimated by Medicaid Database age groups defined by the year of LARC removal (results not shown).

RESULTS

We first compared the characteristics of Delaware Medicaid-insured women whose LARC device was removed in the period 2012 to 2020 (n = 8047) to the characteristics of Medicaid-insured women nationally (using the NSFG data) who discontinued LARC use in approximately the same period (n = 245) and to the characteristics of privately insured women and all women nationally who discontinued LARC use (n = 481; Table 1). Nationally, Medicaid-insured women who discontinued LARC between 2011 and 2019 constituted one quarter (23.0%) of all women who discontinued LARC; two thirds (64.4%) of women who discontinued LARC were privately insured; and 12.7% were uninsured.

Nationally, compared with privately insured women, Medicaid-insured women who discontinued LARC were substantially younger, more likely to be from a disadvantaged minority group (Black or Hispanic), and more likely to have been using an implant than an IUD. More than half (54.6%) of women covered by Medicaid who discontinued LARC were younger than 25 years at the time of discontinuation, compared with only one quarter (23.5%) of privately insured LARC-discontinuing women. In Delaware, women covered by Medicaid who discontinued LARC were also relatively young, with women younger than 25 years constituting 41.6% of this population.

US women covered by Medicaid were also more likely to be Hispanic or non-Hispanic Black than were US privately insured women who recently discontinued LARC. Hispanics made up 27.0% of Medicaid-insured versus 20.3% of privately insured women, and non-Hispanic Blacks made up 16.2% of Medicaid-insured versus 9.7% of privately insured women in the 2011 to 2019 period. Black and Hispanic women together constituted an even higher fraction (54.8%) of women covered by Medicaid who discontinued LARC in Delaware. The Black versus Hispanic composition of women covered by Medicaid who discontinued LARC was reversed between Delaware (42.7% Black and 12.1% Hispanic) and nationally (16.2% Black and 27.0% Hispanic). Implants were more common among women covered by Medicaid who discontinued LARC in Delaware (42.6%) than LARC-discontinuing Medicaid-insured women nationally (28.8%). Approximately equal proportions of implants versus IUDs is a phenomenon that is also common to Colorado's contraceptive access initiative.[15] This may be because implant insertion requires less training for providers than does IUD insertion.[25]

In Figure 1, we show the age distribution comparison of births occurring within the first 3 years after LARC removal to the equivalent maternal age distribution of all Medicaid-covered births (Table 2). Both series are from observed data. Births within 3 years of Medicaid-covered LARC removal were concentrated among women whose LARC was removed in their 20s (63.5%), whereas for all Medicaid-covered births the equivalent fraction was only 53.5% ($P < .001$). The youngest age group (aged 15–20 years) makes up only 17.1% of births following Medicaid-covered LARC removal versus 23.7% of equivalent age all Medicaid-covered births. We saw relatively few births after aged 30 years at LARC removal for both groups: 14.9% following LARC removal at 30 to 34 years and 15.3% for equivalent maternal ages of all Medicaid-covered births.

We next describe the fractions who give birth within 3 years and 8 years of LARC removal (Table 2), by age at removal, for Delaware women covered by Medicaid. We estimated these fractions from the multiple-decrement life table, as described in Appendix A. We describe both the age group–specific fractions giving birth and the contributions of each age group to the overall fraction of LARC-discontinuing women giving birth.

For all 3 age groups of women who were younger than 30 years when their LARC was removed, we estimated that more than half would give birth within the next 8 years: 56.7%, 59.7%, and 51.7%, respectively, for those aged 15 to 20, 21 to 24, and 25 to 29 years when their LARC was removed. These age groups contributed 39.4% of births

TABLE 1— Characteristics of Women at Long-Acting Reversible Contraception (LARC) Discontinuation: Delaware, 2012–2020; United States, 2011–2019

	Medicaid-Insured Delaware, % or No.	Medicaid-Insured US, %[a,b] or No.	Privately Insured US, %[a,b,c] or No.	All US, %[a,b,d] or No.	P: Medicaid-Insured: Delaware vs US[e]	P: Privately Insured vs Medicaid-Insured, US[e]
Age at LARC discontinuation, y					.09	<.001
15–20	17.4	20.9	7.1	11.3		
21–24	24.2	33.7	16.4	21.5		
25–29	29.3	20.5	35.3	31.6		
30–34	17.6	14.1	17.5	16.2		
≥35	11.5	10.8	23.7	19.4		
Race/ethnicity					<.001	.12
White	43.6	48.6	60.9	55.6		
Hispanic	12.1	27.0	20.3	24.7		
Black	42.7	16.2	9.7	10.6		
Other[f]	1.6	8.2	9.1	9.1		
LARC device type					<.01	<.01
IUD	57.4	71.2	83.3	79.7		
Implant	42.6	28.8	16.7	20.3		
Insurance type						
Private/other				64.4		
Medicaid				23.0		
None				12.7		
Sample size	8047	245	481	824		

Source. Delaware Medicaid Database; US 2011–1013, 2013–2015, 2015–2017, and 2017–2019 National Survey of Family Growth (NSFG).
Note. IUD = intrauterine device.
[a]The NSFG (US) estimates are weighted.
[b]NSFG years 2011–2019 refer to the year of the survey. LARC discontinuations are from 0 to 3 years before the survey year.
[c]Includes public insurance other than Medicaid.
[d]Includes uninsured.
[e]χ^2 significance and *P* value.
[f]Includes unknown race/ethnicity.

to the LARC-removal cohort, whereas relatively small contributions to births came from women who discontinued LARC after aged 30 years: 6.1% from LARC discontinuations at aged 30 to 34 years and 1.8% at aged 35 years and older. Across all ages, almost half (47.4%) of LARC removals resulted in a birth within 8 years; it is important to note that some women chose to get a new LARC inserted or opted for sterilization instead, meaning that they would no longer be considered as possibly having a post-LARC birth. Most of these births occurred within the first 3 years of LARC removal (31.4% of the LARC-removal cohort).

Because relatively few births occurred in any given year after 3 years following LARC removal, and to minimize confounding associations through switching to other contraceptive methods following LARC removal, we focused our analyses of birth intendedness on women who had a birth within 3 years of LARC removal (at durations of 0, 1, or 2 years). These results are presented in Table 3. Overall, the intended fraction of births within 3 years of Medicaid-covered LARC removal was 6.4 percentage points higher than the intended fraction for all Medicaid-covered births (65.2% vs 58.8%; *P* = .08). That is, overall there was a 6.4 percentage point greater intended fraction among births following recent LARC removal than among all Medicaid-covered births.

When considering intendedness by age, we observed very similar proportions

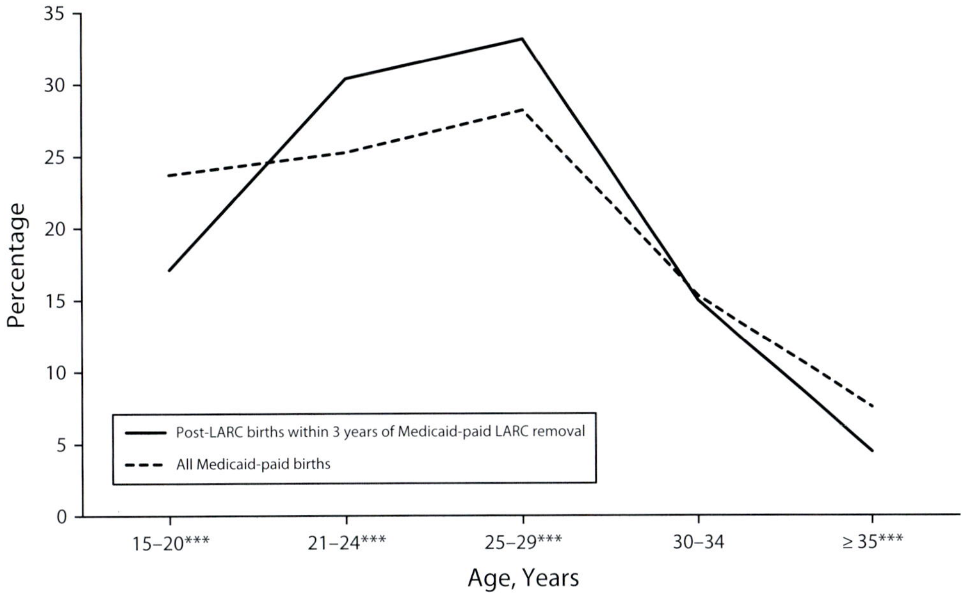

FIGURE 1— Age Distributions of Births by Medicaid-Insured Women: Delaware, 2012–2020

Source. Delaware Medicaid Database with linked Delaware births ("post-LARC births within 3 years of Medicaid-paid LARC removal") and Delaware Pregnancy Risk Assessment Monitoring System Database ("Medicaid-paid births").
Note. LARC = long-acting reversible contraception. We measured age at LARC removal for women with a post-LARC birth and at birth for women with a Medicaid-paid birth (adding 2 years to the latter age groups to match a median duration to birth of 2 years following LARC removal). We rejected the χ^2 test of the null hypothesis of no difference in the overall age distribution between LARC-removal and all Medicaid age distributions at $P < .001$.
***$P < .001$ according to the χ^2 test of the null hypothesis of no difference between the "post-LARC births within 3 years of Medicaid-paid LARC removal" and the "Medicaid-paid births" groups.

intended across age groups for births within 3 years of LARC removal across age groups younger than 30 years: 60.7%, 62.8%, and 64.6%, respectively, of births following a LARC removal at aged 15 to 20, 21 to 24, and 25 to 29 years were intended. The intended fractions by age differed substantially, however, for all Medicaid-covered births. Adding 2 years to the all women age categories to make them equivalent to the median age of women at their births after LARC discontinuation at aged 15 to 20, 21 to 24, and 25 to 29 years, we saw that the intended fractions for Delaware Medicaid-covered births were, respectively, 47.2%, 58.5%, and 64.1%. That is, there was a substantial upward gradient toward higher intended fractions with age through those in their 20s ($P < .001$) among all Medicaid-covered births, whereas there was not for births following Medicaid-covered LARC removals ($P = .73$).

DISCUSSION

Our study broadens the investigation of LARC beyond the focus of previous research on LARC's potential to reduce unintended pregnancy[26] to consider instead LARC's potential to increase intended pregnancies resulting in birth. Central to this broadening is the conceptualizing of intended pregnancy and birth as more than the converse of unintended pregnancy and birth. The distinction between intended and unintended births is seen in the reproductive justice framework, whose first 2 tenets are "(1) the right to have a child under the conditions of one's choosing; [and] (2) the right not to have a child using birth control, abortion, or abstinence."[27(p290)] It is also seen in the definition of reproductive autonomy as "a woman's ability to achieve her reproductive intentions."[28(p20)]

A woman's reproductive autonomy hinges on, among other things, her being able to use (and discontinue) her birth control method of choice as well as her being able to prevent and achieve pregnancy and birth under the conditions of her choosing. With regards to the latter—intended pregnancy or birth—previous LARC studies have included that of Eeckhaut et al.,[11] who found that 45% of women who discontinued LARC use between aged 20 and 34 years were estimated to have an intended live birth within 9 years of LARC discontinuation, and a study[12] that found that the fraction of births from an intended pregnancy for women whose last contraceptive

TABLE 2— **Births After Medicaid-Covered Long-Acting Reversible Contraception (LARC) Removal, With Comparisons to All Medicaid Births: Delaware, 2012–2020**

	Age Distribution of Women, % or No.,				Contribution of Each Age Group to the Total Share of Women Who Had a Birth[e]	
	Births Within 3 y of Medicaid-Paid LARC Removal[a]	All Medicaid-Covered Births[b]	P[c]	Percentage of Women in Each Age Group Having a Birth Within 8 y of LARC Removal, %[d]	Within 8 y of LARC Removal, %[f]	Within 3 y of LARC Removal, %[g]
Age group, y						
15–20	17.1	23.7	.001	56.7	9.9	5.7
21–24	30.4	25.3	.001	59.7	14.4	9.5
25–29	33.1	28.2	<.001	51.7	15.1	10.5
30–34	14.9	15.3	.74	34.6	6.1	4.4
≥35	4.5	7.6	<.001	15.9	1.8	1.4
15–44	100.0	100.0	<.001	47.4	47.4	31.4
Total sample size	2134	3537				

[a]Delaware Medicaid Database with linked Delaware births, 2012–2020.
[b]Delaware Pregnancy Risk Assessment Monitoring System (PRAMS), 2012–2020 Medicaid-covered births, with age + 2 years to match the median duration of births after LARC removal in that series.
[c]χ^2 test for difference between post-LARC removal births and all Medicaid births.
[d]At each duration (years 0–7 for columns 5 and 6 and years 0–2 for column 7, where year 0 is the calendar year in which the LARC device was removed), we derived the percentage having a birth from a multi-decrement life table and then summed it across years to estimate the cumulative % (Appendix A [available as a supplement to the online version of this article at http://www.ajph.org] provides more details).
[e]Contribution of each age group to the total share of women in the LARC-removal cohort who had a birth.
[f]Calculated as the product of the cumulative % in that age group who gave birth within 8 years of LARC removal (Table 2) and the % of all women with a LARC removal who were in that age group (Table 1).
[g]Calculated as the product of the cumulative % in that age group who gave birth within 3 years of LARC removal (not shown) and the % of all women with a LARC removal who were in that age group (Table 1).

method was a LARC was 20 percentage points higher than that for women whose most recent method was either moderately effective (e.g., the pill) or less effective (e.g., condoms). This difference is much higher than our estimated 6 percentage points greater intendedness among Medicaid-covered LARC removals than among all Medicaid-covered births. However, we note that in Eeckhaut and Rendall's study,[12] the estimated difference went down to 15 percentage point greater intendedness after LARC when analyzing only births to women who had used no contraceptive method in the month of conception. Unfortunately, the Medicaid Database does not permit the identification of "no method" periods.

Low-income women (here defined by Medicaid eligibility) who have used then discontinued LARC were considerably younger than were privately insured women: nationally, 55% of Medicaid-insured women were younger than 25 years at the time of LARC removal, and 21% were aged 15 to 20 years at LARC removal. Similarly, among Delaware Medicaid-covered LARC removals, 42% were for women younger than 25 years, and 17% were for those younger than 21 years. By comparison, nationally, only 24% of all privately insured women's LARC removals were for women younger than 25 years, and only 7% for women younger than 21 years.

Despite the overall young ages at LARC removal in the Delaware Medicaid population, more than 60% of Delaware women's births in the 3 years following LARC removal were intended, including 60.7% among those who had removals at aged 15 to 20 years and 62.8% at aged 21 to 24 years. The lack of an upward age gradient in intended proportions in Delaware's Medicaid-insured LARC-discontinuing women is important. Almost by definition, younger women's births are more likely to be unintended, given that most unintended births are those that "occurred too soon" rather than being "unwanted then or at any time."[29] This suggests that the majority of Medicaid-insured women in Delaware who used and then discontinued use of LARC, even though they had births at relatively young ages (in their 20s largely), nevertheless had births that for them were of their desired birth timing. This may be interpreted as a successful use of LARC to enable reproductive autonomy, as that concept includes having births at the time the woman chooses.

TABLE 3— Birth Intendedness After Medicaid-Covered Long-Acting Reversible Contraception (LARC) Removal, With Comparisons of Intendedness to All Medicaid-Covered Births and All Births: Delaware, 2012–2020

	Percentage Intended	
	Births Within 3 Years of LARC Removal[a]	All Medicaid Births[b]
Age group, y		
15–20	60.7	47.2
21–24	62.8	58.5
25–29	64.6	64.1
≥30	72.1	64.8
P^c	.73	<.001
All aged 15–44 y[d]	65.2	58.8
Sample size, no.	187	3537

[a]We used the Delaware Medicaid Database with linked Delaware births and linked Pregnancy Risk Assessment Monitoring System (PRAMS) records for all age at removal results.
[b]Delaware PRAMS data, with age groups defined by age + 2 years.
[c]χ^2 test of difference in percentage intended by age group.
[d]χ^2 test of difference in percentage intended between "births within 3 years of LARC removal" and "all Medicaid births" ($P = .08$). Differences in percentage intended by each age group were not statistically significant ($P > .05$).

There are, however, noteworthy limitations to our study. One is that our study is of women from the time of a LARC removal. That is, we did not consider the conditions of the women at the time of their LARC insertion. An important issue with the use of LARC to facilitate intended pregnancies and births at younger ages is that of pressure by a medical provider either to have LARC inserted or to not have their LARC removed.[30] Additionally, in a study of young women's contraceptive feature preferences,[31] not needing a provider visit to discontinue use and allowing the user to resume fertility immediately after discontinuation were associated with women's lack of interest in IUDs, again emphasizing the critical role of reproductive autonomy in the process of LARC insertion.

Because we did not consider women's characteristics before or at their LARC insertion—including (the strength of) fertility intentions—we were not able to assess if and how these might have shaped women's decision to use LARC. Finally, even though administrative data enabled us to observe the entire population of Medicaid-insured women, we were able to observe birth intendedness for only a relatively small number of women: those who were also included in the PRAMS sample. Our findings on patterns of birth intendedness by age at LARC removal would be more robust if drawn from a larger sample.

Despite these limitations, results indicate that LARC offers a valuable option to enable low-income women to achieve their family planning goals: both of preventing unintended births and of having children at the still relatively young ages of their choosing. Previous work has shown that LARC use increased in Delaware under the no-cost conditions of the Delaware Contraceptive Access Now initiative, especially at younger ages,[18,19] and for postpartum women.[20] For the latter, LARC use enabled longer intervals between births,[32] and longer birth spacing has also been found to be associated with higher intended fractions of those subsequent births.[33] AJPH

ABOUT THE AUTHORS

Michael S. Rendall and Constanza Hurtado-Acuna are with the Department of Sociology and the Maryland Population Research Center, University of Maryland, College Park. Mieke C. W. Eeckhaut is with the Department of Sociology and Criminal Justice, University of Delaware, Newark. Katie Gifford is with the Center for Community Research & Service, University of Delaware, Newark.

CORRESPONDENCE

Correspondence should be sent to Michael S. Rendall, 3139 Parren J. Mitchell Art-Sociology Building, 3834 Campus Dr, University of Maryland, College Park, MD 20742-1315 (e-mail: mrendall@umd.edu). Reprints can be ordered at https://www.ajph.org by clicking the "Reprints" link.

PUBLICATION INFORMATION

Full Citation: Rendall MS, Eeckhaut MCW, Gifford K, Hurtado-Acuna C. Long-acting reversible contraception (LARC) and early childbearing revisited: births and birth intendedness after LARC removal in a state Medicaid population (2012–2020). *Am J Public Health*. 2025;115(1):95–102.

Acceptance Date: August 10, 2024.

DOI: https://doi.org/10.2105/AJPH.2024.307844

ORCID iDs:
Michael S. Rendall https://orcid.org/0000-0001-8541-1033

Mieke C. W. Eeckhaut https://orcid.org/0000-0001-9132-0883

CONTRIBUTORS

M. S. Rendall conceptualized and oversaw all parts of the study and drafted the article. M. C. W. Eeckhaut collaborated on the study design and drafting of the article, conducted the analyses using the National Survey of Family Growth (NSFG), and oversaw the Medicaid Database and Pregnancy Risk Assessment Monitoring System (PRAMS) analyses. K. Gifford conducted all analyses involving the Medicaid Database, including comparisons to NSFG and PRAMS data, and wrote the Medicaid Database sections. C. Hurtado-Acuna conducted the PRAMS analyses and wrote the PRAMS sections. M. C. W. Eeckhaut, K. Gifford, and C. Hurtado-Acuna reviewed the article.

ACKNOWLEDGMENTS

We gratefully acknowledge infrastructural support from the Eunice Kennedy Shriver National Institute of Child Health and Human Development (grant

P2C-HD041041) and from a research grant from a private philanthropic foundation.

Medicaid claims data were provided by the Delaware Division of Medicaid Medical Assistance through a partnership between the University of Delaware and the Delaware Department of Health and Social Services. Birth certificate data were provided by the Delaware Division of Public Health, Vital Statistics. Pregnancy Risk Assessment Monitoring System (PRAMS) data were provided by the Centers for Disease Control and Prevention (CDC) PRAMS Working Group. National Survey of Family Growth data were from public use data made available by the CDC's National Center for Health Statistics.

Note. The funders had no role in the study design or the collection, analysis, or interpretation of data.

CONFLICTS OF INTEREST

The authors have no conflicts of interest to disclose.

HUMAN PARTICIPANT PROTECTION

The analysis of Medicaid claims and linked birth certificate and Pregnancy Risk Assessment Monitoring System (PRAMS) data was approved by the University of Delaware institutional review board and the Delaware Division of Health & Social Services Human Subjects Review Board. The independent analyses of the National Survey of Family Growth and PRAMS data were deemed exempt from review by the University of Maryland, College Park institutional review board.

REFERENCES

1. Kavanaugh ML, Jerman J, Hubacher D, Kost K, Finer LB. Characteristics of women in the United States who use long-acting reversible contraceptive methods. *Obstet Gynecol.* 2011;117(6):1349–1357. https://doi.org/10.1097/AOG.0b013e31821c47c9
2. Daniels K, Abma JC. Current contraceptive status among women aged 15–49: United States, 2017–2019. *NCHS Data Brief.* 2020;388:1–8. Available at: https://www.cdc.gov/nchs/products/databriefs/db388.htm. Accessed October 3, 2024.
3. Trussell J. Contraceptive failure in the United States. *Contraception.* 2011;83(5):397–404. https://doi.org/10.1016/j.contraception.2011.01.021
4. American College of Obstetricians and Gynecologists. ACOG Committee opinion no. 450: increasing use of contraceptive implants and intrauterine devices to reduce unintended pregnancy. *Obstet Gynecol.* 2009;114(6):1434–1438. https://doi.org/10.1097/AOG.0b013e3181c6f965
5. Centers for Disease Control and Prevention. Providing quality family planning services: recommendations of CDC and the US Office of Population Affairs. *MMWR Recomm Rep.* 2014;63(RR-04):1–54. Available at: https://www.cdc.gov/mmwr/preview/mmwrhtml/rr6304a1.htm. Accessed October 3, 2024.
6. Ott MA, Sucato GS; Committee on Adolescence, et al. Contraception for adolescents. *Pediatrics.* 2014;134(4):e1257–e1281. https://doi.org/10.1542/peds.2014-2300
7. Dehlendorf C, Perritt J. Statewide contraceptive access initiatives: a critical perspective. *Am J Public Health.* 2022;112(suppl 5):S490–S493. https://doi.org/10.2105/AJPH.2022.306930
8. American College of Obstetricians and Gynecologists. ACOG Committee statement no. 1: patient-centered contraceptive counseling. *Obstet Gynecol.* 2022;139(2):350–353. https://doi.org/10.1097/AOG.0000000000004659
9. Horvath S, Bumpus M, Luchowski A. From uptake to access: a decade of learning from the ACOG LARC program. *Am J Obstet Gynecol.* 2020;222(4 suppl):S866S868.e1. https://doi.org/10.1016/j.ajog.2019.11.1269.
10. Senderowicz L. Contraceptive autonomy: conceptions and measurement of a novel family planning indicator. *Stud Fam Plann.* 2020;51(2):161–176. https://doi.org/10.1111/sifp.12114
11. Eeckhaut MCW, Rendall MS, Zvavitch P. Long-acting reversible contraceptive use for birth timing and birth stopping. *Demography.* 2021;58(4):1327–1346. https://doi.org/10.1215/00703370-9386084
12. Eeckhaut MCW, Rendall MS. Are births more likely to be intended following use of long-acting reversible contraceptives? An analysis of US births in 2003–2015. *Popul Res Policy Rev.* 2022;41(3):1085–1110. https://doi.org/10.1007/s11113-021-09680-5
13. Ricketts S, Klingler G, Schwalberg R. Game change in Colorado: widespread use of long-acting reversible contraceptives and rapid decline in births among young, low-income women. *Perspect Sex Reprod Health.* 2014;46(3):125–132. https://doi.org/10.1363/46e1714
14. Secura GM, Madden T, McNicholas C, et al. Provision of no-cost, long-acting contraception and teenage pregnancy. *N Engl J Med.* 2014;371(14):1316–1323. https://doi.org/10.1056/NEJMoa1400506
15. Romer SE, Kennedy KI. The Colorado initiative to reduce unintended pregnancy: contraceptive access and impact on reproductive health. *Am J Public Health.* 2022;112(suppl 5):S532–S536. https://doi.org/10.2105/AJPH.2022.306891
16. Moniz MH, Dalton VK, Davis MM, et al. Characterization of Medicaid policy for immediate postpartum contraception. *Contraception.* 2015;92(6):523–531. https://doi.org/10.1016/j.contraception.2015.09.014
17. Choi YS, Rendall MS, Boudreaux M, Roby DH. Summary of the Delaware Contraceptive Access Now (DelCAN) Initiative. 2020. Available at: https://popcenter.umd.edu/delcaneval/summary-init. Accessed September 18, 2024.
18. Boudreaux M, Xie L, Choi Y, Roby D, Rendall M. Changes to contraceptive method use at Title X clinics following Delaware Contraceptive Access Now, 2008–2017. *Am J Public Health.* 2020;110(8):1214–1220. https://doi.org/10.2105/AJPH.2020.305666
19. Boudreaux M, Gifford K, McDuffie MJ, McColl R, Kim T, Knight E. Delaware Contraceptive Access Now and contraceptive initiation among Medicaid enrollees. *Am J Public Health.* 2022;112(suppl 5):S537–S540. https://doi.org/10.2105/AJPH.2022.306938
20. Caudillo ML, Hurtado-Acuna C, Rendall MS, Boudreaux M. Association of the Delaware Contraceptive Access Now Initiative with postpartum LARC use. *Matern Child Health J.* 2022;26(8):1657–1666. https://doi.org/10.1007/s10995-022-03433-2
21. US Department of Health and Human Services. Public-use data file documentation 2017–2019, National Survey of Family Growth. 2020. Available at: https://www.cdc.gov/nchs/data/nsfg/NSFG-2017-2019-UGMainText-08.pdf. Accessed September 18, 2024.
22. Chiang CL. *The Life Table and Its Applications.* Malabar, FL: Robert E. Krieger; 1984.
23. Mosher WD, Jones J, Abma JC. Intended and unintended births in the United States: 1982–2010. *Natl Health Stat Report.* 2012;55:1–28. Available at: https://pubmed.ncbi.nlm.nih.gov/23115878/. Accessed October 3, 2024.
24. Centers for Disease Control and Prevention. PRAMS [data set]. 2019. Available at: https://www.cdc.gov/prams/prams-data/researchers.htm. Accessed September 18, 2024.
25. Skračić I, Lewin AB, Roy KM. Evaluation of the Delaware Contraceptive Access Now (DelCAN) initiative: a qualitative analysis of site leaders' implementation recommendations. *Contraception.* 2021;104(2):211–215. https://doi.org/10.1016/j.contraception.2021.03.015
26. Parks C, Peipert JF. Eliminating health disparities in unintended pregnancy with long-acting reversible contraception (LARC). *Am J Obstet Gynecol.* 2016;214(6):681–688. https://doi.org/10.1016/j.ajog.2016.02.017
27. Ross LJ. Reproductive justice as intersectional feminist activism. *Souls.* 2017;19(3):286–314. https://doi.org/10.1080/10999949.2017.1389634
28. Upadhyay UD, Dworkin SL, Weitz TA, Foster DG. Development and validation of a reproductive autonomy scale. *Stud Fam Plann.* 2014;45(1):19–41. https://doi.org/10.1111/j.1728-4465.2014.00374.x
29. Kost K, Zolna MR, Murro R. Pregnancies in the United States by desire for pregnancy: estimates for 2009, 2011, 2013, and 2015. *Demography.* 2023;60(3):837–863. https://doi.org/10.1215/00703370-10690005
30. Eeckhaut MCW, Hara Y. Reproductive oppression enters the twenty-first century: pressure to use long-acting reversible contraception (LARC) in the context of "LARC First". *Socius.* 2023;9. https://doi.org/10.1177/23780231231180378
31. Gomez AM, Clark JB. The relationship between contraceptive features preferred by young women and interest in IUDs: an exploratory analysis. *Perspect Sex Reprod Health.* 2014;46(3):157–163. https://doi.org/10.1363/46e2014
32. Gifford K, McDuffie MJ, Rashid H, et al. Postpartum contraception method type and risk of a short inter-pregnancy interval in a state Medicaid population. *Contraception.* 2021;104(3):284–288. https://doi.org/10.1016/j.contraception.2021.05.006
33. Ahrens KA, Thoma ME, Copen CE, Frederiksen BN, Decker EJ, Moskosky S. Unintended pregnancy and interpregnancy interval by maternal age, National Survey of Family Growth. *Contraception.* 2018;98(1):52–55. https://doi.org/10.1016/j.contraception.2018.02.013